BIBLE STORYTELLING TOOLS

A Guide for Storying the Bible

Jackson Day

BIBLE STORYTELLING TOOLS

Copyright © 2004 by Jackson Day. All rights reserved.
No part of this book may be reproduced, stored in a retrieval system, or transmitted by any means, electronic, mechanical, photocopying, recording, or otherwise, without written permission from the author.

Bible Storytelling Project
P. O. Box 1248
Ashville, AL 35953

Http://biblestorytelling.org

Published 2007 by
Lightning Source
1248 Heil Quaker Blvd.
La Vergne, TN 37086

Printed in the United States of America

ISBN 978-0-9797324-2-3

TABLE OF CONTENTS

		Page
	Introduction	
1	The Usefulness of Bible Stories	i
	■ Storytelling Is Biblical	1
	■ Types of Bible Stories	2
	■ Different Ways to Use Bible Stories	2
2	Bible Storytelling with Oral Communicators	10
	■ Bible Storytelling with Primary-oral Communicators	10
	■ Bible Storytelling with Secondary-oral Communicators	19
3	Methods of Communicating with Bible Stories	24
4	How to Analyze a Bible Story	26
	■ How to Analyze a Story Comparing Different Narrations of the Same Story	34
5	Telling a Bible Story	40
6	Selecting Life-lessons from a Bible Story to Become the Divisions for a Sermon or Study	49
7	Bible Storytelling with Dialogue	52
8	Narrative Preaching: Bible Storytelling with Preaching	55
	■ Use the Preaching Cycle	55
	■ Bible Storytelling with Preaching after the Story	59
	■ Bible Storytelling with Preaching Inserted	64
	■ Preach the Sermon; Teach the Lesson	70
9	Narrative Teaching: Bible Storytelling with Teaching	75
	■ Bible Storytelling Combined with Questions	75
	■ Bible Storytelling Combined with Using Teaching Cycles	82
	Chart: Three Methods Useful for Communicating Selected Life-lessons from Bible Stories	89
10	Miracles	90
11	Parables	97
12	Biographical Analysis Using Bible Stories	109
13	Biographical Sermon: Biographical Bible Storytelling with Preaching	118
14	Doctrinal Analysis Using Bible Stories in Chronological Order	126
15	Doctrinal Sermon Using Bible Stories	136
16	Using Drama with Bible Stories	143
17	Connecting a Bible Story to the Listeners' Lives	146
18	Chronological Bible Storying Tracks	153
	■ Multiple Storying Track	153
	■ Single Storying Track	162
	■ Fast-storying Track	163
19	Organizing the Storying Track	165
	■ Panoramic View of the Bible	183
20	List of Bible Stories with References	187
	■ List of Miracles	193
	■ List of Jesus' Parables	194
21	Chart of Bible Stories and Doctrinal Objectives	196

INTRODUCTION

My childhood was spent on a farm in Alabama, twelve miles from the small county seat town of LaFayette. I was thirteen when I saw television for the first time. On many Sundays, my father's family went to my grandparents' house and sat on the front porch swapping stories.

When I enrolled in Samford University in Birmingham, I became a barber to pay the bills. I worked for Jimmy Williams, a storytelling barber in Mountain Brook, a suburb of Birmingham. Customers often stayed in the barber shop hours after getting a haircut listening to Jimmy tell his stories. Others would drop by when they did not need a haircut just to hear a good story.

After completing my studies at the university, I attended Southwestern Baptist Seminary in Fort Worth, Texas, where I met and married Doris Herron from Los Angeles, California. I was a pastor in Pagosa Springs, Colorado, and Walla Walla, Washington before going to Brazil.

While storytelling was a part of my growing up, it was on the mission field that I realized its importance in teaching and preaching the Bible. In December 1970, my wife and I were appointed as missionaries to Brazil with the International Mission Board of the Southern Baptist Convention. Our family arrived in Brazil in July of 1971. Since 1974, I have trained church leaders to preach and teach using Bible stories. I was unable to train men with less than an elementary education to preach using methods I had learned in seminary. One of my students was Jairo Lima, an uneducated brick layer, who learned to read after becoming a believer in Jesus. He loved to preach. When he told Bible stories and made applications, his listeners sat on the edges of their chairs with mouths wide open. In sharp contrast, when he tried to preach from one of Paul's letters, no one paid attention. Jairo helped me understand that the uneducated are usually great storytellers and can be effective church leaders when they preach or teach using Bible stories. I also realized that when I myself told a Bible story as part of my sermons, those with limited education understood me.

Through trial and error I kept writing and rewriting a workbook on how to teach and preach using Bible stories. Most of my ideas came while working with my students. While I did obtain some ideas from books, I did not make notes on their sources and am not able to give credit to those who influenced some of my thoughts. In 1992, I discovered the series of books published by New Tribes entitled FIRM FOUNDATIONS by Trevor McLlwain. McLlwain's series presents a plan for telling Bible stories in chronological order for the purpose of evangelizing and planting new churches with tribal people.

I began to incorporate the idea of teaching the Bible stories in chronological order in my teaching and writings. My wife and I have prepared twelve books in Portuguese that are distributed by SOCEP - SOCIEDADE CRISTÃ EVANGÉLICA DE PUBLICAÇÕES LTDA. in Brazil. The books are sold throughout Brazil and Brazilian missionaries take them to other parts of the world. Those books have also been translated into Spanish. We discovered that Bible stories are effective with all social levels and we have used them in starting four churches in upper class communities.

We lived for thirteen years in Brasília, the capital city of Brazil. The Baptist Theological Seminary in Brasília invited me to develop and co-ordinate a Theological Education by Extension Course using Bible stories in chronological order to train lay preachers and church leaders. In this course the students study one night a week for three semesters. The students study the Bible stories in chronological order and learn to teach, preach, and be spiritual leaders. For several years, I was the coordinator of the "Communicating by Means of Bible Stories Extension Course."

In 1998, my wife and I were invited by the regional leadership of Eastern South America (Brazil, Paraguay and Uruguay) of the International Mission Board of the Southern Baptist Convention to promote Bible Storytelling in the region. We did this through preparing written materials and leading training seminars to equip missionaries and nationals who were church leaders to evangelize, teach, preach, train and plant new churches using Bible stories. We had that responsibility until we retired in March of 2003.

ACKNOWLEDGMENTS

My thanks are due to English teachers who discovered many of my grammar and spelling errors and gave valuable suggestions to improve this book. They are Ms. Diane Champion, Ms. Bertha Fagan and Ms. Berdie Hope. Ms. Diane Grill then corrected my final revision and made many suggestions to improve my writing.

The more time I spend writing, the more I understand why so many authors express thanks to their spouses. The person who helped me the most with this book is the one who has been my helpmate since she agreed to marry me. I am thankful for all Doris Day has done to help me with this book.

Each Bible story or summary of a Bible story is a contemporary paraphrase that was crafted by the author of this book.

THE USEFULNESS OF BIBLE STORIES

Many ways exist for storytellers, preachers, and teachers to use Bible stories. Bible Storytelling has great potential because all age groups, cultural groups, nationalities, and educational levels love a good story.

Bible stories include the historical accounts narrated in the Bible and the parables told by Jesus. With some cultural groups, it is wise to refer to Bible stories as *Bible narratives* because some people groups have the idea that a story is similar to a bedtime story or folkloric tale. In Brazil, evangelical Christians prefer to use the term "Bible Narratives." In this book I will be using the terms *story* and *narrative* interchangeably.

Narratives are the most common type of literature in the Bible. Of the thirty-nine Old Testament books, thirty-four contain stories of events. The following Old Testament books primarily contain historical stories: Genesis, Joshua, Judges, Ruth, 1 and 2 Samuel, 1 and 2 Kings, 1 and 2 Chronicles, Ezra, Nehemiah, Esther, Daniel, Jonah and Haggai. Large portions of Exodus, Numbers, Job, Isaiah, Jeremiah, and Ezekiel also contain historical stories. The twenty-seven New Testament books contain a mixture of stories, teachings, exhortations, discourses, warnings and prophecies. Each New Testament book contains stories. The greatest portions of the Gospels of Matthew, Mark, Luke and John are historical stories; almost all of Acts is narrative. Obviously, Bible stories are God's major tools for teaching man his truths.

Bible stories make an impact and communicate truth narratively. Stories open doors for gaining knowledge of God, understanding of man's sinful condition, revealing truths, and having an encounter with Jesus Christ. Bible stories create memories in the listeners' minds.

Storytelling is natural and easy. Storytelling entertains and energizes. Bible Storytelling can change perceptions and worldviews. Bible Storytelling is non-adversarial and bypasses normal defense mechanisms. Stories are also easy to remember.

STORYTELLING IS BIBLICAL

- 70%+ of the Bible is in story form.

- Biblical leaders used Storytelling to communicate God's message:
    - Moses;
    - Joshua;
    - David;
    - Gospel writers;
    - Stephen;
    - Paul sharing his testimony;
    - Author of Hebrews.

- Jesus never spoke without using a parable (Mk 4:33-34).

TYPES OF BIBLE STORIES

In the Bible there are varied types of Bible stories.

1. Heroic

The heroic is a literary style that narrates the lives of great people who are respected and honored by others. Through the narration, their great feats are celebrated. Examples:
- Abraham;
- Gideon;
- Deborah;
- David;
- Daniel;
- Paul.

2. Tragedy

The tragedy is a literary style that narrates the history of a person who had opportunities to become a hero, but forfeited them by making mistakes that resulted in a wretched ending. Examples:
- Samson;
- Saul;
- Solomon.

3. Epic

An epic is a literary style that narrates a long chronicle containing a series of episodes in the life of a person or group. Example:
- The chronological narration of events linked to the 40 years that Israel wandered in the desert.

4. Romance

A romance is a literary style that narrates a love history. Examples:
- Ruth;
- Song of Solomon.

5. Polemic

A polemic is a literary style that narrates a controversy where one person or group attacks another person, group or their convictions. Examples:
- The ten plagues against Egypt (Ex 7-12);
- The prophet Elijah confronts 450 prophets of Baal on Mount Carmel (1 Kn 18:16-46).

6. Satire

A satire is a literary style that narrates events destined to censor or ridicule defects or mistaken convictions. Example:
- Jonah. The book of Jonah ridicules his anger over the plant that withered while having no concern for the people of Nineveh. It is also ironic that God had compassion for Jonah, who had none for Nineveh.

DIFFERENT WAYS TO USE BIBLE STORIES

1. **Use Bible stories with those who are predisposed to reject Bible teaching**

Stories are the best approach to modify the viewpoints of those who are predisposed to reject Bible teaching. Bible Storytelling may gain a hearing with people groups who are hostile to a direct confrontation of the Gospel truths.

A child named Billy couldn't swallow a pill. No matter what his mother tried, it wouldn't go down. Threats of spankings or promises of candy made no difference; the pill always ended up right on the tip of his tongue. Finally, his mother discovered a method that worked. She cut a raisin open, inserted the pill and gave it to Billy. He swallowed the raisin with its hidden pill but had never been able to swallow the pill alone, even though alone it was much smaller. Likewise, stories are excellent "raisins" in which to wrap truths that are hard to swallow. Where frontal attack would certainly fail, the story becomes a raisin which contains the truth that is hard to swallow.

The following are examples of biblical stories used as "raisins" in which to wrap truths that are hard to swallow:
- David committed adultery with Bathsheba. After she became pregnant, David planned her husband Uriah's death to cover up the adultery. Then, he took Bathsheba for his wife. Nathan, the

prophet, told David a story about a rich man with many sheep who stole the only lamb belonging to a poor man. When David became enraged by the imagined injustice, Nathan confronted David with his own sin problem by saying: "You are the man" (2 Sam 12:1-9).

■ David's son Amnon raped his half-sister Tamar. Another son, Absalom, sought revenge by killing Amnon and then fled to another country. King David longed for Absalom. The king's general Joab crafted a story for Tekoa, noted as a wise woman, to tell David. Its purpose was to help him reconsider the conflict with his son Absalom and allow him to return to Jerusalem (2 Sam 14).

■ The Pharisees and the teachers of the law grumbled about Jesus socializing with sinners. Jesus responded with the parables of the lost sheep, the lost coin and the lost (prodigal) son (Lk 15).

■ To some who were confident of their own righteousness and looked down on everyone else, Jesus told a parable of a Pharisee and a tax collector who went to the Temple to pray. The Pharisee stood up and prayed about himself, thanking God that he was better than other men. The tax collector stood up, beating his breast and begged: "God, have mercy on me, a sinner" (Lk 18:9-14).

Bible personalities used storytelling to communicate to those not prepared to accept the truth. Stories are still effective with people who are not prepared to receive the truth. At times confronting someone with the truth might turn the listener into an enemy; whereas, telling him stories may change his life.

2. Use Bible stories with those who are disinterested in Bible teaching

Bible stories are helpful to gain listeners among those disinterested in the Gospel. Some have no desire to hear the Gospel because they are indifferent, not because they are hostile. They may be interested in things such as pleasure, parties, sports, politics, making money, etc., but they have no interest in spiritual things. They seek entertainment, but have no interest in God's truths. One may need to entertain them with Bible stories to draw them to be present to hear God's Word. The Bible story becomes a delicious "raisin." While swallowing the story, God's truth may transform the listener who came only to be entertained.

3. Use Bible Storytelling to make your home a Bible teaching place

3.1 A place for family devotions

Storytelling is a potential source for teaching the Bible to the basic educational community of the Church: the family. Throughout the history of Israel in the Old Testament, as well as the history of the New Testament Church, the family was the primary educational center. Parents were expected to read the Bible or tell Bible stories to the children, talk about the scripture and lead the family in prayer. Regretfully, with the decline of oral recitation and the advent of television, the role of the family and parents in the religious education process declined. An important step in the revitalization of religious education is for parents once again to learn to tell Bible stories to their children. The Church should train parents how to tell Bible stories as a means of revitalization of religious education. Parents with little biblical knowledge should begin learning Bible stories and telling them to the family circle.

Using Bible stories with children is the most effective way to make family devotional time enjoyable. Everyone loves a story. Children pay more attention to a Bible story than to a reading of a doctrinal text such as Paul's letter to the Galatians.

My wife and I used Bible stories during our family devotion with our children. We selected a book of the Bible and told the stories in the order in which we found them. Then we started another book. When the children were small, I prepared in advance by reading the story to myself. Then, during the devotion I told the story in my own words. When the children were five or six years old, I read the story and asked simple questions and explained what they did not understand. After they reached eight or ten years old, they helped lead the devotion time. During holidays and summer vacation time, the children read or told the Bible stories, and we talked about them.

In addition to telling their children Bible stories, parents need to teach their children to tell Bible stories themselves.

A word to the beginning preacher: The best school in which to train to preach is your own home. The man who learns to communicate biblical stories to his own children is able to preach and be understood by adults.

3.2 A place for outreach

Christians have family and friends who are not followers of Jesus and would resist entering a church, but they would enjoy being in someone's home to hear Bible stories and discuss them.

Churches need to have a vision of using the homes of new Christians to teach the Bible and to evangelize. The new Christian most likely has more friends who are outside the church than does a longtime Christian. This new Christian can tell his family members, co-workers and friends that he knows little about the Bible and that someone from the church is going to teach him the basic Bible stories. He invites his non-church friends and family members to study the Bible with him.

The new Christian and his invited friends can be told a series of Bible stories that give them an overview of the Bible. While the new Christian is learning the basics from Bible stories, his family and friends are being evangelized.

3.3 A place for Bible study cell groups

Some churches organize families who live close to each other into cell groups for the purpose of week-day Bible studies. Bible stories provide dynamic, doctrinally sound studies for cell groups.

Other names to describe cell groups are: home Bible study groups, Life-groups, Bible study nuclei, etc. These different programs have in common the fact that church members who live in the same geographic area are organized into cells or small groups and they then invite friends and relatives to study the Bible with them on a regular basis. Usually, the cell groups meet weekly, on the day and hour most convenient for the participants to have Bible Study and to fellowship.

Some cells are organized for people who have things in common other than geographic location. A same-profession cell group may be organized for medical doctors, or school teachers, or truck drivers, etc. A cell may be organized for people with similar life styles such as single adults, prisoners, young couples without children, middle age couples with an empty nest, athletes, etc. Edification cell groups are for Christians who study the Bible together and help one another grow toward spiritual maturity.

3.4 A place to plant new churches

Many Christians live a long distance from any evangelical church. Inviting friends and family to a home to sing and tell Bible stories is an excellent way to begin a new church. God used our family in this way to start one such church in Denver, Colorado, and five in Brazil.

A church planter may find a family willing to open up their home for Bible studies in a community that needs a new church.

4. The inexperienced preacher or Bible teacher should use Bible stories

Anyone who can tell a story or joke can learn to tell a Bible story, discover truths from the story, and make applications to the listeners. It is easier to study and interpret correctly a Bible story than a doctrinal text such as Paul's letters. The easiest sermon or Bible study to prepare has as its text a Bible story. The new leader who tells Bible story is less likely to misinterpret the Bible or fall into error. In addition, everyone loves a story. Consequently, the listeners or students will pay attention and the Word of God will be transmitted and understood. Bible stories should be used by beginning preachers and teachers.

5. Use Bible stories in a storying track, in a series, or as a solitary story

5.1 In a storying track

A **storying track** begins with the creation in Genesis; continues through the Old Testament; focuses on the life, death, resurrection and ascension of Jesus; continues through the Book of Acts; places the Epistles in their chronological order within Acts; and finishes with stories related to the end times.

The **Multiple Storying Track** is a cyclic plan for a group of stories to be told and retold to the same group of listeners for different purposes. Each storying cycle has its own distinct purpose. Stories emphasized in each of the tracks are chosen to meet the needs of the listeners whose spiritual condition places them within that track. The **Multiple Storying Track** develops several tracks. In this book, I emphasize three: the **Evangelistic Storying Track**, the **Discipling Storying Track** and the **Leadership Equipping Storying Track**.

The **Single Storying Track** presents one time a group of Bible stories in chronological order. With each story, truths are emphasized that connect with the needs of the listeners.

5.2 In a series of studies or sermons

Many possibilities exist for using Bible stories in a series. For example:
- Principal characters in Genesis;
- Events in the life of a key-person (for example: Abraham, David, Jesus, Peter or Paul);
- Miracles in the Old Testament;
- Great prophets;
- Key events in the life of Jesus;
- Parables of Jesus;
- Miracles of Jesus;
- People who talked alone with Jesus;
- People praised by Jesus;
- Events recorded in the Book of Acts;
- Events in the life of the early church;
- Events in the life of Paul.

5.3 As a solitary story

Solitary storytelling isolates a story to be presented to a specific group for a specific occasion. For example: on a certain Sunday, the preacher decides to use as the text for his sermon, Joseph in Potiphar's house.

6. Use situational Bible Storytelling

Take advantage of the numerous situations in which Bible Storytelling can be effective such as a funeral, a wedding, an invitation to visit the sick, a birthday party, an anniversary celebration. Tell one or more stories that are appropriate in the situation. For example: a young pastor was asked to speak at the funeral of an elderly lady. He told the story of Peter resurrecting Dorcas (Ac 9:36-42) and stated: "As the widow ladies showed Peter the clothes Dorcas had made, we are here to remember the deeds of Mrs. Bradford. Peter restored Dorcas to life and we are comforted during our grief because Mrs. Bradford's faith in Jesus will result in her resurrection to enjoy a new life."

7. Use Bible Storytelling to minister to specific target groups

Storytelling is effective with specific target groups such as the following:
- Prisoners;
- The uneducated, unskilled working class;
- Immigrant groups;
- The homeless;
- Migrant workers;
- Unchurched;
- Children;
- Yuppy baby boomers;
- Single adults (yet-to-marry and single-again);
- Single-parent households;
- Co-workers of the same profession;
- University students;
- International students;
- Internationals in a cross cultural situation;
- Apartment dwellers;
- Upper class (urban, suburban, or rural);
- Inner city;
- Vacationers in a resort area (beach ministry, campground, park area).

8. Use Bible Storytelling to test the acceptance of the Gospel

When the church plans to begin a new evangelistic outreach (whether a preaching point, home Bible study, or mission church), it is wise to test the openness of the people to the Gospel. Storytelling a series of Bible stories is helpful in discovering the interest of the people who live in the target area. If there is interest in hearing the stories and studying the Bible, then the project needs to go ahead. In the case of little interest, seek another location to plant an evangelistic outreach.

9. Use Bible stories to evangelize

Bible Storytelling is highly effective in evangelizing those with little biblical knowledge. Narrate selected Old Testament stories that emphasize the character of God and the sinful nature of man. Then present New Testament stories from the Gospels about the life of Jesus, people who followed him, his crucifixion and resurrection. Conclude with stories from Acts about those who were converted.

10. Use Bible stories to teach the new believer

Often the new convert has little biblical knowledge and is confused with the words used to explain the Bible at church. Bible stories communicate biblical truths while avoiding problems that create confusion or difficulty in understanding the truth.

In most churches, the only members who have an understanding of the chronological order of Bible stories are those who attended Sunday School as children. Teaching new Christians Bible stories in chronological order will give all believers the privilege of having a panoramic view of the Bible.

A church could create a Sunday School Class or a Weekday Bible Study Class to teach new Christians and new church members the Bible stories in chronological order. This could be a continually rotating class where a new group begins the study every six months, or even once a year.

11. Use Bible stories to resolve specific questions or needs

A Bible story can be used to resolve a specific question or spiritual need. For example:
- A listener believes that a criminal cannot be saved. The storyteller could use the story of the thief converted while on the cross or the story of Saul's conversion to explain that Jesus came to seek and save even criminals.
- A new believer returns to drinking and gets drunk. Some church members don't want to give the backslider another chance. The story of Jesus' encounter with Peter after his betrayal could be applied.

12. Use drama to communicate truths found in Bible stories

Drama can be used to make a Bible story come alive. Actors may act out a story told in the Bible, or they may invent a brief drama related to an incident recorded in the Bible. (See chapter 15, Using Drama with Bible Stories).

13. Use Bible stories to teach, preach and train in a church attended mainly by primary-oral communicators

Primary-oral communicators are those who depend upon the spoken word to receive information and to communicate their thoughts. Included within the oral communicators are the illiterates, those with limited reading abilities, and those who can read, but do so only if required.

Many churches or evangelistic outreach groups composed of primary-oral communicators do not have conditions to organize Sunday School classes with a different class for each age group. There may only be one Bible teacher for all age groups. The published Sunday School literature may not be understood. In an interior rural church in Brazil, I listened to the Sunday School teacher state: "Today we are studying one of the most important doctrines for Baptists, justification. I don't know what justification means, but the author of our quarterly says it is one of the most important doctrines for Baptists." Then the teacher stumbled over the words as he read the lesson from the quarterly. When he finished, neither he nor anyone else in the class understood the meaning of justification.

In such places, Bible stories can be used for the multiple purpose of teaching, preaching and training. I am going to present two plans for using Bible stories for the multiple purpose of teaching, preaching and training. One is for a church that has only one weekly meeting. The other is for the church that has several weekly meetings.

13.1 For the church with one weekly meeting, a multiple-purpose service to teach, preach and train

A single weekly meeting can use different activities in order to train new leaders, to teach the Bible and to preach. I discovered this approach while ministering in a semi-desert area of Brazil. I co-operated with lay preachers who traveled from a city to visit and lead worship services in distant villages. If the preachers from the city were unable to attend scheduled sessions, the congregations had no one to lead them. Although there were local Christians who could read, they had difficulty understanding the Sunday School literature. Therefore, we designed a multiple-purpose meeting using Bible stories.

The order of the weekly multiple-purpose meeting designed to train, teach and preach in one session is:
- The leader selects someone to begin with music and a prayer.
- The local Christian who is being trained is advised beforehand that he will be asked to tell a Bible story at the beginning of the worship service. Another person who is being trained may be invited to repeat the story or read the text where the story is found in the Bible.
- The leader then asks questions for the purpose of teaching the Bible story. An adult who has never been in a Bible study before should be able to answer all the questions. The leader asks most of the questions to the adults, but he includes some for the children.
- The congregation sings several songs that are related to truths taught by the Bible story.
- The leader preaches a sermon using the same Bible story as his text. He begins his sermon by retelling the story, then continues by explaining and applying life-lessons discovered in the story.

A WEEKLY MULTIPLE-PURPOSE MEETING TO TRAIN, TEACH AND PREACH	
GOAL	ORDER OF THE WORSHIP SERVICE
TRAIN	The one who is being trained to preach and teach is invited beforehand to tell the chosen Bible story. - The worship service begins with a song and a prayer. - The worship leader invites the one being trained to stand in front of the congregation and tell his Bible story. - Others may be invited to repeat or read the Bible story.
TEACH	The leader becomes a teacher by asking his listeners questions about the Bible story. He teaches by asking questions. The questions should be easy, so if someone is hearing the story for the first time, he will be able to answer.
PREACH	The congregation sings some songs, and then the leader preaches a sermon having as its text the Bible story that has been told and discussed.

13.2 For the church with multiple weekly meetings, the same Bible story can be used at each gathering, but each time for a different purpose

The church attended by oral communicators may have multiple weekly meetings. One encounter may be for Bible study, another for worship and preaching, another for prayer, and yet another for training. The same Bible story can be used at each meeting. I will give two examples of churches in Brazil using this approach.

One of the churches is led by Durval who has less than an elementary school education. Durval participated in a training program studying Bible stories in chronological sequence. Durval follows a plan for presenting the Bible in chronological order. His church schedules three weekly meetings. During the first meeting, on Sunday morning, Durval leads a one room Sunday School class. Great-grandparents are in the same class with their great-grandchildren. For Bible study he tells the Bible story featured for the week. Then he asks questions about the story. Some questions are for the children; others are for the adults. The second weekly meeting, on Sunday night, is for worship and preaching. After a time of prayer, testimony and singing, Durval retells the Bible story explored that morning, then he preaches his sermon using it as his text. The third weekly meeting is on Wednesday night, a time for prayer and review. After prayer, Durval invites those present to retell the Bible story featured the previous Sunday. After the story is retold by two or three people, other stories are retold by those present.

The other church has a seminary-trained pastor and is located on a large island in the Amazon region of Brazil. The church is pursuing the Bible stories in chronological order. The church has weekly Sunday morning Sunday School with separate classes for children and adults, but all study the same Bible story. That way the entire family is studying the same story. For the evening worship, the pastor retells the story utilized on Sunday morning and then preaches, using the story as his text. For the Tuesday night prayer meeting at the church building, various people retell the story emphasized the previous Sunday, and other stories previously examined. On other week-nights, church members go to neighboring villages to teach or preach the Bible story adopted for the week.

14. Use a Church-Planting Multiple Bible-Storying Track

A Church-Planting Bible-Storying Track is used to begin an evangelistic outreach for the purpose of planting a new church. A **Storying Track** begins with the creation in Genesis; continues through the Old Testament; treats the life, death, resurrection and ascension of Jesus; continues through the Book of Acts; places the Epistles in their chronological order within Acts; and finishes with stories related to the end times.

The **Church-Planting Multiple Storying Track** is a plan for a group of stories to be told and retold to the same group of listeners for different purposes. It is cyclic in that some stories are told more than one time. Each storying cycle has its own distinct purpose. The **Church Planting Multiple Storying Track** develops at least three tracks: the **Evangelistic or Basic Storying Track**, the **Discipling Storying Track** and the **Leadership Equipping Storying Track**.

TRACK # 1:   Evangelistic or Basic Storying Track

The Evangelistic or Basic Storying Track uses stories that give a general vision of the Bible, and serve as a foundation for non-follower of Jesus to understand the Gospel.

The church planter with one Bible Storytelling encounter per week should prepare to spend between two and nine months with the first Track. Summarize, without entering into details, several stories in one storytelling session. For example during one storytelling session, the church planter could give a summary of the lives of Abraham, Jacob and Joseph and briefly refer to principal life-lessons discovered in each life.

TRACK #2:   Discipling Bible Storying Track (for new believers and Christians with limited biblical knowledge)

New converts and Christians with limited biblical knowledge receive a more detailed telling of the stories with more time spent on life-lessons discovered from them. With the first Storying Track, several stories would have been summarized during a single encounter. For the Second Storying Track, the church planter will retell many of the stories already narrated while entering into more details with each one. For example: if during the first Storying Track he gave a summary of Abraham, Jacob and Joseph's lives during one encounter, with the second Storying Track he could take more than one encounter to consider each of their stories. Some stories not mentioned the first time around could be inserted into their proper chronological order. Likewise, greater details will be given to treat life-lessons discovered from each story.

The church planter could plan on spending from six months to two years with the Second Storying Track.

TRACK #3:   Maturing Christians and Leadership Equipping Bible Storying Track (for maturing Christians and leaders)

The Maturing Christians and Leadership Equipping Bible Storying Track brings together a group of stories for teaching doctrine and training mature Christians. Bible text not presented in story form will be taught to give complete knowledge of the Scripture. Special attention will be made to train mature Christians with leadership abilities to evangelize, teach, preach, organize Bible study groups and plant new churches.

During the third Bible Storying Track, review stories already told while adding new ones as needed. Introduce Old Testament poetic literature, New Testament Epistles and Revelation. Provide doctrinal studies using Bible stories, and then provide analytical doctrinal studies using all of the Bible.

When the church planter begins the Third Storying Track, he is faced with an open-ended opportunity to teach or preach God's Word, using all the Scripture and different approaches. But if he is working with predominantly oral communicators, following the chronological storying tracks will always be the principal method used. Repeatedly following chronological storying tracks preserves the integrity of the Bible for people with limited or no reading skills.

NOTE: For more information on communicating Bible stories in chronological order, see the chapters in this book on (17) **Chronological Bible Storying Tracks**, (18) **Organizing the Storying Track**, and (19) **List of Bible Stories with References**.

CONCLUSION

Bible stories communicate God's messages. There are many ways that storytellers, preachers, and teachers can use Bible stories. Some uses for Bible stories were mentioned in this chapter. Use Bible stories, and you will discover other uses as well.

BIBLE STORYTELLING WITH ORAL COMMUNICATORS

BIBLE STORYTELLING WITH PRIMARY-ORAL COMMUNICATORS

Basically, two types of oral communicators exist in the world today: primary-oral communicators and secondary-oral communicators. Primary-oral communicators cannot read. Secondary-oral communicators can read but only do so for work or study; seldom for pleasure. Primary-oral communicators sit around a flickering fire listening to stories and telling stories. Secondary-oral communicators sit in front of a flickering screen, watching and listening to a story.

1. Types of Primary-Oral Communicators

Different classifications of primary-oral communicators exist, but they all learn orally and they communicate orally. They gain knowledge through hearing the spoken word; they communicate their ideas through the spoken word.

1.1 Illiterate-illettered

The illiterate-illettered lives in a culture without a written language and is untouched by writing in any form. He has never been exposed to the letters of the alphabet and has yet to see a written word. The illiterate-illettered includes tribal people, without a written alphabet. Also included would be people who belong to a culture with education and books available, but they personally do not have access to the written word. They live in rural, isolated communities away from the conveyances of civilization. Their homes do not contain cans with the words: NESTLE or MILK. They don't live close to buildings that have signs with the words: POST OFFICE, POLICE, PHARMACY or RESTAURANT.

1.2 Illiterate-lettered

A culture with a written language also has a residual oral-culture operating within it. The illiterate-lettered does not read, but lives among people who read and write. Letters and words are constantly within sight, even if they are not understood. A group of letters cannot be read, but certain letters when grouped together serve as symbols. The group of letters *POST OFFICE* symbolizes the place where friends send letters. The group of letters *BANK* symbolizes the place where a check is exchanged for money. The group of letters *DRUG STORE* symbolizes the place where medicine is bought.

1.3 Semi-literate Oral Communicator

The semi-literate has some education but reads poorly. He is able to read and write on an elementary level. He has difficulty understanding unfamiliar written material and communicates poorly when writing. He is able to read when working with familiar documents and familiar ideas. He only reads and writes when required or if the subject has special interest. He will fill out forms, write checks, copy recipes, sign his name, occasionally write a letter, and read when the subject has special interest. The semi-literate communicator prefers to learn through hearing the spoken word and to communicate his ideas through the spoken word.

My father went to a school that only offered the first five grades. He could read and write. He read a weekly newspaper and a monthly magazine for farmers. He would fill out his tax forms once a year, make notes when a farm worker borrowed money, and write checks. But he would read only when required, or if the subject were of special interest. I never saw my father reading a book.

Some literates have regressed to become semi-literates. In school they learned to read. When they left school, they avoided reading. Lack of contact with the written word resulted in their regressing to where they function like an illiterate. The semi-literate may be able to pronounce words on a written page, but has difficulty explaining what was read.

2. Some Characteristics of the Oral Communicator

Many oral communicators are highly intellectual. They hear better than the literate and remember more details of what they hear. The oral communicator is forced to develop his memory in order to survive.

2.1 The primary-oral communicator knows only what he can recall

In an oral-culture, one knows what he can recall. What is not remembered is not known. A fact exist only if someone is able to recall it. A story exists only when it is being told or if a local storyteller is capable of narrating it. Two of my ancestors fought in the Civil War. One wrote letters that are still in the family, the other did not write. Though the latter did not write, my grandparents kept his memory alive through stories. My grandparents died when I was a child, and I have forgotten their stories. Since no one wrote down my grandparents' stories, the life of that civil war ancestor is forgotten, and little is known about him other than the information on his tombstone.

2.2 Oral Communicators often express thoughts through word-picture proverbs

Oral communicators express thoughts through stories and word-picture proverbs. Word-picture proverbs are short sayings that paint pictures. "One picture is worth a thousand words," and the oral communicator can paint a picture with short sayings. Examples of word-picture proverbs:
- The person who was bitten by a snake is afraid of a short rope.
- He is as hard to find as a goose in a snow storm.
- He was caught with his pants down.
- Love is like the sun. A cloud can hide it, but can't put it out.
- Women are like highways: the more curves, the more danger.
- He's so low down he can sit on a cigarette and dangle his feet.
- He is like a match: when he gets hot he loses his head.
- I would rather be called "square" than see my daughter rounded out.
- Give your tongue a vacation and work with your head.
- The man who beats his horse will soon be walking.

Much wisdom is expressed in word-picture proverbs. In fact, the wisest man of his time sought to discover proverbs and write them down. Solomon, the author of Ecclesiastes, called himself "The Teacher." "The Teacher" pondered and searched out and set in order many proverbs" (Ec 12:9-10). The result is the book of Proverbs.

2.3 Oral communicators use concrete-logic

People who use concrete logic talk about people, things, events and experiences that can be seen, felt, heard, touched, tasted or smelled. Concrete-logic refers to an event, thing or person that is either real or fictitious. The concrete element may be some ingredient from nature; it may be an allegory or it may still be a reference to behavior. Concrete-logic works more or less in the following way:
- Subjects are known in connection with life experiences. *Examples of life experiences: experiences from pain to well-being, from sadness to happiness, from fear to courage, from good to the evil, from sickness to good health, from experience of sin to experience of a holy life, and so on.*
- Subject matter is emphasized by relating it to a life experience. *An example: people need to resist temptation.*
- A story is told involving people who illustrate the subject, and life-lessons are extracted from the story. *Examples of stories that relate to people's need to resist temptation: Eve's experience with the snake in the Garden; Joseph with Potiphar's wife; Daniel in Babylonia; Peter during Jesus' trial.* Instead of a story, a comparison to an event or an example from nature may be used to illustrate the subject.
- Then life-lessons related to the subject are formulated. *Examples of life-lessons that relate to people's need to resist temptation: always be ready to resist temptations;* or *knowing how people in the Bible faced temptation helps us resist temptation.*
- Usually life-lessons are applied to the reality of life. *For example: during these times of financial stress we must resist the temptation to make easy money by selling drugs or stolen material;* or *don't have sex outside of marriage.*

2.4 Oral communicators are storytellers

Oral communicators are storytellers. Thoughts are expressed in stories of actions and events. An oral communicator was asked if a man named William could be trusted. The oral communicator told about William's finding a billfold with money. William had a friend read to him the name and address of the owner. Then he went to the owner's home and refused to give the billfold to anyone but the owner. William felt insulted when he was offered a reward.

An oral communicator giving a speech would probably mention some word-picture proverbs, mention some event and tell some stories. The educated communicator may think that the stories have casual connections or he sees no connection between the stories. However, other oral communicators will see some connections. The oral communicator will use repetitions. Two or three stories may illustrate the same truth. Some sentences will be repeated, or the same ideas will be repeated using different words.

An oral communicator will express religious beliefs with stories and/or short proverbs. An evangelical would tell the story of his conversion, describe what he does at church, tell how he practices his religion and describe the traditions of his church. An oral communicator would probably emphasize such activities as family devotions, prayer before meals, church attendance, prayers God answered, and he would tell about God helping him in time of need. He would rarely mention convictions and doctrine in the form of propositions.

2.5 Oral communicators talk about feelings in connection to life stories

The oral communicator doesn't speak about feelings as abstract entities. He expresses feelings in connection with life histories that emphasize actions and events. For example, subjects such as love, faith, patience, truth, falsehood, pain, desire, hope and others are translated into actions, stories, and concrete verbal experiences. Thus, an oral communicator would not speak about a mother's love as an abstract subject. He would tell a story about a mother who is loving. An oral communicator does not speak about faith as an abstract subject, but about a person experiencing faith or how a certain person shows he has faith. The subject of patience is not talked about, but the conduct of a certain person who has patience is discussed.

An oral communicator talking about an abusive father might mention his hostility when his father beat him, and his reaction of running away. However, he would not mention the fact that he hated his father without describing his father's abusive behavior. It would be rare for him to speak about an emotion outside the context of a story.

2.6 Oral communicators depend upon the redundant

An oral communicator depends upon the redundant. He will repeat the same thing or something similar several times. This helps both the speaker keep on track and the hearer remember the key thoughts. Example of being redundant: "It was raining hard. It was pouring down rain. You couldn't see because of the rain."

Repetition is essential to retain knowledge in an oral-culture. Files, notes, and books are not available to help preserve acquired knowledge. In an oral culture, information, once acquired, must be constantly repeated or it will be lost. Knowledge not repeated aloud soon disappears. Thus, the oral communicator must invest great energy in repeating new data.

The person who teaches or preaches to oral communicators should repeat new information several times, and he should help his listeners repeat the same new knowledge. A Bible story that is told for the first time needs to be repeated soon afterwards, and the listeners need to be given opportunity to repeat the same story.

2.7 Oral communicators are trained by apprenticeship

Oral communicators are trained by apprenticeship instead of going to school, studying a book or listening to teachers' explanations. A youth learns hunting by hunting with experienced hunters. The apprentice cabinet maker learns by observing a master cabinet maker, helping the master cabinet maker, and making cabinets while the master watches and makes suggestions.

Oral communicators do not retain information by note-taking. They learn by apprenticeship: by watching, participating and being observed. In apprenticeship, the expert shows the apprentice how to do a task, watches as the apprentice practices portions of the task, and then the expert turns over more and more responsibility until the apprentice is proficient enough to accomplish the task by himself. Trades are learned by apprenticeships, which means observation and practice, with only minimal verbalized explanation.

Steps to apprenticeship training:
- **Modeling**: the master performs a task with the apprentice observing. Some explanation is given to help the apprentice understand how the task is being done. The master shows the apprentice how to do a task.
- **Coaching**: the master becomes a mentor who coaches the apprentice through different activities necessary to do the task. When coaching, the master observes the apprentice carrying out a task and offers hints, feedback, modeling, reminders, and new tasks aimed at improving his performance. Coaching is the process of overseeing the apprentice's learning.
- **Fading**: as the apprentice improves his skills, the master decreases his coaching and gives the apprentice more and more responsibility. The apprentice receives responsibilities away from the watchful eyes of the master.

The steps to apprenticeship training: modeling, coaching and fading are repeated with each new skill taught. They are repeated and repeated and repeated. Repetition is essential to the apprentice training. File systems, written notes and books are not available to help retain knowledge. Knowledge or a skill, once acquired, must be constantly repeated or it will be lost.

The steps to apprenticeship are taught in a social setting. The apprentice has the opportunity of observing other apprentices perform their task, and when the master coaches one, all are learning.

3. Literate Communicator

The literate communicator depends upon the written word. He learns by study. Study includes reading, making notes when listening and organizing thoughts on paper. He makes notes to remember important facts. He reads to discover facts.

Thoughts are analytically based. Presentations are outlined and structured. Items are usually connected. The literate communicator uses theory, propositional thought and discourse. Discussion is usually about ideas. Beliefs are usually expressed through doctrinal statements.

The educated literate communicator usually uses logical reasoning. The logical reasoning is also known as lineal reasoning. Logical reasoning treats the subjects based on ideas, concepts, beliefs, or qualities. The following is an example of the way logical reasoning works:
- A person makes for himself a classification of subjects *(for example: systematic theology)*.
- Each aspect of the subject is given an abstract title *(for example: justification)*.
- One elaborates on the subject in an abstract manner *(for example: definition of justification)*.
- A series of rationalizations to explain the subject are given, all in an abstract nature *(for example, what justification is, what it is not, reasons the subject justification is important to the Christian, and so on)*.

With the passing of time, logical reasoning began to characterize the thought process of western society. The Greek and Latin culture, especially the Greek, influenced the Western society to depend upon logical reasoning. This resulted in the educational system, from kindergarten through the university being based on logical reasoning. The same applies to systematic theology and the curriculum used in Sunday School literature, in Bible colleges, in seminaries, and in Bible institutes.

The literate communicator is oral-dysfunctional. The more he studies in school, the more oral-dysfunctional he becomes.

4. Oral communicators and literate communicators use different thought processes

The oral communicator and the literate educated-communicator don't think alike. They don't elaborate ideas, structure their reasoning, or organize data in the same way.

The oral communicator uses concrete-reasoning and works with stories, history, facts, events and real things, while the literate communicator generally uses logical reasoning and works with ideas. Thus, the oral communicator navigates the world of stories and concrete objects or events, while the educated literate communicator navigates the world of ideas.

ORAL COMMUNICATOR VERSUS LITERATE COMMUNICATOR

ORAL COMMUNICATOR	LITERATE COMMUNICATOR
Experience-oriented. What has been experienced by oneself, one's community and one's elders is what is real. Emphasis is on doing what one can do and enjoying the moment.	Task/Goal-oriented. Emphasis is on achieving specific objectives that have been clarified in writing.
Story based	Analytical based: thought / idea
Speech: Stories and/or proverbs. Stories and happenings mentioned, often with casual connections.	Speech: Outlined. Structured. All items usually connected. Uses theory, propositional thought and discourse.
Uses lots of repetition.	Critical of repetition.
Functional-knowledge. Information is desired that will enable one to maintain relationships, be accepted in the community, and complete the job at hand.	Factual-knowledge. Seeks the facts that will enable the person to understand details, analyze, organize, control, manage; and if needed, change the structure or system.
Concrete: people, things, events and experiences that can be seen, felt, heard, touched or smelled	Logical: abstract ideas, concepts, beliefs, or qualities
Intuitive	Logical
Relational. Seeks to achieve what is expected or required by the community.	Pragmatic. Seeks to get the assigned or desired task done. Values what works, or what was agreed in writing.
Word is bond. A person's identity is related to doing and being what he says.	Put focus on specific written agreement. Written promises can be renegotiated. What is written is more important than what was said or meant. What is written is not binding because it can be renegotiated.
Life stories: action / events. "What happened to you? What did you do?"	Thoughts, feelings, introspection. "How do you feel about what happened?"
Learn by apprenticeship.	Learn by study.
Beliefs expressed by stories.	Beliefs expressed through doctrinal statements.
Concerns: concrete life based	Concerns: psychological / feelings based
Morality: Personal integrity is important. Relational obligations are determined by what ones culture and community expect.	Morality: It is essential to fulfill formal, stated legal agreements that are dependent upon what is known at the time. More information, or a change in the situation, can change the obligation. Then legal agreements can be renegotiated.
Religion: emphasizes traditions, practice and actions.	Religion: emphasizes verbal expressions and doctrinal statements.

A detailed analysis of the communication styles of Jesus and Paul shows that Jesus was an oral communicator while Paul was an educated literate communicator.

Jesus started with illustrations and stories when he taught. Usually, when Jesus was asked a question about abstract concepts, he began his answer with concrete reasoning.

Jesus was asked: "Is it lawful to give a poll tax to Caesar, or not?" Jesus answered: "Show me the coin used for the poll-tax ..." and then concluded: "Render to Caesar the things that are Caesar's; and to God the things that are God's" (Mt 22.17-19). A doctor of the Law asked Jesus: "Who is my neighbor?" Jesus didn't give a logical and finished answer. He narrated the parable of the Good Samaritan (Lk 10.25-37).

However, Paul's writings were clearly the language of a well educated literate communicator. It seems that Paul worked at translating the Gospel written in the storytelling rhetoric of oral communicators into logical reasoning language used by educated literate communicators. He translated the ideas expressed in the Gospel stories into logical categories of Greek philosophy, in a contextualization effort. Today, those who work with oral communicators need to do the opposite: take Paul's writings and convert them to stories and/or proverbs, and use repetition.

An analysis of the speech styles of Jesus and Paul could be summarized as following:

SPEECH OF JESUS (Mt 13)	SPEECH OF PAUL (Gal 4:1-7)
Focus: Images, stories	**Focus:** Ideas
Argument: Concrete events and objects	**Argument:** Abstract ideas
Development: Circular	**Development:** Linear
Speech: Starts with stories about events, objects, and/or people to illustrate thoughts.	**Speech:** Starts with an abstract idea and argues his thoughts using analytical reasoning.

In sketch form, the structure and the development of both speech styles are presented like this by the author:

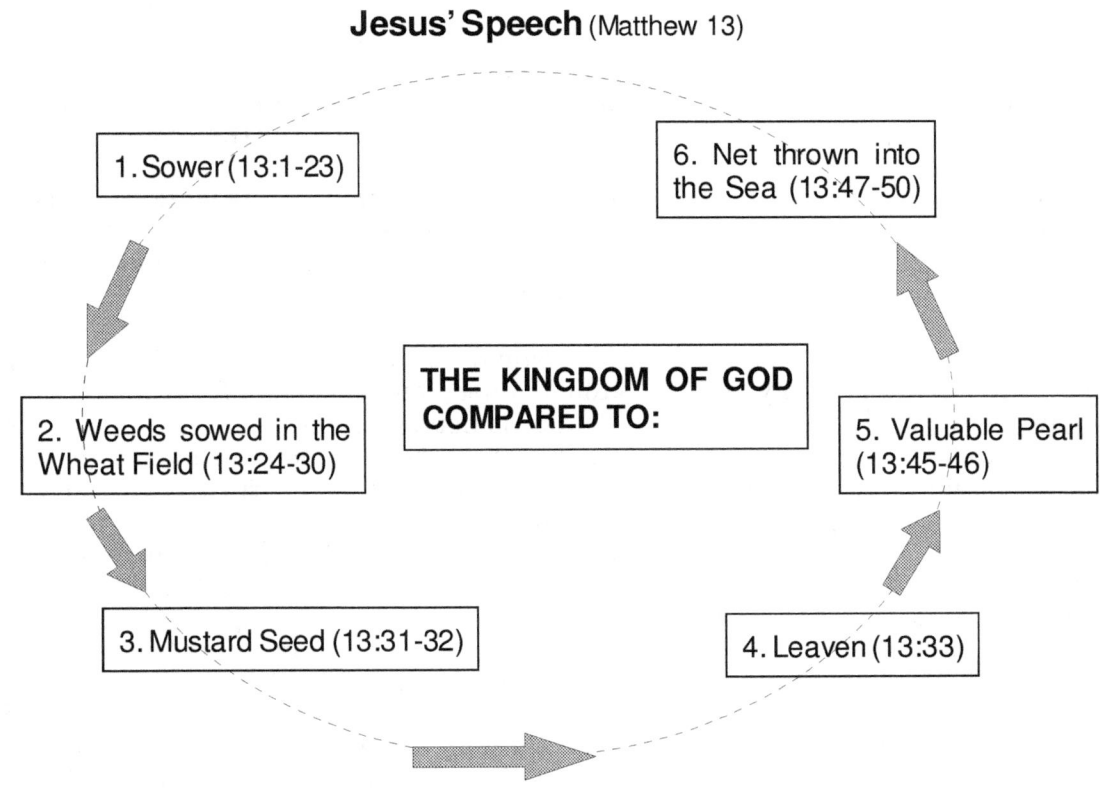

Bible Storytelling Tools © Jackson Day

Paul's Speech (Galatians 4:1-11)

Theme: **THOSE WITH FAITH IN JESUS ARE SONS AND NOT SLAVES**

1. Man's condition under the Law (4:1-3)
   - 1.1 The man under the Law is a slave (4:1)
   - 1.2 The man under the Law is subject to the elemental things of the world (4:3)

2. The condition of the man who is in Christ (4:4-7)
   - 2.1 When the fulness of time came, God sent His Son (4:4)
   - 2.2 The man in Christ is redeemed from slavery (4:5)
   - 2.3 The man in Christ is an adopted son (4:5-6)
   - 2.4 The man in Christ has the Spirit (4:6)
   - 2.5 The man in Christ calls God "Father" (4:6)
   - 2.6 The man in Christ is an heir (4:7)
   - 2.7 The man in Christ knows God and is known by God (4:9)

3. Argument: it is absurd to return to slavery (4:8-11)

Jesus' speech is circular. He told stories about concrete objects, events and people, and he uses repetition, which is characteristic of the reasoning of an oral communicator. However, Paul's speech is lineal, basically composed of analytical thoughts, abstract logical reasoning. This is characteristic of a well educated literate communicator.

The oral communicator works with objects, facts and events while the literate communicator works with ideas. Thus, the oral communicator navigates the world of stories while the literate communicator navigates the world of ideas.

5. The oral communicator needs to be taught the Bible

Primary-oral communicators make up about 70% to 80% of the world's population. Primary-oral communicators learn orally and communicate orally. Primary-oral communicators gain religious beliefs mainly through hearing stories that express convictions and hearing others narrate personal religious experiences.

The dependence upon the printed page; the use of printed books and tracks; and the use of the copier and the computer printer has resulted in the church neglecting primary-oral communicators. Most evangelical churches depend upon the written word to evangelize, teach, and train. Therefore, primary-oral communicators have few opportunities to be evangelized; if evangelized, they have little opportunity to be taught the doctrines of the church; and they have almost no opportunity to be trained as leaders.

Primary-oral communicators need to hear the Bible stories. God reveals himself through stories. Theology lives in the stories about God and his interactions with people.

Repetition is essential to retaining a Bible story in an oral-culture. The primary-oral communicator will not refer to the Bible to refresh his memory. In an oral culture, a Bible story, once acquired, must be constantly repeated or it will be lost. Therefore, spiritual leaders who minister to oral communicators must repeat over and over the same stories.

6. Topical studies organized in outline form are inappropriate for communicating with the primary-oral communicator

Primary-oral communicators can be taught and trained, but the use of outlined topical studies is not an adequate method to use with them. Primary-oral communicators can learn any doctrine that is illustrated with stories, narrative accounts of historical events, and parables. An oral communicator can be a leader of others; he can learn and then teach any doctrine through storytelling.

Primary-oral communicators have difficulty understanding topical and outlined studies. The western culture uses a topical outline analysis to explain all subjects. Those who studied in a school, learned abstract topics organized in outline form. Educated evangelical Christians tend to use the outline method for Bible study, teaching and preaching. Pastors who studied in a Bible institute or seminary were taught to analyze a text and organize it in an outline. Those who write Sunday School literature use topical outlines about abstract ideas. The result is that most preaching and Bible study use a method that is difficult for oral communicators to comprehend.

7. Primary-oral communicators can be evangelized, taught and trained using Bible stories

Primary-oral communicators can understand any doctrine that is explained using Bible stories, narration of historical events and stories relevant to their culture. Primary-oral communicators hear better than the literate. Their memory records details that pass unperceived to the literate who studied in a school. This gives the primary-oral communicator unique abilities to learn and recount stories to others. Evangelical Christians need to realize that primary-oral communicators are capable of understanding any biblical truth that is illustrated orally with Bible stories.

The number of primary-oral communicators in the world is great. Civilized, first-world countries have large numbers of illiterates, semi-literates and others who are primary-oral communicators. In most third-world countries the number of primary-oral communicators is much higher.

The preacher/teacher who presents the Gospel to primary-oral communicators in the same way as he does to literate communicators is using wrong methods and insulting his target group. Evangelicals need to realize that primary-oral communicators have a different style to express wisdom, to think and to decide on the important things of life. Where people use logical-reasoning, the Gospel proclamation can start with Paul's writing that uses logical-reasoning. However, with people who use concrete-reasoning, it is essential to begin the proclamation of the Gospels with biblical stories.

The teacher's skill is not based upon what he articulates but on what the students learn. The effectiveness of the sermon is not determined by the preacher's words, but by biblical truths the listeners learn, understand, and apply to their lives. When the oral communicator does not understand, the blame should be placed upon the teacher/preacher for not communicating effectively instead of accusing the oral communicator of having inferior intellect. When I was a boy on my father's farm I learned to hunt rabbits. When I shot above the rabbit, I was not considered smarter than the rabbit, but was accused of being a poor shot. The preacher/teacher who communicates above the understanding level of his listeners is not intelligent; he is a poor shot.

The secret to communicating biblical truths to primary-oral communicators is to seldom use analytical texts and topical outlined studies. Use Bible stories and illustrate abstract biblical truths with contemporary stories about objects and events.

8. Bible stories told in chronological order give the primary-oral communicator an Oral Bible

The best method to transmit truths to primary-oral communicators is to follow the historical sequence presented in the Bible. Tell the stories in the order that the events took place. Begin with the creation in Genesis and proceed through the Old Testament. Then present the birth, life, death, resurrection and ascension of Jesus. Move ahead through the Book of Acts. Present the Epistles, explaining how they fit into the chronological order of events recorded in the Book of Acts. Finish with stories related to the end times. The Christian faith is based upon the great acts revealed by God himself, beginning with the creation and climaxing with the life, death, resurrection and ascension of Christ, continuing with the expansion of the Church, and firming up by the expectation of the second coming of Christ. The primary-oral communicator receives an Oral Bible when stories are narrated in the chronological sequence.

To give the primary-oral communicator an Oral Bible, it is necessary to separate Bible Storytelling from Bible interpretation. Most educated preachers and teachers explain the story while narrating it. They must separate Bible Storytelling from explanation, teaching or preaching.

The reason for narrating without interpretation is to enable the oral communicators to discern between the biblical story and the interpretation done by the preacher/teacher. After telling the story, discuss it, interpret it, explain it, teach it, or preach it. The only Bible the primary-oral communicator can use is an Oral Bible. The primary-oral communicator gains an Oral Bible when he hears Bible stories told in chronological order.

Observations

Academic study of faith and theology is essential to expressing one's faith in a literate culture. It is an outcome of loving God with all one's heart, mind and soul. However, expressing theology with academic expressions escalates the Gospel to a level where only those who are at home in the literate culture understand it.

My childhood years were spent on my father's farm. Henry, an illiterate farm hand, worked for my father and was our closest neighbor. As a child, I would sit on Henry's front porch and listen to his stories. When I was 14 years old, my father died and we moved from the farm to my mother's home town. After I graduated from a university, I returned to my childhood home and visited Henry. He could not understand me; neither could I understand him. My visit embarrassed both of us. While I was studying, I lost the ability to communicate to an illiterate who had been a close friend. I had become a deficient oral communicator.

A Brazilian pastor friend of mine came from a rural village that only had an elementary school. My friend left home to continue studying and now has a doctoral degree in philosophy. He regrets that when he returns to visit his home place, his family and former friends are unable to understand him. His education has eliticized his speech, and his family can't understand him when he talks about his faith.

A seminary professor in Brazil stated: "Regretfully, the more education some pastors receive, the fewer people are saved by their preaching." He was not accusing educated pastors of losing their evangelistic zeal. He was saying that the more some pastors study, the more complicated words they use. As a result, preaching that is not understood does not produce transformed lives. Some educated pastors forget how to speak the common lingo of oral communicators.

I do not intend to belittle education nor to criticize theological education. I give thanks to God for my university and seminary education. I value theological teaching and was a professor for eleven years at the Baptist Theological Seminary in Brasília, the capital city of Brazil. I have been a guest professor at other seminaries. Evangelical church leaders need to study and read books. However, preachers with academic training need to understand that teaching methods used in an academic institution are inappropriate for listeners who seldom read. Methods that communicate to high school and university graduates fail when used with oral communicators. Those who preach and teach the Bible to oral communicators need to adapt and use means that put across biblical truths to them.

Evangelical primary-oral communicators need to be trained to teach and preach. Jesus chose fishermen with limited education and trained them using the apprentice method. He mainly taught by telling stories. He used much repetition. The apostles lived and traveled with Jesus, observing everything he said and did. Later he sent them out to minister. The educated pastor who teaches primary-oral communicators by imitating his seminary professors will be frustrated. However, a pastor can train oral communicators by using the apprentice method.

I have prepared a book in Portuguese, the English title of which would be: BIBLICAL NARRATIVES: TRAINING GUIDE. The book gives suggestions to pastors on methods for training evangelical oral communicators. It uses Bible stories, the apprenticeship approach, and lots of repetition. Many spiritual leaders with limited education have been trained using those suggestions. Some are church planters; others are the primary spiritual leaders of their churches. Oral communicators can be trained to function as spiritual leaders if methods appropriate to their communication style are used.

NOTE: For more information on communicating Bible stories in chronological order, see the chapters in this book: (17) **Chronological Bible Storying Tracks**; (18) **Organizing the Storying Track**; and (19) **List of Bible Stories with References**.

BIBLE STORYTELLING WITH SECONDARY-ORAL COMMUNICATORS

The post-modern cultural shift has moved many educated people into oral communication styles. The primary-oral communicator cannot read. The secondary-oral communicator can read but only does so for work or study, seldom for pleasure. Secondary-oral communicators do not read the news; they watch the news or get it off the internet. They do not read books; they listen to a CD recording or wait to see the movie.

Many who are able to read and write have been swept into the electronic-oral culture. They depend upon the telephone, radio, television, computer and DVD for communication. Electronic-oral communicators avoid writing letters but send e-mails, faxes, use phones, or send text messages. Electronic-oral communicators can read and write; however, they prefer to communicate with oral or visual forms of communicating.

The terms post-literate, aliterate, and secondary-oral communicator are used to describe the person who is capable of reading with understanding but seldom reads for pleasure.

Many people who are called "literate" and who are part of the technological world are preferred oral-communicators. Recently, I was in the home of a young man who has a master's degree. He said: "After I graduated from the university, I have not read a book. I only open a book if my job requires me to read something." The young man has six monitors attached to his computer so he can do multiple tasks at the same time. The television is always on when he is at home.

Another professional man with multiple university degrees told me: "If you see me reading, you can know that I am studying."

We live during a period of history and technology where a majority of the world's population is still in the pre-literate oral communication era. However, many high school and university graduates are in the post-literate information age. They have a base of literacy, but their primary means of learning has shifted back to oral and visual media.

The primary-oral communicator is unable to read or write. The secondary-oral communicator is found in a high-technological culture that depends upon the existence of the printed word. Reading and writing is necessary for the high-technological culture to function. The secondary-oral communicator depends on electronic audio and visual communications (multimedia). The electronic media sustains and encourages orality with devices such as the telephone, radio, television, VCR, DVD, etc.

The printed word (books, newspapers, magazines, etc.) is no longer the primary means of obtaining and dispensing knowledge for secondary-oral communicators. The electronic media (radio, television, computer, phone, etc.) is now their primary means of obtaining and sharing knowledge. The result is that many who have years of formal education are post-literate.

The literate person who is not getting information from a face-to-face encounter is getting it from the printed word – from newspapers, magazines, and books. The post-literate person who is not getting information from a face-to-face encounter is getting it from the electronic media. Telephones, radios, televisions, and computers have replaced the printed word as the secondary-oral communicator's major means of non-face-to-face communication.

The human race has lived in four communication eras:

1st Oral: The primary form of communication in the oral era was the human voice.
2nd Script: The invention of the alphabet enabled people to communicate through the written word.
3rd Printed word: The printing press was invented by Gutenberg in the 1450's. The printing press utilized alphabetic moveable type and machinery, and made it possible for the printed word to be mass produced.
4th Electronic media: The invention of the telegraph in 1837 marked the first invasion into the world of print. Inventions that have moved this era forward include devices such as the telephone, the phonograph, the photograph, radio, movies, television, computers, VCR, DVD, etc.

We are living in the third communication change in the history of mankind.

1st	The first communication change was from an oral culture to an alphabetic and manuscript culture, where only a privileged minority was literate. The change took thousands of years.
2nd	The second communication change was from the age of the alphabetic and manuscript culture to mechanism and print. The change began with the invention of the Gutenberg Press in the 1450's and took hundreds of years.
3rd	The third communication change was from the literate world of print to the age of electronic communication. This change started with the invention of the telegraph in 1837. The change began to move rapidly in the 1960's with the increased popularity of television. The year 1985 is significant as the year of a major shift from the printed culture to the electronic culture. The shift is marked by it being the first year when more videocassettes were checked out/rented from video stores than there were books checked out of libraries.

THE RELATIONSHIP BETWEEN COMMUNICATION FORMS AND THE JUDEO-CHRISTIAN RELIGION			
Culture	**Worship**	**Communication System**	**Architecture**
Oral	Animal sacrifices	Storytelling	Outdoor altars
Oral/Script, literacy for privileged few	Animal sacrifices	Storytelling and prophecy	Tabernacle/Temple
Oral/Script, emerging literacy	Animal sacrifices	Scroll	Centralized Temple
	Scripture reading and teaching by literate men		Local communities meeting in small groups at synagogues
Oral/Script, literacy restricted to the elite	Scripture reading, chanting, and mass	Manuscript	Cathedrals in urban centers
Literate, dependence upon the printed word	■Small discussion Bible study groups ■Scripture reading and sermon for a larger group	Printed books, magazines, and newspapers	Small church buildings
Post-literate (electronic media)	■Pre-packaged Bible study on life-issues or ethical-issues ■For worship: storytelling and screens	■Programed workbooks or digital programs for Bible study ■Electronic digital for worship	■Large church building to mega-church campuses ■Alternative church: life-style or like-minded community cell groups that don't utilize buildings ■People who stay home and watch a church service on TV

Children who were entertained at home by watching television instead of listening to parents read and who played with video games instead of reading comic books, grew up to become the post-literate generation. They learn and process knowledge in terms of media, such as television, radio, telephone, and computer. The media involves basic literacy, but requires more visuals, graphics and click-skills. In the post-literate society, writing and reading are of value, but only because they facilitate manipulation of electronic media equipment.

The literate person is able to read, understand, and express himself with the written word. The post-literate person has not lost these abilities. The post-literate prefers the electronic media to receive information and to express himself. The post-literate can read but is disinclined to seek information from literary sources. He seldom reads for pleasure. He only reads when required to do so or if the subject is of great interest. The post-literate is able to read, but increasingly chooses not to do so. The post-literate is a secondary-oral communicator.

A growing number of Americans associates reading almost exclusively with the drudgery of school assignments or job requirements. They see little connection between reading and what they perceive to be "real life." Many post-literates would consider that "reading for pleasure" is comparable to "brushing your teeth for pleasure." Reading for pleasure is not an option for them.

LITERATE	POST-LITERATE
MODERNIST	**POST-MODERNIST**
The literate world is a child of typography.	The post-literate digital-world is a child of electronic media.
The printed page (books, magazines, papers) is the dominant medium. Print is a culture of the eye.	Electronic media (telephone, radio, TV, computers, DVD, VCR, etc.) is the dominant medium. Digital is a culture of the eye and ear.
The printed page is silent.	Return to oral communication. The electronic media is oral and visual.
Printed language is guided by rationality, deductive organization and logic.	Digital is the language of image, suggestions, story and emotion.
Print, is high in data and ideas, low in physical/sensate participation.	Digital is high in physical/sensate participation (sight, sound).
Factual knowledge involves the facts that will enable the person to understand details, analyze, organize, control, manage; and if needed, change the structure or system.	Functional knowledge involves information that will enable the person to maintain desired relationships, advance in chosen career, obtain desired possessions and acquire recognition.
Speech is outlined linear development of ideas. All topics are related. It emphasizes abstract ideas, concepts, beliefs, or qualities. It's linear, logical, and analytical.	Speech stitches stories together. It uses concrete logic about people, things, events and experiences that can be seen, felt, heard, touched or smelled.
Is task/goal-oriented. Emphasis is on achieving specific objectives that have been clarified in writing.	Is experience-oriented. Emphasis is on enjoying the desired experiences.
The speaker explains ideas so that the hearer understands. The burden is on the hearer to do something with the ideas.	The speaker tells stories so the hearer experiences them. The hearer participates in the life of a story.
Does serial processing of information, one piece at a time.	Does parallel processing of multiple pieces of information simultaneously.
International news travels slowly.	The world is a global-village. International news is instant.
Truth is absolute. It is objective and relates to rational analysis of facts, descriptions, repeatable events and patterns. Truth is presented using linear logic.	Truth is relative. Experience is what is real. Truth in one situation may not be truth in another. One person's truth differs from another person's truth.
Faith is believing the right doctrine.	Faith is experiencing the reality of the storied gospel. Believers participate in the story by counter-pointing Bible stories with their own story.
Religion emphasizes verbal expressions and doctrinal statements. It emphasizes right information.	Religion emphasizes stories, practice, actions, ethics and worship style. It emphasizes life transformation.
Literate churches	Electronic media churches
Pastor is respected as one of the most literate persons in a community.	Children and youth are the most skilled people in the world of electronic communication.
Christians are committed to denominational affiliation.	Christians are non-denominational. They are committed to a local congregation, and, beyond that, to a networks of like-minded groups. They are unified over ethical issues or worship style.

It is estimated that most people spend 80% of their non-working and non-sleeping time watching TV.

The secondary-oral generation has much in common with primary-oral communicators. The secondary-oral generation is less "linear" in their thinking processes. Logic is more associative and dynamic, creative and imaginative, not so much deductive and sequential.

The western, literate linear thinker has a high cultural value on factual knowledge. This affects the priority in learning, planning and the underlying sense of truth. Truth is seen as consisting in facts. Facts are specific descriptive statements about an objective, perceivable reality. Knowledge is the accumulation of facts.

The oral culture, on the other hand, places priority on relationships and experiences. This produces a concept of dynamic truth, not a focus on facts. Truth is seen as consisting in functional knowledge that focuses on relational skills. Truth is seen in terms of knowledge that gets a people to where they want to be, personal integrity, and fulfillment of relational and family obligations. Functional knowledge seeks information that will enable the person to maintain desired relationships, advance in a chosen career, obtain desired possessions and acquire recognition.

Post-literates place a high value on relationships and interaction, similar to oral traditional cultures. Personal experience is more important than objective fact and established knowledge.

The post-literate technology requires traditional literacy skills, but the typical post-literate is a passive-literate. The literacy skills needed for the visual dramatic portrayal on the TV or a music DVD, for example, are more for perception. There is less concern for a high skill in self-expression, associated with writing or public speaking. Literacy is assumed and even necessary; however, it is not in focus. Literacy serves more as an adjunct to the event oriented, dynamic visual world of interactive media.

Many post-literate individuals do not feel it is important or have the patience to give attention to spelling or style. General understanding and dynamic communication is of primary value. This makes them more like dynamic, relational members of oral cultures. Post-literates favor an oral-visual learning style. Thus many post-literates have more in common with pre-literates than with literate westerners.

In the emerging digital post-literate age, main-line churches have become side-lined churches. Old main-line churches are decreasing in number. The emerging churches are those with oral roots. Most of their preachers mastered storytelling on the "sawdust tent revival trails" or in store front churches and have adapted to the new electronic media. They did not learn to preach in highly academic seminaries.

Preachers and Bible teachers, who were shaped by the literate world's approach to communicating, need to experience a paradigm shift if they are to communicate to post-literates. They need to tell stories, especially Bible stories, so that God's Word might come alive for the post-modern post-literate society. The missionary who leaves the United States and goes to Southeast Asia, expects that the styles of preaching and teaching which are powerful for communicating the Bible in the USA may not communicate in Asia. However, many Christian leaders who are shaped by the literate culture are unaware that their listeners have experienced a paradigm shift to a post-literate culture. Most Christian leaders live in a literate culture while their listeners live in a secondary-oral culture. Leaders are often unaware that their literate preaching and teaching style no longer communicate in this new cultural age. Christian leaders need to learn to tell Bible stories and to craft stories that communicate Biblical truths in response to a deep need to communicate God's Word to post-literates.

METHODS OF COMMUNICATING WITH BIBLE STORIES

Different methods can be used to communicate Bible stories. In some settings the story is told, and that is all; in others, the story is utilized as a teaching or preaching tool. This chapter mentions some of the principal methods used; other chapters explain how to use these methods.

1. Bible Storytelling

Pure **Bible Storytelling** narrates a Bible story, being faithful to biblical facts. When the story is finished, the storyteller is finished. The storyteller avoids distorting any facts recorded in the Bible; however, he takes the liberty of using his own words, and he briefly explains facts unfamiliar to his listeners.

When pure Bible Storytelling is used in the worship service, the storyteller begins where the story begins and ends where the story ends.

2. Bible Storytelling with Dialogue

The narrator who uses **Bible Storytelling with Dialogue** relates the Bible story and then discusses it with his listeners. He may ask such questions as:
- What catches your attention in the story?
- Is there anything in the story that is hard to understand?
- Who are the main characters in the story?
- What problems did the characters face?
- How did the characters face their problems?
- How have you faced similar problems?
- Is there someone in the story who is similar to you or who is different from you?
- What does the story tell about God?

The storyteller may ask a few questions and encourage his listeners to discuss the story, but the discussion is open-ended and takes the direction the listeners desire, as long as it is in some way related to the story.

3. Bible Storytelling with Teaching (Narrative Teaching)

The teacher narrates the story and then teaches truths extracted from it. The story is the text for the lesson plan. The Bible story receives the main focus but it is framed with teaching emphasis. This book discusses two primary methods that may be used for **Narrative Teaching**.

3.1 Bible Storytelling with Questions

In **Bible Storytelling with Questions**, the teacher narrates the Bible story and then asks questions designed to help listeners discover life-lessons from the story. The storyteller does not explain the story nor explain life-lessons he discovered in the story. He asks questions that guide the listeners to discover biblical life-lessons for themselves.

3.2 Bible Storytelling with an Outlined Teaching Plan Using the Teaching Cycle

The teacher who uses **Bible Storytelling with an Outlined Teaching Plan** selects life-lessons discovered in the story, cites the selected life-lessons, explains them, and guides discussion by asking questions about the story and the chosen life-lessons.

4. Bible Storytelling with Preaching (Narrative Preaching)

Bible Storytelling may be coupled with preaching. The storyteller tells the story and then uses the story as a basis for preaching. The story is the text for the sermon. The Bible story receives the main focus, but it is framed with a sermon and application. This book presents two basic methods for preaching with Bible stories:

4.1 Bible Storytelling with Preaching after the Story

Using this approach, the storyteller-preacher tells the Bible story that is the text to his sermon. Then he develops the life-lessons discovered in the story as the points of his sermon. The preaching application is delayed until after the telling of the entire story.

4.2 Bible Storytelling with Preaching Inserted

Using this approach, the storytelling preacher narrates the Bible story. When he comes to an episode that inspires a life-lesson he wishes to develop, he stops storytelling, inserts his life-lesson and develops it as a sermon point. Afterwards, he continues storytelling until he reaches another episode that inspires a life-lesson he wishes to develop. He continues narrating and inserting life-lessons transformed into sermon points until the story is finished.

5. Contemporizing the Bible Story

The storyteller who contemporizes Bible stories tries to transport the Bible story to actual times and tells the story as it could have happened today.

Here is an example of contemporizing the Parable of the Good Samaritan (Lk 10:25-37):
- The man going to Jericho becomes a traveling salesman in his new Honda Accord;
- The traveling salesman stops at a filling station and robbers put a nail under a tire;
- The salesman stops to change his tire, and the robbers clobber him, steal his car and leave him beside the road;
- The priest becomes a pastor on his way to church. He continues on his way so he will be on time for a prayer meeting;
- The Levite becomes a deacon going to a home to make an evangelistic visit. He continues on his way, afraid to stop to help the man beside the road;
- The Samaritan becomes an illegal migrant worker driving a 1979 Ford pick-up. He stops to help the salesman.

I recommend that contemporizing the Bible story be used with caution. There is a danger that the storyteller may alter the Bible story. Another danger is that he may give the impression that the Bible must be updated before it communicates.

6. Non-Biblical Stories can Help Communicate Scriptural Truths

The Bible storyteller should listen to contemporary stories and develop a habit of making a connection between them and biblical stories. He should also use stories from his own life experiences to illustrate divine truths.

The storyteller can likewise craft stories for the purpose of illustrating biblical truths. However, stories crafted by today's storyteller are on a different level from biblical stories and parables crafted by Jesus. Biblical stories are God's Word. One can craft stories that illustrate biblical truths; however, the crafted story will never have the authority of being God's Word. The storyteller should never try to use his crafted story to substitute God's Word as recorded in the Bible. Nevertheless, evangelicals need to constantly craft stories that illustrate biblical truths or help listeners to understand them. They should use contemporary stories that help listeners understand Bible stories and help their listeners to make a connection between contemporary stories and biblical ones.

CONCLUSION

Other chapters will explain and give directions on developing the methods mentioned in this chapter.

HOW TO ANALYZE A BIBLE STORY

The effective storyteller or preacher/teacher who uses storytelling, must become a story-analyst. This chapter explains how to analyze a Bible story.

1. Read, reread and read again

Read the biblical passage that contains the chosen Bible story several times. Read the same passage, using different translations of the Bible.

2. Identify the structure of the story

The typical story adheres to the following structure:
- The initial sequence in which a problem or need is set up, created or identified.
- The sequence of episodes in which the story develops with its pattern of problems, conflicts, outside interference and aborted attempts at resolution.
- The final sequence in which the outcome of the story is reached.

2.1 Consider the context of the Bible story

The context establishes the place and time in which the story occurred and who are the characters in the story. The context considers the background of the story: who told the story, what was the historical setting for the story, and what episodes took place beforehand that relate to the story.

Bible passages, before the text that contains the story, establish the background for the story. Consider what Bible passages, before the text with the story, reveal about the historical circumstances, the characters in the story, and the purpose for telling the story. Other research may be needed to gain an adequate understanding of Bible customs and historical background of the story being analyzed. The context establishes the initial situation at the beginning of the story.

2.2 Determine the key-person or persons

Identify the key-person or persons in the story. Determine who is the chief character in the story. Some stories only have one chief character; in others, more than one stand out.

2.3 Determine the key-location

Identify the principal location where the events took place. In some stories it is essential to identify the location where the events took place if the story is to be clearly understood. In others it is not.

2.4 Determine key-repetitions

Events in a Bible story are often tied together by words, themes, facts or ideas that are repeated, either exactly or with minor variations. Repetitions are made in biblical stories in order to emphasize truths, to build a climax or to express strong emotions. Since repetition is done purposely, it is important to discover what is repeated.

The Bible passages that come before and after the story need to be examined to determine if the chosen story repeats words, themes, facts or ideas that are emphasized in the context of the story.

Examples of repetitions in Bible stories:

#1 In the story of Joseph in Potiphar's house:
- The Lord was with Joseph (Gen 39:2, 21, 23);
- Joseph was the overseer of all in Potiphar's house (Gen 39:4, 6, 8, 9);
- Potiphar's wife invited Joseph to go to bed with her (Gen 39:7, 10, 12).

#2 In the story of God speaking to the boy Samuel:
- Three times the Lord called Samuel, who ran to Eli, thinking it was he who called (3:4-5, 6, 8);
- The boy Samuel was ministering before the Lord (2:18; 3:1);
- The sins of Eli's sons (2:12-17; 2:22-25; 3:13);
- The sin of Eli in not disciplining his sons (2:27-30; 3:13-14);
- The boy Samuel grew (2:21, 26, 3:19).

2.5 Determine the key-attitudes expressed in the story

Stories express attitudes, feelings and emotions. A story may express a positive or negative attitude. Resignation, cynicism, hostility, shock, horror, sorrow, pain, love, joy, surprise and wonder are some of the attitudes expressed through stories. The storyteller needs to express the same attitudes as those expressed in the Bible. He needs to help his listeners feel the same emotions as those expressed in the Bible story. Therefore, it is important to detect the attitudes expressed in the story being analyzed.

2.6 Determine the initial-problem

The context establishes the initial situation of the story. The initial-problem is the episode that disturbs the initial situation established in the context.

A characteristic of Bible stories is that some problem or need at the beginning of the story will disturb the initial situation. Something happens that requires an adjustment to the initial situation. Stories begin with a problem or need which intensifies with a series of episodes until a final-situation is reached. Therefore, identifying the episode that brings the initial disturbance is a key to understanding the story.

The initial-problem identifies an event or happening that disturbs the initial situation. Given this definition, a positive change or a decision to change disturbs the initial situation as much as a negative event or an outside interference over which the Bible character had no control.

Examples of problems found in Bible stories are many: enemies, opposition, conflict, oppression, contradiction, danger, unmet need, more than one seeking a goal that can be obtained only by one, and God's will in conflict with man's desires. The story-analyst needs to determine the initial-problem presented in an episode at the beginning of the story.

2.7 Identify the sequence of events

The context establishes the initial situation. The initial-problem disturbs the initial situation. The initial-situation and the initial-problem are followed by a series of episodes or events as the story develops with its pattern of problems, conflicts and aborted attempts at resolution until final-situation. Each event that complicates the problem or each attempt at finding a resolution is an episode within the story. Some stories are complex with subdivisions that contain plots within plots. Some episodes reveal outside divine or human intervention. Complex stories have many twists and turns of the plot. Each subdivision, plot, plan, turn of events or new development is an episode within the story. The story-analyst should observe the sequence of events in the order narrated.

While identifying the series of episodes from the beginning until the end of the story, pay special attention to dialogue, conflict, contrast and divine intervention. The Bible uses dialogue for emphasis. Conflict is the spice of every story. Contrast often reveals evidence about character and choices. Jacob and Esau serve as contrasts to each other. In some stories, two people who are similar serve to contrast each other. Jacob and his father-in-law, Laban, serve as a contrast to one another. The attitude of God toward Nineveh is viewed in contrast with Jonah's attitude.

After determining the initial-problem, note the sequence of events until the story reaches a final-situation.

2.8 Discover the final-situation of the story

Stories begin with an initial-problem which intensifies with a series of episodes until a conclusion is reached that establishes a final-situation. The final circumstance may be similar to or completely different from the initial one. Usually a connection exist between the initial-problem and the final-situation. Some stories have a positive ending, others a negative one. Discover what happened as a result of the person's seeking to solve the initial-problem or satisfy the need that was established at the beginning of the story. Find answers to questions, such as the following:
- How did the story end?
- How was the initial-problem solved or key-need met?

- What were the results of improper action taken to attempt a resolution to the problem?
- What was the outcome of the story? What is the connection between the initial-problem that disturbed the initial situation and the final-situation that established the outcome?

SIMPLIFIED STRUCTURE OF A BIBLE STORY			
CONTEXT	**INITIAL-PROBLEM**	**SEQUENCE OF EVENTS**	**FINAL-SITUATION**
The context considers essential background information that establishes the initial situation.	The initial-problem presents the episode that disturbs the initial situation.	A series of episodes happen as the story develops its pattern of problems, conflicts, outside intervention and aborted attempts at resolution.	The outcome of the story establishes the final result, a new situation.

3. Discover life-lessons expressed by the story

A life-lesson is a truth drawn from the Bible story that applies to our relationship with God, others, and ourselves. It serves to guide, warn and/or encourage us in our life journey.

Discover important life-lessons taught by the story and write them down. Try to extract all of the obvious life-lessons taught by the story.

It is helpful to understand differences exist between a historical fact, a conclusion reached, a life-lesson taught and an application made.

HISTORICAL FACT:	A fact mentioned in the story
CONCLUSION:	A fact that is implied even though the Bible story doesn't mention it
LIFE-LESSON:	A truth that is discovered from the facts told in the story
APPLICATION:	An explanation of how the life-lesson discovered in the story should make a difference in the lives of people today

SEE THE FOLLOWING EXAMPLES:

EXAMPLE #1	
HISTORICAL FACT:	Joseph is taken to Egypt and sold as a slave (Gen 37:36; 39:1).
CONCLUSION:	Joseph is forced to live in a place that is undesirable to him.
LIFE-LESSON:	One who serves God may be required to live in an undesirable location.
APPLICATION:	In order to work, study, have medical treatment or serve God, we may be required to live in a location that is undesirable to us.

EXAMPLE # 2	
HISTORICAL FACT:	Potiphar's wife invited Joseph to go to bed with her (Gen 39:7).
CONCLUSION:	That was a hard temptation for a 17-year-old with a strong sexual appetite and an opportunity to satisfy it.
LIFE-LESSON:	The person who is faithful to God may suffer strong temptations to have sex outside of marriage.
APPLICATION:	We all are subject to sexual temptations.

Bible Storytelling Tools © Jackson Day

With each life-lesson discovered, the person analyzing may make a note of other biblical passages (parallel texts) that teach the same life-lesson. // is a signal for a parallel text.

4. Mark the life-lessons that are most important for the students or listeners

Underline or otherwise mark life-lessons that are most important to communicate to one's students or listeners. One can discover many important life-lessons in any Bible story. It is impossible to use all of them in one sermon or Bible study. Select and mark those to be used.

ANALYSIS OF A BIBLE STORY

STORY:

TEXT:

STRUCTURE:

    Context (the initial situation):

    Key-person:

    Key-location:

    Key-repetitions:

    Key-attitudes:

    Initial-problem:

    Sequence of events (a series of episodes as the story develops):

    Final-situation (the conclusion of the story):

LIFE-LESSONS TAUGHT BY THE STORY:

EXAMPLE # 1: ANALYSIS OF A BIBLE STORY

STORY: Joseph in Potiphar's House

TEXT: Gen 39:1-23

STRUCTURE:

Context:
Israel loved Joseph more than all his other sons. Joseph's brothers hated him. Joseph dreamed that his father, mother and brothers would bow down before him. Joseph's brothers sold him to slave merchants (Gen 37).

Key-person: Joseph

Key-location: Egypt, Potiphar's home

Key-repetitions:
- "The Lord was with Joseph" (39:2, 3, 21, 23).
- Potiphar put Joseph in charge of everything he owned (39:4, 5, 6, 8).
- Potiphar's wife invited Joseph to go to bed with her (39:7, 10, 12).
- Potiphar's wife accused Joseph of trying to have sex with her: to the servants (39:14-15) and to Joseph's master (39:17-18).

Key-attitudes:
- Hope in the midst of despair is expressed:
  - Joseph, the slave, became a blessing (39:1-5).
  - Joseph was tempted but resisted (39:9-12).
  - Joseph was falsely accused but prospered in prison (39:14-23).
- Potiphar's wife desired to have sex with Joseph (39:7-11).
- Joseph feared sinning against God (39:8-12).
- Potiphar burned with anger when he heard his wife's accusation against Joseph (39:19-20).

Initial-problem:
Slave merchants took Joseph to Egypt and sold him to Potiphar, an Egyptian officer who was captain of Pharaoh's bodyguard (Gen 39:1).

Sequence of events:
- Joseph was taken to Egypt and bought by Potiphar (39:1).
- The Lord was with Joseph (39:2).
- Joseph gained Potiphar's favor, who made Joseph the overseer of all he owned (39:4-6).
- Joseph was handsome. His master's wife invited Joseph to go to bed with her (39:7).
- Joseph refused. He said his master had entrusted everything in the house, except his wife, to Joseph's care. Joseph asked how could he do such a wicked thing and sin against God? (39:8-9).
- Daily, she spoke to Joseph, but he refused to go to bed with her or even to be with her (39:10).
- One day when Joseph was alone in the house with her, she caught him by his garment. He left his garment in her hand and fled (39:11-12).
- The woman called her household servants and accused Joseph of trying to sleep with her. She said that when she screamed, he left his cloak and ran out of the house (39:13-19).
- When Potiphar returned home she told him that Joseph tried to make sport of her. When she screamed, he left his cloak and ran out of the house (39:17-18).
- Potiphar burned with anger and put Joseph into the jail with the king's prisoners (39:19-20).
- In prison, the Lord was with Joseph (39:21).

Final-situation:
Potiphar put Joseph in prison, but God was with Joseph and extended kindness to him (39:20-21).

LIFE-LESSONS TAUGHT BY THE STORY:

1. The person who serves God may suffer injustice. Joseph was sold into slavery (39:1), and later jailed because of false accusations (39:20).

2. God is always present with those who are faithful to him. God was with Joseph (39:2, 21, 23) // (Ps 46:1-2).

3. A believer in God is giving a good testimony when those who don't believe in God are aware that God is blessing the believer. Potiphar saw that God was with Joseph (39:3).

4. Those who do not serve God may become blessed because of their relationship with a believer in God. The Lord blessed Potiphar because of Joseph (39:5).

5. The one who serves God is subject to strong temptation. Seventeen-year-old Joseph was tempted to have sex with his master's wife (39:7, 10-12).

6. A person may become blind to moral values. Potiphar's wife was blind to the importance of moral values in the home (39:7).

7. Belief in God gives a person a reason to resist temptation. Joseph's belief in God gave him the conviction that betraying his master would be sin (39:9).

8. Wrong done to another person is sin against God. Joseph realized that to betray his master would be to sin against God (39:9).

9. The one who tempts others to sin may retaliate toward the person who resists temptation. Potiphar's wife tempted Joseph to have sex with her. When Joseph refused, she sought revenge against him (39:13-19).

10. The person who yields to temptation places the blame on others. Potiphar's wife did not assume her responsibility for attempting to seduce Joseph. She used Joseph's garment to falsely accuse him (39:13-14).

11. God's servants live in a corrupt world and may suffer injustice as a consequence of doing what is right. When Joseph resisted sexual temptations, he was falsely accused and jailed (39:20).

12. God is present with his servant who suffers injustice. God was with Joseph (39:2-5, 23).

EXAMPLE # 2: ANALYSIS OF A BIBLE STORY

STORY: God Speaks to the Child Samuel

TEXT: I Samuel 3:1-19

STRUCTURE:

Context:
During the time when the judges governed Israel, there was no king in Israel, and everyone did what was right in his own eyes (Jdg 21:25). The result was that the sins of each generation were worse than those of the previous.

Eli and his sons were priests at the Tabernacle at Shiloh. Eli was old and his sons sinned against God. They were disrespectful to those who brought sacrifices to offer to God, and they disobeyed God's plans for the cooking of the offerings (1 Sam 2:12-17). They had sex with the women who served at the Tabernacle (1 Sam 2:22-24). They refused to listen to their father when he warned them of the consequences of sinning against God (1 Sam 2:25).

A man of God told Eli that, because he honored his sons above God, his family would be punished, but God would raise up a faithful priest (1 Sam 2:27-36).

Hannah had been unable to have children. She prayed asking God for a son, promising to dedicate him to the Lord. She had a son and named him Samuel. When he was weaned, she took him to the Tabernacle for him to stay and be given over to the Lord.

Key-person: Samuel

Key-location: The Tabernacle where Samuel slept

Key-repetitions:
- Three times the Lord called Samuel, who ran to Eli, thinking it was he who had called (3:4-5, 6, 8).
- The boy Samuel was ministering before the Lord (2:18; 3:1).
- The sins of Eli's sons (2:12-17; 2:22-25; 3:13).
- The sin of Eli in not disciplining his sons (2:27-30; 3:13-14).
- The boy Samuel grew in stature and before the Lord (2:21, 26, 3:19).

Key-attitudes:
- Disgust toward Eli's sons.
- Pleasure in the boy Samuel.
- Samuel's affection for Eli.
- God's anger toward Eli.
- Samuel's fear of telling Eli what God had said.

Initial-problem:
In those days a word from God was rare (1 Sam 3:1).

Sequence of events:
- The boy Samuel was ministering to the Lord before Eli (3:1).
- A word from the Lord was rare in those days (3:1).
- Samuel did not yet know the Lord nor had the word of God been revealed to him (3:7).
- Eli was lying down in his place, and Samuel was lying in the Tabernacle where the Ark of God was (3:2-3).

- The Lord called Samuel, who ran to Eli and said: "Here I am, for you called me." Eli answered: "I did not call, lie down again." This was repeated three times (3:1-9).
- Eli discerned that the Lord was calling the boy and told him that the next time he heard the voice to answer: "Speak Lord, for your servant is listening" (3:8-9).
- When God called again, Samuel answered: "Speak, for your servant is listening" (3:10).
- God advised that he was going to judge and punish Eli's family (3:11-14).
- Samuel was afraid to tell the vision to Eli (3:15).
- Eli asked Samuel what was the word from God, and Samuel told him everything (3:16-18).
- The Lord was with Samuel, and all Israel knew that Samuel was a prophet (3:19-21).

Final-situation:

Samuel grew, the Lord was with him, and all Israel knew that he was a prophet of the Lord (3:19-20).

LIFE-LESSONS TAUGHT BY THE STORY:

1. A certain times in history, God avoids revealing himself to people. A word from God was rare in the days when Eli was priest (3:1).

2. God chooses whom he desires to serve him, regardless of the age of the person. Samuel was a little boy when God first spoke to him (3:4).

3. Sometimes people do not understand when God is speaking to them. The boy Samuel did not recognize that God was speaking to him (3:5-6).

4. God makes repeated attempts to reach the person he has chosen for a specific task. When Samuel was confused and thought Eli was calling him, God kept repeating his call to Samuel (3:6-8).

5. A person with knowledge about God may help another understand when God is dealing with him. Eli understood that God was calling Samuel and advised him how to respond (3:9-10).

6. A person needs to be open to hear God speak. Samuel responded to God: "Speak, for your servant is listening" (3:10).

7. God is a judge, and he judges and punishes those who are unfaithful to him. God told Samuel of his judgment on Eli's family (3:11-14).

8. Sometimes, God's messenger will be required to announce truths that are disagreeable, both to the messenger and to the listener. Samuel was afraid to tell Eli that God was going to punish his family (3:15-18).

9. God's presence is constant with the person who serves him. The Lord was always with Samuel (3:19).

HOW TO ANALYZE A STORY COMPARING DIFFERENT NARRATIONS OF THE SAME STORY

OBSERVATION: It is my counsel that the beginning storyteller have several months' experience of analyzing Bible stories contained in only one book of the Bible before he is taught to compare different tellings of the same story. When I was training storytellers in Brazil, I observed students who had less than an elementary school education analyze different tellings of the same story, if they had experience in analyzing stories contained in only one book of the Bible. But, if comparing different narrations of the same story is introduced too soon, the students may become confused and discouraged.

Some stories are repeated in more than one book of the Bible. In the Old Testament some episodes registered in Exodus, Leviticus and Numbers are repeated in Deuteronomy. Many of the events of First and Second Kings are retold in First and Second Chronicles. The episodes in the life of Jesus Christ are recorded in the four Gospels: Matthew, Mark, Luke and John. Especially Matthew, Mark and Luke relate many of the same stories and give us a synopsis or summary of the life of Jesus. Because of this, Matthew, Mark and Luke are called the Synoptic Gospels. Mark has 678 verses, and, of these, the contents of 606 verses are retold by Matthew and Luke. Sometimes they abbreviate; whereas, other times they expand on Mark's contents.

A story that is retold will not be repeated with exactly the same words. Stories that were repeated in different books of the Old Testament were not repeated exactly the same way. Each telling would emphasize different truths and include details not included in the other telling. The three Synoptic Gospels contain many of the same stories of the life of Jesus. Each Gospel gives a different emphasis to the same story. Therefore, by comparing the story told in different books, it is possible to acquire more details about the same event.

EXAMPLE: COMPARING DIFFERENT TELLINGS OF THE TEMPTATION OF JESUS

The story of the temptation of Jesus is found in each of the three Synoptic Gospels: Mt 4:1-11; Mk 1:12-13; Lk 4:1-14.

- Matthew (Mt 4:1-2) and Luke (Lk 4:1) relate that Jesus was led by the Holy Spirit into the wilderness.
- Matthew (4:2), Mark (Mk 1:13) and Luke (Lk 4:2) relate that he was in the wilderness for forty days and nights when he was tempted.
- Only Mark relates that Jesus was with the wild beasts in the wilderness (Mk 1:13).
- Matthew (Mt 4:2) and Luke (Lk 4:2) relate that Jesus fasted forty days and forty nights.
- Matthew (4:3-11) and Luke (Lk 4:3-13) relate the three episodes of the temptation.
- After the temptation, Matthew relates that the devil left Jesus (Mt 4:11), and Luke adds that when the devil had finished the three temptations, he departed until an opportune time (Lk 4:13).
- Matthew (Mt 4:11) and Mark (Mk 1:13) relate that, after the temptation, angels ministered to Jesus.
- Only Luke relates that Jesus left the wilderness and returned to Galilee in the power of the Spirit (Lk 4:13-14).

<u>Sequence of events of the temptations of Jesus in their chronological order:</u>

- Jesus was led by the Spirit into the wilderness (Mt 4:1; Lk 4:1).
- Jesus was with the wild beasts (Mk 1:13).
- Jesus fasted forty days and forty nights in the wilderness (Mt 4:1-2; Lk 4:2), being tempted by Satan (Mk 1:13; Lk 4:2).
- After the forty days of fasting, Jesus became hungry (Mt 4:2; Lk 4:2).
- The three episodes of the temptation:
  - Transform stones into bread (Mt 4:3-5; Lk 4:3-4).
  - Jump from the pinnacle of the Temple (Mt 4:5-7; Lk 4:9-12).
  - Worship the devil (Mt 4:8-10; Lk 4:5-8).

- After the temptation, the devil left Jesus (Mt 4:11); departing from him until an opportune time (Lk 4:13).
- Angels came and ministered to Jesus (Mt 4:11; Mk 1:13).
- Jesus returned from the wilderness to Galilee in the power of the Spirit (Lk 4:13-14).

*****

It is important to make comparisons of stories told in the four Gospels in order to understand the life of Jesus and to place the events in chronological order. Such understanding is essential to study, teach or preach the Bible.

Two resources that will help the story-analyst make comparisons are:
1) **The Bible.** Most published Bibles contain references which mention other texts that tell the same story.
2) **A Harmony of the Gospels.** A Harmony of the Gospels is most helpful to make comparisons of stories told in the Gospels. A Harmony of the Gospels organizes the material of the four Gospels in chronological order. Episodes are told in the order that they happened and the text from each of the Gospels is included for each event. Each episode mentioned in more than one Gospel is published in parallel columns. This facilitates the comparisons of the events and the different styles of each author.

In order to analyze a Bible story while making comparisons of different authors that tell the same narrative, follow the same plan as **ANALYSIS OF A BIBLE STORY**. For "Text," note each text that tells the story. For "**Sequence of events**", note the events in chronological order making a comparison of all the texts that tell the story.

EXAMPLE # 1:   ANALYSIS OF A BIBLE STORY USING COMPARISONS

Matthew (1-2) and Luke (1-2) describe various episodes related to the birth and infancy of Jesus. However, both authors relate different events. To put the events in chronological order, the storyteller should make a comparison between Matthew and Luke, noting some events from Luke, then going to Matthew, returning to Luke, and then returning to Matthew. See the events in chronological order.

STORY: The Birth of Jesus

TEXT: Mt 1:18 - 2:23; Lk 1:5 - 2:39

STRUCTURE:

Context:
Throughout the Old Testament, there were prophecies about a "Promised One." It had been over four hundred years since a person had received a revelation from God through a vision or a visit from an angel. The Jewish nation was dominated by a foreign power, the Romans. The Jews desired for God to send the "Promised One" to liberate them from Roman oppression.

Key-persons: The Angel Gabriel, Zacharias, Mary and Joseph

Key-locations: Jerusalem, Nazareth and Bethlehem

Key-repetitions:
- Angels: the Angel Gabriel visited Zacharias (Lk 1:11-20) and Mary (Lk 1:26-38); an angel appeared to Joseph in a dream before Jesus' birth (Mt 1:20-24) and afterwards (Mt 2:13, 19); angels visited the shepherds the night Jesus was born (Lk 2:8-15).
- People were frightened by the angels, and the angels told them not to be afraid (Lk 1:11-13; 1:26-30; 2:9-10).
- Mary pondered or meditated on what was happening (Lk 1:29; 2:19, 51).
- Expressions of praise or worship were offered by: Mary (Lk 1:49-55); Zacharias (Lk 1:68-79); the angels (Lk 2:14); the shepherds (Lk 2:20); Simeon (Lk 2:29-33); Anna (Lk 2:38); and the wise men (Mt 2:11).

Key-attitudes:
- Fear;
- Amazement;
- Acceptance of God's will.

Initial-problem:
After four hundred years of God not sending a prophet or visiting his people in a special way, an angel appears to Zacharias when he was in the Temple.

Sequence of events:
- The angel Gabriel announced to Zacharias the birth of John the Baptist (Lk 1:5-25).

- Elizabeth became pregnant (Lk 1:24-25).
- The angel Gabriel announced to Mary the birth of Jesus (Lk 1:26-38).
- Mary visited Elizabeth (Lk 1:39-45).
- Joseph faced a dilemma when he discovered Mary was with child (Mt 1:18-19).
- An angel told Joseph about Mary and the child (Mt 1:18-23).
- Joseph took Mary as his wife but did not have sexual relations with her until after the child was born (Mt 1:24-25).
- The government required a census; Mary and Joseph traveled to Bethlehem (Lk 2:1-5).
- Jesus was born (Lk 2:1-7).
- Angels proclaimed the birth of a Savior to the shepherds (Lk 2:8-14).
- The shepherds visited the baby in Bethlehem (Lk 2:15-20).
- Jesus was circumcised and named (when 8 days old) (Lk 2:21).
- Mary kept the forty days of purification (Lk 2:22 with Lv 12:1-4); then they traveled to and from Jerusalem (Lk 2:22-39).
- The wise men sought Jesus in Jerusalem (Mt 2:1-8).
- The wise men visited the Child Jesus in a house (Mt 2:9-12).
- Joseph fled to Egypt with Mary and the Child (Mt 2:13-15).
- Herod ordered the slaying of all boys under two years old in and around Bethlehem (Mt 2:16-18).
- Joseph, Mary and Jesus returned from Egypt to Nazareth (Mt 2:19-23; Lk 2:39).
- The Child Jesus continued to grow and the grace of God was upon him (Lk 2:40).

Final-situation:
The Child Jesus continued to grow and the grace of God was upon him (Lk 2:40).

LIFE-LESSONS TAUGHT BY THE STORY:

1. God keeps his promises. He fulfilled all the prophecies of the Old Testament related to the birth of a "Promised One" (Is 9:9 with Mt 1:1; Is 7:14 with Mt 1:20, 25 and Lk 1:34; Mk 5:2 with Mt 26; Ho 11:1 with Mt 2:15). God fulfilled his promise to Zacharias and gave him and Elizabeth a son (Lk 1:57).

2. God is all-powerful. He has the power to do his will. For God, nothing is impossible (Lk 1:37). He enabled an elderly couple to have a baby (Lk 1:15-25). He caused a virgin to become pregnant (Lk 1:26-38). He helped Joseph, a confused and baffled man, understand the Lord's will (Mt 1:19-24).

3. God is all-powerful; he has power over:
   - Nature. He enabled a couple of senior adults to have a child (Lk 1:18, 57). He caused a virgin to become pregnant (Lk 1:31-35) and he announced the birth of Jesus with a star (Mt 2:1-12).
   - Governments. He had Caesar Augustus announce a census that required Mary and Joseph to go to Bethlehem (Lk 2:1).
   - Satan. Satan and his human instrument Herod could not kill the child Jesus (Mt 2:16-18 with Rev 12:1-6).
   - Material needs of his servants. A conclusion of the author is that God used the presents of the wise men to finance the trip to Egypt (Mt 2:11-15).

4. God is all-knowing. Before the birth of both John and Jesus, he knew their future. God's angel foretold the future of Zacharias' son before he was conceived (Lk 1:15-17).

5. A couple who lives righteously in the sight of God, obeying biblical teachings, has a potential for raising children who will serve God. God chose Zacharias and Elizabeth, a couple who were both righteous in the sight of God, to be the parents of John the Baptist (Lk 1:6).

6. The person who doubts God's promises will not testify of God's great deeds. When Zacharias doubted the angel's promise, he lost the ability to speak (Lk 1:20).

7. The person who has honest doubts and seeks an answer from God is not punished. Mary wanted to understand how a virgin could have a child, and God answered her question (Lk 1:34-35).

8. A person must believe in God's Word in order to do his will. For Joseph to marry Mary, he had to believe the message of the angel (Mt 1:20-24).

9. Jesus is both completely man and completely God. The angel advised Mary that her son would be both man and God (Lk 1:32).

10. Several circumstances made Jesus' birth supernatural:
    - His birth was predicted by the prophets of the Old Testament centuries before it happened (Is. 7:14, 9:6-7; Mk 5:2);
    - An angel prophesied the birth of Jesus (Lk 1:30-33; Mt 1:20-21);

- The Holy Spirit, and not a man, made Mary pregnant (Lk 1:35; Mt 1:20);
- Mary was still a virgin when Jesus was born (Lk 1:28-37; Mt 1:24-25);
- The birth of Jesus was announced by angels (Lk 2:8-14);
- Nature in the form of a star announced the birth of Jesus (Mt 2:1-2).

11. Jesus was born Savior. The angel advised Joseph that Jesus would save the people from their sins (Mt 1:21-23). An angel told the shepherds that their Savior was born (Lk 1:11).

12. Leaders who desire to protect the privileges that come with their positions will not accept the right for God to lead. Herod did not accept the right of anyone to rule over him. He feared losing the privileges of being king when the child Jesus became a man (Mt 2:3-4).

13. The person who fights God is cruel. Herod ordered the murder of boys under two years old (Mt 2:16-18).

14. It is possible to have knowledge of the Bible's teaching and yet not be involved in God's work. The chief priest and scribes knew that the Messiah would be born in Bethlehem, yet they did not go there to worship the Child (Mt 2:4-6).

EXAMPLE # 2: ANALYSIS OF A BIBLE STORY USING COMPARISONS

STORY: Temptation of Jesus in the Wilderness

TEXT: Mt 4:1-11; Mk 1:12-13; Lk 4:1-13

STRUCTURE:

Context:
The Bible gives us information about the birth of Jesus and some facts about when he was a baby and a little boy. Then the Bible is silent about his life until he was twelve years old and went on a trip to Jerusalem. Jesus stayed in the Temple without his parents' knowledge, and for three days they thought he was lost. From the time he was twelve until he was thirty, the Bible does not narrate facts about his life. During this time, Jesus lived in the village of Nazareth, working as a carpenter and was unknown beyond his home town.

When Jesus was thirty, John the Baptist was popular with the multitudes. John dressed in a garment made of camel's hair with a leather belt and ate locusts and wild honey. He was preaching and baptizing in the wilderness of Judea and called the people to repent and make ready the way of the Lord. Those who repented of their sins were baptized. John proclaimed: "I baptize you with water; but One is coming who is mightier than I. I am not fit to untie the thong of his sandals. He will baptize you in the Holy Spirit and fire."

Jesus came to the river Jordan to be baptized by John. John resisted, saying: "I have need to be baptized by you."

Jesus answered: "Permit it at this time; for in this way it is fitting for us to fulfill all righteousness."

John baptized Jesus. When Jesus came up from the water, the heavens were opened, and he saw the Spirit of God descending as a dove, and coming upon him.

A voice out of the heavens proclaimed: "This is My beloved Son, in whom I am well pleased."

Key-persons: Satan and Jesus

Key-location: The Wilderness

Key-repetitions:
- Two of the three temptations began with Satan telling Jesus: "If you are the Son of God" (Mt 4:3, 6; Lk 4:3, 9).
- Jesus answered each temptation with: "It is written" and quoted an Old Testament text (Mt 4:4, 7, 10).

Key-attitudes:
- Satan expressed doubt that Jesus was the Son of God.
- Confidence was manifested by Jesus in the Scripture.
- Conflict and hostility existed between Satan and Jesus.
- The physical weakness of Jesus was in contrast with his strength to resist temptation.

Initial-problem:
Jesus was led by the Spirit into the wilderness to be tempted by Satan (Mt 4:1).

Sequence of events:
- Jesus was led by the Spirit into the wilderness (Mt 4:1; Lk 4:1).
- Jesus fasted forty days and forty nights in the wilderness (Mt 4:2; Lk 4:2), being tempted by Satan (Mk 1:13; Lk 4:2).
- Jesus was with the wild beasts (Mk 1:13).
- After forty days of fasting, Jesus became hungry (Mt 4:2; Lk 4:2).
- The three episodes of the temptation:
  - Transform stones into bread (Mt 4:3-5; Lk 4:3-4).
  - Jump from the pinnacle of the Temple (Mt 4:5-7; Lk 4:9-12).
  - Worship the devil (Mt 4:8-10; Lk 4:5-8).
- After the temptation, the devil left Jesus (Mt 4:11). The devil departed from Jesus until an opportune time (Lk 4:13).
- Angels came and ministered to Jesus (Mt 4:11; Mk 1:13).
- Jesus returned from the wilderness to Galilee in the power of the Spirit (Lk 4:13-14).

Final-situation:
After the temptation, Jesus returned from the wilderness to Galilee in the power of the Spirit (Mt 4:11; Mk 1:13).

LIFE-LESSONS TAUGHT BY THE STORY:

1. Satan is a lying and deceiving tempter who fights against God and his will. He tempted Jesus to rebel against God as he had tempted Adam and Eve.

2. The person who has faith in God does not need to prove his position with God. God the Father called Jesus "My Son" (Mt 3:17). Satan challenged Jesus to prove he is the Son of God (Mt 4:3, 6). He asked Jesus to do something that God did not request. Jesus had no reason to prove anything to Satan.

3. Satan tempts God's servant to please people instead of obeying God. Satan tempted Jesus to become the political and warring Messiah that the Jewish nation was expecting. The Jews were waiting for a fighting warrior king who would expel the Romans and restore the throne of David.

4. Satan knows the words of God and even uses the Bible in a distorted manner in order to deceive people. He made a slight change in the words of God to deceive Eve in the garden, and he distorted the Bible to deceive Jesus in the wilderness (Gen 2:16; 3:1, 4; Mt 4:6).

5. The desire to seek a solution to human problems without considering God, or by using a plan that does not follow God's will is a temptation from Satan. The temptation to transform stones into bread was a temptation to satisfy physical hunger outside of God's plan.

6. The three episodes of Jesus' temptation are faced by all:
   - The wilderness: Jesus suffered the temptation of the flesh; to have bread without God. He was tempted to satisfy the appetites and desires of the physical body. He was tempted to use his own power to satisfy the physical need for food.
   - The pinnacle of the Temple: Jesus suffered the temptation of the world, to have position and prestige without God; to live by the standards of the world. He was tempted to impress people, to use his abilities to gain glory for himself. He was tempted to put on a spectacular show to impress the people, to call attention to himself and gain prestige for himself.
   - The high mountain: Jesus suffered the temptation to serve Satan, to have power without God. This was the temptation to do anything necessary to gain power, to be able to force others to obey and serve his every desire.

7. Since Jesus was tempted as a man, he is able to help those who are being tempted (Hb 2:18) and to have compassion toward them in their weakness (Hb 4:15). Because Jesus was a man, he experienced hunger like any other. He did not win over temptation with divine power but with resources available to every person.

8. Jesus was tempted the same as every human being, but he did not yield. He remained without sin (Hb 4:15). Eve was tempted in the Garden of Eden in the presence of abundance and yielded. Jesus was tempted in the wilderness, experiencing hunger and resisted. Jesus resisted stronger temptations than any other person.

9. Temptation may be resisted with two resources: the Holy Spirit and God's Word used correctly. Jesus used these two resources available to anyone: the Holy Spirit and the Word of God.

■ At his baptism, the Holy Spirit descended upon Jesus (Mt 3:16). The Holy Spirit led Jesus into the wilderness (Lk 4:1) and accompanied him throughout his battle with Satan (Mt 4:1). The Holy Spirit was with Jesus until the end of his battle (Lk 4:14).

■ In each of the three episodes of his temptation, Jesus used the armor of the Word of God, answering Satan with words from the Bible (Mt 4:4, 7, 10).

10. The tempted person should resist Satan with the Word of God. Satan flees from the person who resists him with God's Word (Ja. 4:7). The Bible teaches us to resist Satan (Ja. 4:7; 1 Pet 5:8-9). Jesus resisted Satan when he ordered: "Go away from here, Satan" (Mt 4:10). It is important to resist Satan formally, ordering him with God's authority to leave us alone, giving Satan reasons found in God's Word.

TELLING A BIBLE STORY

There are three different ways to tell a Bible story:
1st Memorize word for word the story as told in the Bible.
2nd Summarize in order to condense the story, skipping some of the details that the storyteller does not consider important for his listeners. Then memorize the condensed version, always using the same words with each narration of the story.
3rd Paraphrase the Bible story. The storyteller uses his own words to tell the story; however, he is cautious to always be true to the biblical facts.

In my opinion, in South America, North America and Europe, the best approach is to paraphrase the story. This is the method that is emphasized in this book. However, in some places the story needs to be memorized, or to be told using the very same words each time it is retold.

A Brazilian missionary who has a ministry with the Muslims told about a Muslim youth who had recently converted to the Christian faith. The youth stated that when he was a Muslim, he had memorized all of the Koran, and he had begun the process of memorizing all of the whole Bible. Those who tell Bible stories to Muslim groups who give importance to memorizing the Koran, need to memorize word for word the Bible stories they tell.

Most tribal people tell their religious myths with slight variations with each telling. However, in a few tribal groups, religious myths are always repeated word for word, and the same gestures are always used in retelling the myth. Missionaries who work with such tribal groups could summarize or condense the story, and even skip some of the details. Then they would need to memorize the condensed version, always using the same words with each narration of the story.

In some places, Bible stories need to be memorized and repeated with the same words. However, in most places, the storyteller can paraphrase the story, using his own words.

One of the most difficult things for most preachers and Bible teachers to do is to tell the story rather than preach or teach. Most of the training in seminaries, Bible colleges and even churches support a preaching or teaching approach to Bible stories. Therefore, one must make a conscious effort to change former habits in order to become a storyteller.

1. Bible stories are organized to be understood orally

It is important to understand that Bible stories were told orally before they were written. The story was repeated by mouth many times before it was written in a book. The story was perfected and organized to be understood by hearing. At first, Bible stories were not written to be studied from a book. Few people had books or were able to read. Even the written story was for the purpose of being understood and remembered when read aloud. The one who heard the story read would be able to return home and tell it to family members, friends and neighbors.

2. When telling a Bible Story, do not invent facts beyond those found in the Bible

The Bible storyteller should not exaggerate and recreate the story, inventing facts, situations and events not found in the biblical story. The storyteller needs to be exact in order not to deceive the listener. He needs to be certain of his facts, from the least to the most important. Avoid recreating what took place. Do not use your imagination to invent senses, events, situations or characters not found in the Bible story. Be careful neither to repress or increase facts.

An example: Recreating the story of the woman caught in adultery (Jn 8:2-11):

The sun rose with Diana cuddled up next to Benjamin, her new lover. She awoke with horror hearing the bang of the bedroom door being kicked in. She screamed with fear expecting to see bandits with knives and swords. But the men in the doorway were the teachers from the temple plus the Pharisees from the synagogue where she attended on the Sabbath with her parents.

The Pharisees told Benjamin to get lost. He grabbed his clothes, throwing them on as he jumped out the window. Then they pulled Diana off the bed, not even giving her time to put on her clothes. In desperation she grabbed the sheet and wrapped it around herself as they forced her out the door. Diana couldn't

Bible Storytelling Tools © Jackson Day

understand why they were exclaiming: "We've got him now. Let's see him get out of this!"

Diana was dragged to the Temple and made to stand in front of the carpenter-turned-teacher, who was called Jesus. The men said to Jesus: "Teacher, this woman was caught in the act of adultery. In the Law, Moses commanded us to stone such women. Now what do you say?"

But Jesus bent down and started to write on the ground with his finger. When they kept on questioning him, he straightened up and said to them, "If any one of you is without sin, let him be the first to throw a stone at her."

Again he stooped down and wrote on the ground: "Jacob and the widow Sarah; Simon cheating the widow Hannah out of her home; Saul abandoning his elderly parents..." Jesus kept on writing as those present began to go away one at a time, beginning with the oldest until only Jesus was left with the woman still standing there. Jesus straightened up and asked her, "Woman, where are they? Has no one condemned you?"

Diana answered: "No one, sir."

Then Jesus declared: "Then neither do I condemn you. Go now and abandon your life of sin."

A mistake usually made by beginner storytellers is to "recreate" the Bible story, inventing facts, situations, events and people not mentioned in the text. The results are often counterproductive. Listeners become bored and stop paying attention, or the listeners may love the storyteller's recreation of the story, when in fact, they are receiving a contaminated version of the Bible. Bible stories were perfected and freed of unnecessary baggage by constant retelling throughout many generations. The Holy Spirit inspired and guided the human authors to write the stories in a manner to be understood by hearing.

Bible stories are the most powerful stories in the history of literature. They are recorded in the Scripture in the best manner to be understood orally. Every time a Bible story is retold, it becomes a sacred occasion and the presence of the Holy Spirit is active in communicating God's Word. Therefore, the storyteller does not need to improve on biblical stories.

While it is not recommended to have a rote recitation of exactly the same words as your Bible translation, the storyteller should learn the story as close to word for word as possible. He must be true to the facts presented in the Bible story. Storytelling does invite some degree of improvisation. This is evident in the variations of the same stories in the Gospels themselves. But each telling of the same story must be true to the biblical facts!

3. The storyteller may need to include complementary facts to make the story understood by today's listeners

The listeners of today live in a different country, have a different culture and speak a different language than the original listeners to the story. Facts that the original listeners understood may leave today's audience confused. The storyteller may remain true to the biblical story and include complementary facts to enable his listeners to clearly understand the Bible story. Adding complementary facts in order to help today's listeners is different from inventing and making up new facts. Therefore, complementary facts may need to be included in order to clarify biblical facts. Complementary facts describing the historical arena where the action of the story took place may be essential for your listeners to understand the story.

For example:

#1 When telling the story of God speaking to Moses through the burning bush and referring to God telling Moses to remove his sandals, the storyteller could include the complementary fact that slaves went barefooted (Ex 3:4-5).

#2 Exodus narrates the Israelites' leaving Egypt and mentions there were about six hundred thousand men on foot, aside from children (Ex 12:37). In those times, only men of age to fight in battles were counted. Today all the population is counted. Therefore, one could give the complementary fact that there were about two million, five hundred thousand Israelites leaving Egypt.

#3 The first listeners to the narrative of the birth of Jesus would understand that a Jewish couple who was engaged to be married had a legal commitment that could only be terminated by divorce. The engaged couple was called husband and wife even though the marriage ceremony that initiated the couple's living together would only happen in a distant future. Today they would be called fiancees. These complementary facts need to be explained today.

#4 The first listeners to the narrative of Jesus healing the ten lepers (Lk 17:11-19) understood the racial hatred that existed between the Jews and Samaritans, but today's audience may not. Therefore, it would be helpful to include the complementary fact that the Jews had strong racial prejudice against the Samaritans.

#5 All those who heard Jesus tell the parable of the pharisee and the publican who went to the Temple to pray (Lk 18:9-14) understood who the pharisees and the publicans were. Only the longtime church-goers of today would know, and many of them could not explain who the pharisees and publicans were. It would be helpful to include the complementary facts that the pharisees were respected Jewish spiritual leaders who were faithful but legalistic in following the religious traditions of their ancestors. The publicans were corrupt Jewish tax collectors who became wealthy by overcharging their fellow citizens. They were despised and called traitors by fellow Jews.

While the Bible storyteller should not exaggerate and make up facts not found in the biblical story, it may be necessary to include explanations not mentioned in the Bible that complement and clarify the story for his audience.

4. The storyteller needs to prepare in advance

The following suggestions will help the storyteller prepare in advance for telling his story.

4.1 Begin preparation by identifying the structure of the story

Key-elements that help identify the structure of a Bible story are:
- **Context.** The context establishes the place and time in which the story occurred and the characters who begin the story.
- **Key-person(s).** These are the important characters in the story.
- **Key-location**. This is the principal location where the events took place.
- **Key-repetitions.** Events in a story are often tied together by words, themes, facts or ideas that are repeated, either exactly or with minor variations. Repetitions are made in biblical stories in order to emphasize truths, to build a climax or to express strong emotions.
- **Key-attitudes.** Stories express attitudes and emotions. To be true to scripture, one must express the same attitudes as those expressed by the original storyteller. For example, in telling the parable of the prodigal son (Lk 15:11-32), the storyteller should express the following attitudes:
  - The selfishness of the younger son who wanted to receive his inheritance before his father died;
  - The hopelessness of the prodigal in the pigpen;
  - The compassion and joy of the father receiving his son home;
  - The anger of the older brother when confronting his father;
  - The compassion of the father when dealing with the older brother.
- **Initial-problem.** Almost all Bible stories begin with an event that is related to a problem or necessity that changes the initial situation.
- **Sequence of events.** The sequence of events is the outline of the story and will help the storyteller learn and remember the structure and main plot points.
- **Final-situation of the story**. Understand the state of affairs at the ending of the story.

Telling a Bible story is similar to flying an airplane. If one knows how to take off and how to land, he can usually find the way to his destination. If the storyteller knows the problem that begins the story and how it is solved, he can remember to tell the events that happened along the way.

People who are good at telling jokes have both the beginning sentence and the punch line in mind before telling the joke. The storyteller needs to have in mind both how the story begins and how it ends. The Bible storyteller needs to have in mind the initial-problem and the final-situation.

The storyteller should not explain the key-person, the key-location, the initial-problem, the attitudes expressed by the story, the facts and ideas repeated, and the final-situation of the story. However, once he is aware of these things, he vividly communicates them to his listeners.

4.2 The storyteller should prepare for several days in advance for the telling of his story

The storyteller should refer to the analysis of the structure of the story on a daily basis before the telling of the story. Each day review the sequence of events. He should also read the story in the Bible again and again and again. It is helpful to read the story in different translations of the Bible.

In order to have a story firmly in the memory, the narrator should repeat it often on a regular basis. In order to retain it, the storyteller must continue to repeat the narrative. The best preparation is the telling and retelling of the story.

4.3 The storyteller should avoid memorizing the story

Many beginning storytellers prepare to tell a story by memorizing the words used to tell the story. They repeat the story, word for word, over and over. Memorization is hard on the storyteller and on the listeners. It is more effective to think, and rethink, and rethink the story, rather than mindlessly repeating words!

Memorization for storytelling becomes a hindrance. The act of memorizing the story instills the fear of forgetting it. Memorization inhibits and removes freedom and joy from storytelling. Most memorized stories sound like they were chipped out of granite. Memorization also produces fear in the listeners. Once listeners realize that the storyteller is reciting lines that were memorized, they start to worry if he is going to make it through to the end. Every pause presents the unsettling possibility that the storyteller has forgotten lines in the story.

4.4 The storyteller may find it helpful to memorize a few key parts of the story

It is helpful for the storyteller to memorize a few key parts of the story: the first few sentences; the final-situation; any repetitive phrases or sentences that are important to keep the meaning or the flow of the story; and any list that is contained within the story.

Memorize the opening sentences in order to know how to begin. Memorize the final-situation to know how to end the story. That keeps the storyteller from fumbling for a way to get out of the story. Preparation helps the storyteller both start and end strong.

Phrases or sentences that are repeated throughout the story should be memorized. For example: in the creation story, the phrase: "And there was evening, and there was morning; the (1st, 2nd, 3rd ...) day" is repeated six times. The phrase: "And God saw that it was good," is repeated seven times.

Lists that are contained within the story need to be memorized. For example, the creation story has a list of things that were created each day (Gen 1). Another example, the list of ten plagues when God freed the Israelites from slavery in Egypt (Ex 7:14 - 12:29).

A guideline for the storyteller: do not memorize the story. But it is helpful to memorize the beginning, the final-situation, phrases that are repeated, and lists contained within the story.

5. Visualize and imagine the story before telling it

For a story to come alive, the teller must "see" the story taking place in his imagination, in the same way that he experiences a dream. Then he conveys the sense of vitality to his listeners. To do this, the storyteller needs to use his imagination to help him understand what happened, to experience the emotions of the story and to communicate them without being theatrical. Using the imagination beforehand helps the storyteller vibrate with emotions while telling the story. The storyteller uses his imagination in order to understand what happened and feel the emotions of the story, but not to reinvent what happened!

The more the story is internalized, imagined, and felt, the easier it is to remember and the more details the teller will include.

Thinking through a story can be done in the dead spaces of time or when engaged in activities that require little mental attention. Take advantage of spare time: before and after bedtime, when riding in the car, or while waiting for an appointment. Take advantage of activities that require little mental attention: taking a shower, beautifying the face before the mirror with a razor or makeup, driving in little traffic, washing dishes or mowing the grass.

5.1 Rethink the story using the imagination to experience the events that took place

The storyteller needs to use his imagination to experience the story he will be telling:
- The sights;
- The sounds;
- The smells;
- The tastes;
- The feelings;
- The emotions.

The storyteller should mentally experience the story with his five senses: sight, smell, sound, taste, and touch.

EXAMPLE # 1: USING IMAGINATION TO EXPERIENCE A BIBLE STORY

Suggestion for using your imagination to experience the story of Joseph and his brothers (Gen 37).

- Imagine Joseph telling his father: "Daddy, you will never believe what my brothers did!" In the background Joseph's brothers are sneering; "There goes that tattle-tale again."
- Imagine Joseph exclaiming: "Daddy, this coat is gorgeous!" However, Joseph's brothers are complaining among themselves: "That kid is spoiled rotten. The old man never gave us anything like that." Try to feel the joy that Israel felt for his young son; the happiness that Joseph felt at getting a special gift from his father; and the jealous hatred the brothers felt for their spoiled, tattle-telling brother.
- Imagine Joseph telling the family at breakfast: "Listen to this dream I had." Imagine how Israel looked up with a smile on his face while Joseph's brothers clenched their teeth complaining: "Oh not again. Another dream about his lording it over us. Somebody ought to put that kid in his place."
- Imagine the terror Joseph felt when his brothers threw him into the dry well. He was accustomed to special privileges from his father. He didn't understand why his brothers hated him. He begged and pleaded. Imagine the whining crybaby telling his brothers: "Just wait until I tell Daddy what you did to me. You are going to be sorry. This time you went too far."
- Try to feel the cool dampness of the deep dry well. Smell the damp earth. Feel the darkness around Joseph while he sees a distant light at the top. Feel his fear of insects, snakes and crawling creatures that he can't see in the dark, deep well. Imagine what he is feeling when his attempts at climbing out loosen the damp earth that caves in over him.
- Imagine Joseph's terror when he realized his brothers were not joking and that he has been sold as a slave. Try to imagine his cries as he pleaded with his brothers while the slave traders laughed and slapped him around.

The storyteller preparing to tell the story of Joseph and his brothers should use his imagination to experience the event told in the story. He should try to feel the emotions felt by each character mentioned in the story. The storyteller's imagination should produce the story on the screen of his mind so that he has a "virtual reality experience."

EXAMPLE # 2: USING IMAGINATION TO EXPERIENCE A BIBLE STORY

To use your imagination to experience the story of Jesus' birth, reflect on:
- The reaction of Mary's mother when Mary returned from a three-month visit with cousin Elizabeth and she realized Mary was pregnant. Imagine her reaction when she learned that Joseph was not responsible and heard Mary trying to explain her visit with the angel and that God himself was the father of her child;
- Joseph's confusion when realizing his fiance was pregnant and knowing he couldn't be the father;
- The reaction of the neighbors when they heard Mary's story that the "Holy Spirit" was the father of the child;
- The quickly planned wedding ceremony, with all knowing the bride was with child;
- The reality of being married six months and the first child was due any day;
- Imagine the reactions of family members and neighbors;
- The reaction of Joseph and Mary when they arrived in Bethlehem and found only a stable to sleep in;
- The smell of the stable;

- The sounds made by the animals;
- How it was to have a child born in a filthy place with poor lighting at night;
- How Joseph felt when he put the newborn baby into an animal's feed trough.

The storyteller preparing to tell the story of Jesus' birth should use his imagination to produce the story on the screen of his mind. This will enable him to experience the smells, tastes, feelings, and emotions of everything connected with the episode. His imagination should give him a "virtual reality experience."

If the storyteller uses his imagination to see the image vividly, the story will be remembered easily. The storyteller who experiences the events of the story in his imagination will enable his listeners to do the same. By experiencing the events in his imagination as if he were seeing a video on the screen of his mind, the storyteller does not worry about remembering the events in their chronological order; he will narrate the story he experienced using his thought process.

5.2 Rethink the story using the imagination to make a connection between the biblical narrative and one's own experiences.

The storyteller needs to use his imagination to make a connection between his own experiences and the events that took place in the Bible. Making a connection between one's own experience and the biblical event helps one experience the proper emotions when telling the story.

EXAMPLE # 1: CONNECTING A BIBLE STORY TO PERSONAL EXPERIENCES

In order to make a connection between Joseph and his brothers, I remember:
- Joseph told his father about his older brothers' wrongdoings. I remember the anger I felt when my younger sister told my parents about the things I did wrong.
- Joseph must have felt lonely when he was sent to Egypt. The time I felt most alone was when I was a university student and had to work during the Christmas holidays. It was the first time I was away from my family during the holidays.
- Joseph was betrayed by his brothers. I remember the deception I felt after my father's death, and we discovered that a relative had helped dishonest business men "con" my mother. Another time I felt betrayed was when I realized that my university roommate was also dating the girl I wanted to marry.
- When Joseph was shipped to Egypt as a slave, he was forced to adapt to a new culture. It was difficult for me to adjust when I left the small town of Enterprise, Alabama, to go to Samford University in the big city of Birmingham. When my wife and I left the USA to go to live in Brazil, I suffered humiliation and embarrassment learning to speak Portuguese.

EXAMPLE # 2: CONNECTING A BIBLE STORY TO PERSONAL EXPERIENCES

In order to make a connection between the birth of Jesus in the manger and my experiences, I remember:
- The smell of the barnyard on the farm where I was raised;
- The disgust I felt when I stepped in fresh cow manure;
- The most disagreeable night of my life. I was traveling with my wife, three small children and many pieces of baggage through a semidesert area of Brazil. The car motor quit. After we waited on the side of the road for three hours, a lady gave my wife and children a ride into town, but she did not have room for our luggage, so I slept in the bushes by the car. The only hotel in town had no rooms available, and my wife and children slept on the floor of a restaurant-tavern with no mattresses;
- The difficulty of traveling with my wife when she was pregnant. She was more sensitive at that time;
- My first son was born in a sterilized room in a hospital; even so, I was afraid something would go wrong. I can imagine the fear Joseph must have felt in a filthy barnyard, without medical help and with poor lighting.

Making a connection between one's own experience and the biblical event helps the storyteller experience the proper emotions when telling the story. The storyteller does not mention the connections he made between the story and his own experiences, but those connections help him express the proper feeling while telling the story.

5.3 Use visual symbols to map out the Bible story

Mapping out the Bible story by using stick line drawings or simple pictures is one of the best tools to help the storyteller visualize and remember it. Instead of writing words and sentences, the storyteller represents each episode of the story with a design or a stick line drawing.

The storyteller begins making visual designs for the context or initial-situation, other designs for the initial-problem, he continues with drawings for each of the sequence of events, and finishes with drawings for the final-situation. He makes visual notes for each episode. At times the map may include a word or phrase; however, it is mostly drawings.

A story-board is similar to mapping out the story. The storyteller uses simple line drawings or simple pictures to represent what's happening in each sequence of events. Then he uses the story-board to jolt his memory as he tells the story. The Bible storyteller does not memorize the words that tell the story; but he remembers the pictures of the events mentioned in the story.

If the storyteller needs notes to help him tell the narrative, he uses the visual map or story-board instead of notes using words and phrases.

EXAMPLE: ***MAPPING A BIBLE STORY*** (Gen 37)

5.4 Pantomime the Bible Story

Pantomiming is an excellent tool for learning a Bible story without memorizing it. Many storytellers have found that pantomiming the story helps them to experience the story with their entire body.

I have been in countries where I did not speak the language. On several occasions I was able to communicate to a sales person by pantomiming and was able to understand the sales person who pantomimed to me. To buy eggs, I put my fingers from my two hands together to form an oval shape. Then I put my hands by my side and flapped them as if they were wings, and I clucked like a chicken.

The pantomimic communicates through bodily movement instead of the spoken word. To express by pantomime, is to communicate a thought, action, object, or event by means of bodily movements, gestures, facial expressions and attitudes. For example, one would pantomime the idea of a "baby" by cradling an imaginary infant.

To pantomime a story, the storyteller practices the story without using his voice. However, he will use the full range of movement allowed by the human body to express each thought, attitude, dialogue, object, and event found in the story.

I suggest that the storyteller pantomime the Bible story in two stages:

1st <u>First stage</u>: While reading the story, use gestures and facial expression to express each sequence of event in the story.
2nd <u>Second stage</u>: Remember the details of the story without memorizing it. At this point, minimize the spoken word by saying few words while concentrating on pantomiming each event and dialogue with gestures and bodily movement.

6. Follow the structural order of the biblical story and utilize the sequence of events

Many pastors and teachers within the church are accustomed to teaching or preaching the Bible stories and must make a conscious effort to change habits and tell the story without stopping to explain, teach or preach.

Storytelling is a natural process where the story is told, following its natural structure in chronological order. The storyteller emphasizes the words and facts emphasized in the Bible story while emotionally experiencing the story being told. The storyteller should economize his words, staying close to the words used in a first-rate contemporary translation.

The storyteller should follow **the sequence of events**, telling the story in chronological order:

- <u>Consider the context</u>. Explain the background of the story with a few words that would help the listeners understand the historical circumstances surrounding the story.
- <u>Follow the sequence of events</u>. Start at the beginning of the story. Continue following the sequence of events until concluding with the final-situation of the story.

7. Rehearse the story

The storyteller should practice telling his story out loud. Rehearsing helps him know which parts come easily and which need more work. Telling the story out loud helps fix the story in his mind and gives him opportunity to work on his voice and gestures.

8. Making mistakes is a reality

The only places where perfect people exist are in books and films. The reason: mistakes are edited out. In the real world, the Bible Storyteller must speak without an editor to remove his errors. And, he will make mistakes. Those willing to make errors are the only ones who will improve. The best plan to improve one's ability to tell Bible stories is: tell stories, tell stories and tell more stories. Keep telling Bible stories and the mind will become sharper at remembering details. The one who constantly tells Bible stories will never become perfect; however, he will constantly improve. Therefore, seek and take advantage of opportunities to tell Bible stories.

A small child learning to speak makes his father happy when he tries to say: "Daddy," but comes out with "Da-Da." In the same way our Heavenly Father will be pleased with one who is learning to tell Bible stories and at first doesn't get it perfect.

9. Trust the story

Trust the story! Bible stories are God's stories. His power is present and manifested by the storyteller who understands the story, is faithful to the story, and has internalized the story by making a connection between it and his own life. The storyteller can have the certainty that the power of God is active when a Bible story is told in a straightforward, simple and clear manner.

The storyteller can trust the story to produce fruits beyond his expectations. One can never predict the results of a well-told story, but the storyteller should expect the results to surprise him with joy. A Bible story can be compared to the seeds of Jesus' parables that grow in their own manner and produce fruits beyond what is expected. A well-told story will produce fruit. Trust the story! Tell the story!

OBSERVATION:

The literate person, who had opportunity to study, is the one who needs training in how to tell a story. The oral communicator uses storytelling naturally as a principal means to express his ideas. Therefore, the teacher who trains oral communicators must work **with**, not **against** the narrative style of local storytellers. The teacher must not undo an oral communicator's natural storytelling discourse style.

The teacher should work with the oral communicator to help him tell Bible stories using his cultural method. For example, rap is a narrative device common in American Black communities. The Christian who knows how to rap should be encouraged to use that skill to tell Bible stories. In the semi-desert *Sertão* of Northeast Brazil, storytellers tell rhymed stories while strumming on a guitar. There, Christians should be encouraged to rhyme Bible stories and strum the guitar while narrating them. I would encourage teachers who train oral communicators to:

- Discover within the Christian community people of good reputation who are recognized storytellers (either in songs, poems, rap, etc.), by their own people;
- Encourage them and work with them to prepare Bible stories in their cultural format, using poems, songs, or rap, etc.;
- Help them use their own cultural methods to tell the story while remaining true to biblical facts;
- In this way the trainer becomes a facilitator, working with local talent to produce a desired message.

SELECTING LIFE-LESSONS FROM A BIBLE STORY TO BECOME THE DIVISIONS FOR A SERMON OR STUDY

The storyteller who couples Bible Storytelling with preaching or teaching must select appropriate life-lessons for his listeners or students. When analyzing a Bible story, the story-analyst discovers many life-lessons. One story may yield ten, twenty, thirty or more life-lessons. It would be unwise to present so many life-lessons on one occasion. He must choose the life-lessons most appropriate for the needs of his listeners or students.

Choosing life-lessons from a Bible story to use in preaching or teaching can be compared to the man who is building a house and has a 3/4 ton pick-up to transport building material. He goes to the building supply store that has all the material he needs to build his house. However, he can not take all the wood, cement, plumbing pipes, electrical wiring, sheetrock and roofing material in one trip. He must know where he is in the building of the house and determine the material he most needs to do the task at hand.

The storytelling preacher or teacher has a limited amount of time. He doesn't have time to present all the precious life-lessons he finds in a single Bible story during one occasion. Listeners can only take in a limited the amount of information in at one session. The more life-lessons that are sent out, the less true communication there will be. The preacher/teacher must select the life-lessons that are most needed for his listeners in their present circumstances.

The builder who uses his pick-up to take all the building material in one trip will damage the body of his truck and overheat the engine. The preacher or teacher who tries to present all the life-lessons he discovered from a story on one occasion will confuse and tire his listeners or students.

1. **Consider if the story is part of a Storying Track or if it is a Solitary Story**

Three types of Storying Tracks have been mentioned: Multiple Storying Tracks, Single Storying Track and Fast Storying Track (Fast Tracking). The Solitary Story stands alone. It is not part of a Storying Track.

Multiple Storying Tracks and Single Storying Track are usually used for different types of people groups. Therefore, different criteria are needed for selecting the life-lessons.

The **Multiple Storying Track** is usually applied with pre-literate tribal people and people groups hostile to Christianity. The **Multiple Storying Track** is a plan for a group of stories to be retold or recycled to the same group of people. It is cyclic in that some of the same stories are repeated more than one time. Multiple Storying Tracks make use of Storytelling Cycles which have different purposes. The spiritual condition of the people within the target group determines the Storying Track used with them. Each track is a chronological group of stories selected to meet the needs of the hearers.

Each Storying Track stresses a certain emphasis. Therefore, it is necessary to consider:
- ■The emphasis of the Storying Track;
- ■The life-lessons discovered in the story;
- ■The needs of the listeners and how they connect to the Storying Track emphasis;
- ■The life-lessons that most relate to the emphasis of the Storying Track and the needs of the listeners.

The following chart shows the emphasis of each of the Multiple Storying Tracks.

MULTIPLE STORYING TRACK

TRACK I Evangelistic Bible Storying Track *Selective stories to give an overall view of the Bible to non-evangelicals.*	TRACK II Discipling Bible Storying Track *Essential stories for new Christians or those with little Bible knowledge.*	TRACK III Leadership Equipping Bible Storying Track *Stories selected to teach doctrine and train mature Christians*
Tell Bible stories beginning with the creation in Genesis through the life, death, resurrection and ascension of Jesus until the first converts recorded in Acts.	Review the stories in their chronological order. Begin with the creation in Genesis and continue until the first converts presented in Acts. Add new stories as needed. Then increase other stories from the Book of Acts.	Review stories already told while adding new ones as needed. Summarize the New Testament Epistles and Revelation, do doctrinal studies using Bible stories and then do analytical doctrinal Bible studies.
Emphasize: ■Who God is; ■Character of God; ■Inability of man to please God; ■Man's desperate situation; ■Man's need for a liberator; ■Life of Jesus Christ; ■first believers.	Emphasize: ■God's relationship with his people; ■God's provision for his people; ■Importance of obeying biblical commands; ■Ministry of the Holy Spirit; ■Expected behavior of a follower of Jesus; ■Organization and function of a local church; ■How the Gospel of Jesus is spread.	Emphasize: ■Fellowship within the family of faith; ■Life and character of spiritual leaders; ■Methods God uses to sanctify and mature his children; ■Importance of obeying God; ■Methods God uses to evangelize; ■Methods God uses to plant and grow churches.

The **Single Storying Track** is usually used with a literate people group familiar with Christianity. The Single Storying Track is a group of Bible stories presented once and, with each story, truths are emphasized that connect with the needs of the listeners. The storyteller begins with the creation in Genesis and goes through the Old Testament, treats the life, death, resurrection, and ascension of Jesus; continues through the Book of Acts; places the Epistles in their chronological order within Acts; and finishes with stories related to the end times.

A group participating in the Single Storying Track may contain any or all of the following:
■Nonbelievers in Jesus who know nothing about the Bible;
■Nonbelievers familiar with the Bible;
■New believers;
■Mature Christians;
■Church leaders.

For selecting life-lessons to be used in the Single Storying Track, consider:
■The life-lessons discovered in the Bible story;
■The greatest needs in the lives of the listeners or students;
■The life-lessons that connect with the greatest needs of the listeners or students.

Life-lessons are not selected for the **Fast Storying Track**. In **Fast Tracking**, the storyteller is limited for time and tells a series of Bible stories in one session in order to give a panoramic view of the Bible. He tells the stories without comment or exposition.

Solitary Bible Storytelling isolates a story to be presented to a specific group for a specific occasion. Solitary Bible Storytelling narrates a story that is not part of a Storying Track or series. The story stands alone.

For selecting life-lessons to be used when Solitary Storytelling is coupled with preaching or teaching, consider:
■The life-lessons discovered in the Bible story;
■The greatest needs in the lives of the listeners or students;
■The life-lessons that connect with the needs of the listeners or students.

2. **Consider worldview issues of the target group and life-lessons that connect to bridges or barriers**

It is important to learn what the target group believes, to encourage their beliefs when correct, and to correct with biblical truths when wrong. As the storyteller gains an understanding of the worldview of his target people, he should determine elements that serve as bridges and barriers. Barriers found in the local worldview will hinder the target group from accepting biblical truths. Bridges found in the local worldview will help the target group hear and understand biblical truths. Both barriers and bridges need to be considered when selecting life-lessons. In the same way that the storyteller should consider those elements in choosing a Storying Track, he should consider them in selecting the life-lessons discovered in the stories.

3. Consider the time available when selecting life-lessons

The time available to the preacher or teacher will influence the number of life-lessons that can be presented in one session.

In most churches in the United States, Sunday School teachers have an hour to teach and the preacher has thirty minutes to preach. In most churches the congregation becomes restless after thirty minutes of preaching.

In my experiences in Brazil, most Bible studies in homes should not exceed a forty-five minute teaching time. I did lead one home Bible study group where the participants desired more discussion, and we extended to one hour and thirty minutes.

In the cities, most preachers who hold their congregation's attention preach less than thirty minutes. But I have been in some rural areas where people walked for several hours to get to church, and they expected a two to three-hour worship service including more than an hour-long sermon. I once had a lady in the semi-desert area of Brazil tell me: "I didn't walk two and a half hours to church to only hear a thirty-minute sermon."

Consider the time available and choose life-lessons that can be treated adequately within that time frame. It is better to communicate thoroughly a few life-lessons than to superficially pass over many. The life-lessons selected to be communicated become the divisions of the Bible study or sermon.

BIBLE STORYTELLING WITH DIALOGUE

The person who uses **Bible Storytelling with Dialogue,** narrates the Bible story and then discusses it with his listeners. The dialogue is open-ended and takes the direction the listeners desire, as long as it is in some way related to the story.

If the storyteller has only one encounter with a group, he may tell one story and then help his listeners discuss it. However, if the storytelling session can last several hours, he should tell a cluster of Bible stories in chronological order, switching back and forth between storytelling and discussion.

If the storyteller will be with a group for several days and then be absent for an extended time, he may have several Bible storytelling sessions. He may have only one storytelling session a day, or he may have multiple storytelling sessions each day. After each session, he helps the listeners discuss the story just told.

If the storyteller will be with a group over an extended period of time, I recommend chronological Bible storytelling. The storyteller may have weekly or monthly encounters with a group of listeners. At each encounter, he will tell a new story and then help his listeners discuss it.

Bible Storytelling with Dialogue is widely used by missionaries ministering to tribal people without a written language who have little or no knowledge of biblical teachings.

Bible Storytelling with Dialogue is the most effective method of gaining an audience among people groups hostile toward Christianity. Some people groups would kill the Christian who confronts them with biblical truth. However, people hostile to Christianity will often listen to Bible stories and discuss them. While discussing Bible stories, the Holy Spirit can confront them with the truth.

Bible Storytelling with Dialogue is a simple, effective method to train potential leaders who are beginners in communicating God's Word. If the trainee is unable to read, he is told the Bible story at least twice. Then he is asked to repeat the story in the presence of the trainer. The trainee is taught a set of generic questions that can be asked about any Bible story. After learning the story, the trainee is sent out to tell the Bible story and ask the generic questions.

If the trainee is able to read, he is given the Bible stories in writing and a list of generic questions. He is taught to tell Bible stories and to lead discussions by asking generic questions. As the trainee becomes proficient in storytelling, he will make adaptations and will develop his own generic questions.

Bible Storytelling with Dialogue includes:
- The Bible story;
- Generic questions to help create dialogue.

THE BIBLE STORY

Bible Storytelling with Dialogue begins by telling the Bible story. The story is told following its natural structure in chronological order. Each telling of a story must be true to the biblical facts even when complementary facts are included in order to help today's listeners understand the Bible story. The storyteller should economize his words and stay close to the words used in a first-rate contemporary translation. He should have the certainty that the power of God is active when a Bible story is told in a straightforward, simple and clear manner. After the storyteller has identified **the sequence of events,** he should follow that structure and tell the story in chronological order:

- Consider the context. Explain background information that would help the listeners to understand the historical circumstances surrounding the narrative, to understand the initial situation, and to identify characters in the story.
- Follow the sequence of events. Start at the beginning of the story, making sure to include the facts that enable the listeners to identify the initial-problem. Continue following the sequence of events until the final-situation of the story has been told.

GENERIC QUESTIONS THAT HELP CREATE DIALOGUE

After telling the story, the storyteller dialogues with his listeners. He becomes a facilitator who helps story-listeners talk about the story. Using the dialogue method, the storyteller, is not the teacher who controls the life-lessons his students will learn. He help his listeners talk about the story without determining what they discuss. He should release control over the discussion and let the story-listeners discover for themselves life-lessons from the story to apply to their lives. The storyteller is on a story-journey as a fellow traveler with his story-listeners.

SOME DOS AND DON'TS FOR DIALOGUING ABOUT A BIBLE STORY	
Don't	**Do**
1. Don't expect everyone to like every story you tell.	1. Do engage the story-listeners in activities and discussions that help them grasp the meaning of the story.
2. Don't expect everyone to see the same life-lessons you do.	2. Do allow the story-listeners to express their opinions without being made "right" or "wrong."
3. Don't control, but guide and allow the story-listeners to discover the life-lessons for themselves.	3. Do pay attention, listen, and allow viewpoints to be expressed and respected.
4. Don't give the story-listeners the life-lessons you want them to discover. Let them find life-lessons for themselves.	4. Do expect the Holy Spirit to guide your story-listeners to the life-lessons they need.
5. Don't say, "No, you're wrong." Do say, "Why do you say that?"	

I am suggesting some dialogue questions; however, the storyteller needs to have the conviction that Bible stories speak for themselves, and they touch his listeners in ways that the he can never know nor guess. Therefore, if the listeners start talking about a story as soon as they hear it, the storyteller should give them the freedom to head in the direction they wish to go.

The following dialogue questions are generic. They may be asked about any Bible story, and they may be used with any group. All story-listeners will be able to participate in the dialogue, including those who have little biblical knowledge, and mature Christians with much biblical knowledge.

1. What catches your attention in the story?

This question has no right nor wrong answers. Each listener should feel free to express his opinion. Allow the story-listeners to express their opinions without being made "right" or "wrong."

2. Is there anything in the story that is hard to understand?

This is another question that allows the story-listeners to express their opinions without being made "right" or "wrong." Listening to the answers will help the storyteller discover the needs of his story-listeners. When you disagree with an answer, don't say, "No, you're wrong." Do say something similar to, "Why do you have problems with that?"

3. Who are the main characters in the story?

This question allows the listeners to discuss the characters in the story. Stories are character driven. Characters act, experience conflict and undertake the struggles in a story. The events in the story are generated by the key-character's predicament.

4. **What problems did the characters face?**

This question allows the story-listeners to identify problems faced in the story. Stories are about characters, their struggles and their conflicts.

5. **How did the characters face their problems?**

This question helps the story-listeners identify the reactions of the key-characters to their problems. Pay attention to how the story-listeners make judgement on the rightness or wrongness of the character's actions and choices.

6. **How have you faced similar problems?**

This is a question to help the story-listeners identify with the story. It will help the listener counter point the Bible story with their own experiences.

7. **Is there someone in the story who is similar to you or who is different from you?**

This question helps the Holy Spirit have freedom to guide the story-listeners to life-lessons they need to apply to their own lives.

8. **What does the story tell about God?**

This question helps the story-listeners see God in each Bible story. Bible stories are not the stories of Adam, Eve, Cain, Able, Noah, Abraham, Joseph, David, Mary, Peter and Paul. They are the stories of God's involvement in the lives of Adam, Eve, Cain, Able, Noah, Abraham, Joseph, David, Mary, Peter and Paul. God is the key-character of the Bible and each story is about God.

Suggested generic dialogue questions:
- What catches your attention in the story?
- Is there anything in the story that is hard to understand?
- Who are the main characters in the story?
- What problems did the characters face?
- How did the characters face their problems?
- How have you faced similar problems?
- Is there someone in the story who is similar to you or who is different from you?
- What does the story tell about God?

NARRATIVE PREACHING
BIBLE STORYTELLING WITH PREACHING

Bible Storytelling may be coupled with preaching. The **Bible Storytelling with Preaching** approach may also be called **Narrative Preaching**. The storyteller tells the story and then uses the story as a basis for preaching. The story is the text for the sermon. The main emphasis is the Bible story, but it is framed with a sermon and applications. Two basic methods for preaching with Bible stories are presented:

■ **Bible Storytelling with Preaching after the Story**

The storyteller preacher narrates the Bible story that is the text to his sermon. After telling the story, he develops selected life-lessons discovered in the story as sermon points. The preaching application is delayed until after the telling of the story.

■ **Bible Storytelling with Preaching Inserted**

The storyteller preacher narrates the Bible story until he comes to an episode that inspires an important life-lesson. At this point, he stops storytelling, inserts his life-lesson and develops it as a sermon point. Then he continues storytelling until he reaches another episode that inspires a life-lesson he wishes to develop. He continues storytelling and inserting life-lessons until the end of the story.

I. USE THE PREACHING CYCLE WITH EACH LIFE-LESSON SELECTED FOR THE SERMON

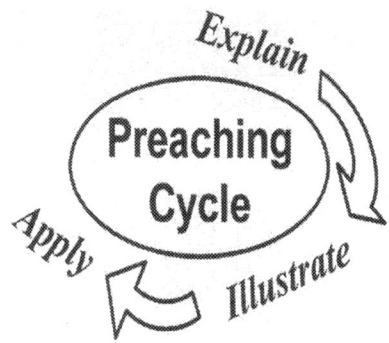

The storytelling preacher should begin to prepare his sermon by analyzing the Bible story that is to be his text. While analyzing the story, he will discover many life-lessons taught by the story. He must select the life-lessons he wishes to employ in his sermon. Each selected life-lesson becomes a division of the sermon. While there are two basic plans for coupling storytelling with preaching, both use the **Preaching Cycle** to develop life-lessons chosen to become sermon divisions.

The **Preaching Cycle** requires three activities for each life-lesson selected to become a sermon division:
■ Explain the life-lesson;
■ Illustrate the life-lesson;
■ Apply the life-lesson to the lives of the listeners.

1. **Explain the life-lesson**

Some of the things the storyteller preacher does while explaining the life-lesson are:
■ He reveals how the life-lesson was discovered in the Bible story;
■ He explains the historical and cultural context of the Bible story;
■ He clarifies details and presents facts about the Bible story that makes the life-lesson more understandable;
■ He presents facts that may not be known, which help his listeners understand the life-lesson;
■ He throws light upon the life-lesson by offering details or motives previously unclear or only implicit;

Bible Storytelling Tools © Jackson Day

- He clarifies the reason for emphasizing the life-lesson;
- He defines or clarifies words to make them better understood;
- He shows the logical development of the life-lesson;
- He uses other Bible texts that explain and reinforce the life-lesson.

Events from the story that is the text to the sermon help explain the life-lesson. Show how the events within the story inspire and communicate the life-lesson.

The Bible interprets itself. Therefore, the preacher can use other teaching texts to explain the story and life-lesson being emphasized. Psalms, Proverbs, the Prophets, the teachings of Jesus, Paul's letters, the General Epistles, and Hebrews can be used to explain a life-lesson. While teaching texts, such as the teachings of Jesus and Paul's letters, help explain a life-lesson, other Bible stories help illustrate it.

2. Illustrate the life-lesson

The storyteller-preacher needs a story, or an anecdote, or a joke, or a description of an event that illustrates the life-lesson. The life-lesson may be illustrated with events from other Bible stories or from stories outside the Bible. Illustrations, beyond the story text, may be:
- Examples;
- Other Bible stories;
- Stories outside the Bible;
- Jokes;
- Anecdotes;
- Comparisons;
- Personal experiences;
- Sports events;
- Historical events;
- Contemporary events.

A good sermon illustration is usually short and simple. Take time to simplify stories used for illustrations. Most illustrations should take less than a minute to tell. Many stories can be told in less than 15 seconds. Nothing kills an illustration like unnecessary length. Avoid dragging out illustrations by giving unnecessary information or going off in tangents.

Illustrations do not replace the explanation, but they serve to reinforce and confirm it. Stories, jokes, and anecdotes are only selected for the purpose of clarifying the life-lesson. Stories, jokes, examples, and anecdotes that do not clarify or support the life-lesson become weak elements in the sermon. Likewise, illustrations just entertain when they don't clarify the life-lesson being presented. A good illustration turns on a light that clarifies the explanation. Illustrations also make the sermon more interesting for the listeners. A good story used as an illustration also gives listeners a memory hook to recall the sermon point.

A storyteller is successful when entertaining, but a preacher is effective only when stories help communicate biblical truths.

The storytelling-preacher needs to develop the habit of searching for stories and making notes to help him remember useful ones. He should make notes to retain any event he experiences or any story he hears or reads that could be useful. The first rule to finding good stories is simple: "If you like it, save it." The faintest pencil is better than the best memory. Write down anecdotes and stories that could be used in sermons. The one who starts looking for good stories will find them everywhere. Soon he will experience stories popping into his mind.

Stories can be adapted in order to best illustrate a life-lesson. Don't simply use a story the way it was found. Update it, personalize it, and shape it so it best illustrates the biblical life-lesson. However, the preacher must be truthful. He should not recreate biblical stories, nor should he alter historical facts; however, he may condense the stories to mention only details that help illustrate the biblical truth.

Humor and jokes can offend listeners; therefore, they should be used with caution. Types of humor to avoid using in sermon illustrations:
- **SARCASTIC HUMOR:** Sarcastic humor brings laughter at the expense of others. Sarcasm is often used like a knife, inserting it quickly, turning it for effect and then pulling it out before the victim realizes he or she has been stabbed. Sarcasm may work with close friends, but it is dangerous to use in public.
- **ETHNIC HUMOR:** Ethnic humor may be interpreted as prejudice. Prejudice is easy to ignite and hard to kill. If the preacher uses ethnic humor, he should make his own race or ethnic group the brunt of the joke. The church of a famous pastor in the United States broadcasted their Sunday morning services on television. A Jewish

evangelical was the pastor's close friend and a popular church member. One Sunday, the pastor made a joke about his Jewish friend's long nose. The Jewish friend and the church audience liked the joke. However, many in the TV audience accused the pastor of being biased against Jews.

■ HUMOR THAT OFFENDS SOMEONE: If the brunt of a joke is a fat person, some who are overweight may be offended. A joke that leaves even one person close to tears should be avoided.

■ HUMOR THAT BELITTLES THE SACRED: Avoid jokes that belittle the sacred or that distract from the seriousness of the occasion. When my first son was born, I remained in the delivery room until he was born. During the delivery the medical doctor told jokes to the nurse. The birth of a baby was a common event to the doctor. However, for me the birth of my first child was a sacred experience. Bible storytellers should not treat the Bible as common, nor should they use biblical stories and texts as the thrust of jokes.

■ HUMOR THAT USES PROFANITY: A joke that requires profanity to make it funny should never be told by the preacher. It certainly does not belong in the sermon.

■ HUMOR RELATED TO SEX THAT EMBARRASSES THE SENSITIVE: Jokes that are accepted by the youth and young couples could create embarrassment to some of the older generation. Such jokes should be avoided.

■ HUMOR THAT IS UNRELATED TO THE SERMON: A joke should be used in a sermon only if it helps the listeners understand the truth being preached. If a joke has no point, leave it to the comedians or save it for the dinner table. Humor that is on target in a sermon progresses the message of the preacher.

Use illustrations that link to things the listeners already know and have experienced. Listeners can only understand illustrations that relate to their experiences. It would be difficult for Brazilians living in equatorial jungles to understand an illustration describing children having a snowball fight.

3. Apply the life-lesson to the listeners' lives

An application establishes what God desires the listeners to know, to be, or to do as a result of understanding the life-lesson discovered in the Bible story. Applications show how the listeners should put the life-lesson to use in their own lives. They explain what the listeners need to do or how they need to change in order to practice the life-lesson communicated from the Bible story.

Three types of applications:
1st   General application: one that is external and serves for all people in all locations at all times in history.
2nd   Specific ecclesiastical or external application: one that applies biblical teaching to specific other people or a local church.
3rd   Personal application: a biblical truth applied to oneself.

All life-lessons presented in a sermon should have as a common goal: to get the listeners to change! Preaching without change as its prime objective is useless. It is a waste of the preacher's and listeners' time. The change may be emotional, intellectual, behavioral, physical or a combination of all four, but it must occur for the sermon to be successful. The preacher wants his listeners to change in one or more of the following:

■ Believe a truth they haven't believed;
■ Trust a promise they haven't trusted;
■ Understand a truth they haven't understood;
■ Obey a command or law they haven't been obeying;
■ Become something they haven't been;
■ Do something they haven't been doing.

Application explains how the listeners should change by putting the truths presented into action. It is not enough to mention, explain and illustrate a life-lesson. Listeners should apply them to their lives. Appeal for the listeners to apply the life-lesson presented to their own lives. Clarify how the listeners should change and appeal for them to change.

4. Develop only one life-lesson at a time using the Preaching Cycle

Some preachers make the mistake of starting to explain one life-lesson, switching to another, leaving the Bible story, or deviating from the sermon division without finding their way back. One deviation becomes the taking-off point for a series of detours. When that happens, the divisions of the sermon become irregular, and confusion reigns in the mind of the listeners. Sometimes a preacher begins explaining one life-lesson, illustrates another, and makes application for still another. To use the **Preaching Cycle**, state the life-lesson that is transformed into a sermon division, then stick with it until it is explained, illustrated and applied. Don't jump from one life-lesson to another, without completing the **Preaching Cycle**.

A Bible story has many life-lessons, but when one is chosen, the preacher should stick with it until it is developed. A Bible story is similar to a passenger train. A train has many passenger cars, just as a Bible story has several life-lessons. Nobody can travel in two cars at the same time. When the preacher chooses a life-lesson, he should stick with it until it is developed. Each sermon division contains the **Preaching Cycle** elements, just as each passenger car contains different seats. The **Preaching Cycle** should develop one life-lesson at a time.

Example of the Preaching Cycle:

Story: The Temptation of Jesus
Text: Matthew 4:1-11

Example of a life-lesson converted into a division of the sermon: Satan is the one who schedules the temptation.

Explanation:
Satan is the one who schedules the temptations that each person must face. He schedules the time, place and kind of temptation without informing the person to be tempted.
After Jesus had fasted forty days, Satan came to tempt him.

Illustrations:
■The Dallas Cowboys have a schedule of their football games and are able to prepare in advance for each game. Yet, if Satan were scheduling the games, the Cowboys could be preparing to play the Denver Broncos on Sunday, but on Wednesday receive a call, "Time to suit up. The game begins in thirty minutes." To the Cowboys' surprise, when they suit up and run out to play, the playing field is a basketball gymnasium and their opponents are the Chicago Bulls.

Application:
Satan is going to schedule temptations for each one of you. You need to be prepared at all times because you never know when the temptation will come nor what the temptation will be. You can know only that Satan is scheduling temptations for you, and you always need to be prepared.

CONCLUSION TO PREACHING CYCLE

Using the **Preaching Cycle** helps with communication. It touches the listener's brain (explanation), his heart (stories that illustrate), and his personal life (application). The preacher who touches all three in a rhythm that explains, illustrates and applies will keep his listeners tuned in to his sermon.

The **Preaching Cycle** always includes explanation, illustration, and application. It does not matter whether explanation or illustration comes first. But application always comes last. Yet in most situations, the **Preaching Cycle** makes an *Illustration Sandwich*. The life-lesson is emphasized at least three times. First it is explained, then repeated in the form of stories which illustrate it, and finished off with applications. Redundancy built into the **Preaching Cycle** helps hammer home the life-lesson.

II. BIBLE STORYTELLING WITH PREACHING AFTER THE STORY

Using this approach, the storyteller preacher tells the Bible story that is the text to his sermon, and then he develops the life-lessons discovered in the story as the points of his sermon. The preaching application is delayed until after the telling of the story.

1. **How to prepare a sermon for Bible Storytelling with preaching after the story**

   1.1 Analyze the Bible story

   Before the storytelling preacher can preach, coupling Bible Storytelling with preaching, he must study the Bible story. He should follow the steps in the chapter **How to Analyze a Bible Story**.

   1.2 Select the most important life-lessons for the listeners

   The storyteller who couples Bible Storytelling with preaching needs to select appropriate life-lessons for his listeners. When analyzing a Bible story, many life-lessons are discovered. The preacher must choose the life-lessons most appropriate for the needs of his listeners. Practical suggestions on choosing life-lessons are found in the chapter: **Selecting Life-lessons from a Bible Story to Become the Divisions for a Sermon or Study**.

   If the sermon will be part of a **Storying Track**, the storytelling preacher will consider the following when selecting the life-lessons for the listeners:
   - The emphasis of the Storying Track;
   - The life-lessons discovered in the story;
   - The needs of the listeners and how they connect to the Storying Track emphasis;
   - The life-lessons that most relate to the emphasis of the Storying Track and the needs of the listeners.

   If the sermon will not be part of a Storying Track, the storytelling preacher will consider the following when selecting the life-lessons for the listeners:
   - The life-lessons discovered in the Bible story;
   - The greatest need in the lives of the listeners;
   - The life-lessons that connect with the needs of the listeners.

2. **Prepare the selected life-lessons, using the Preaching Cycle with each one**

   With each life-lesson discovered from the story that is chosen to become a division of the sermon, the storyteller preacher will develop the **Preaching Cycle**. The preacher must perform three activities with each life-lesson selected to become a division of the sermon:
   - Explain the life-lesson;
   - Illustrate the life-lesson;
   - Apply the life-lesson to the lives of the listeners.

3. **Prepare the Preaching Plan**

   The Preaching Plan is often called the sermon outline. Those who know how to write should make notes on paper concerning their Preaching Plan.

   The Preaching Plan will include:
   - <u>The Bible story</u>: the telling of the Bible story, utilizing the sequence of events;
   - <u>Sermon divisions</u>: life-lessons chosen from the story and developed, following the Preaching Cycle;
   - <u>Conclusion</u>: a summary of the story, life-lessons presented, and appeal for change that would come from putting the life-lessons into practice.

THE BIBLE STORY

Bible Storytelling, with preaching after the story, begins by telling the Bible story. The story is told following its natural structure in chronological order. Each telling of the story must be true to the biblical facts even when complementary facts are included in order to help today's listeners understand the Bible story. The storyteller should economize his words and stay close to the words used in a first-rate contemporary translation. He should have the certainty that the power of God is active when a Bible story is told in a straightforward, simple and clear manner. This would be a good time to review the chapter: **Telling a Bible Story**.

Storytelling is a natural process. After one has identified **the sequence of events,** he should follow that structure and tell the story in chronological order:

- <u>Consider the context</u>. Explain background information that would help the listeners to understand the historical circumstances surrounding the narrative, to understand the initial situation, and to identify characters in the story.
- <u>Follow the sequence of events</u>. Start at the beginning of the story, making sure to include the facts that enable the listeners to identify the initial-problem. Continue following the sequence of events until the final-situation of the story has been told.

In making his Preaching Plan, the storytelling preacher will adapt notes made when analyzing the story. He will copy or abbreviate the notes from the context and sequence of events.

DIVISIONS: Selected Life-Lessons from the Story Are Transformed into Preaching Cycles

I use the following numbering system to outline my sermon divisions:
1. The first life-lesson transformed into a sermon division.
2. The second life-lesson transformed into a sermon division.
3. The third life-lesson transformed into a sermon division, etc.
   If a division has subdivisions, number as following:
   3.1 The first life-lesson that is a subdivision of the third life-lesson.
   3.2 The second life-lesson that is a subdivision of the third life-lesson.

Each division will be developed using the Preaching Cycle. For each division, prepare notes for: explanation; illustration; application.

It does not matter whether explanation or illustration comes first. However, application always comes last.

1st DIVISION — The 1st life-lesson selected to be presented becomes the 1st sermon division.

The First Preaching Cycle
- EXPLAIN the life-lesson.
- ILLUSTRATE the life-lesson.
- APPLY the life-lesson to the lives of the listeners.

2nd DIVISION: — The 2nd life-lesson selected to be presented becomes the 2nd sermon division.

The Second Preaching Cycle
- Explain.
- Illustrate.
- Apply.

Continue until each life-lesson selected is developed using the Preaching Cycle.

CONCLUSION:

The storytelling preacher needs to plan how to conclude the sermon. This helps him to stop talking when it is time to quit. The preacher who does not prepare his conclusion often has trouble finishing his sermon.

The conclusion should review the main aspects treated in the sermon and call for action on the part of the listeners.

The conclusion should summarize:
- The principal facts of the Bible story;
- The principal life-lessons (divisions of the sermon) treated.

The conclusion should associate the main life-lessons with the content of the Bible story. The content of the story, associated with the life-lessons, strengthens the power of God's Word to convict the hearer.

All sermons should have a common goal: to get the listeners to change. Failure to elicit a response to change is failure to communicate. Therefore, the conclusion should invite the listeners to change by putting the truths and applications presented into action. It is not enough to tell a Bible story and persuade the listeners that the life-lessons presented are true. Appeal to the listeners to apply the life-lesson presented to their own personal lives. Clarify how the listeners should change and appeal to them to change.

The conclusion should be short and powerful! Similar to the Brazilian "cafezinho" (little cup of coffee) or the "Espresso coffee" served in New Orleans. Those little cups of coffee are strong, hot, sweet and little. The conclusion should be strong (powerful), hot (animated), sweet (leave a good taste), and little (short).

The conclusion should be short. It should consume no more than ten percent of the total sermon. A thirty-minute sermon should not have more than a three-minute conclusion. Make your conclusion short.

A little girl was making whipped cream. She was so excited with whipping the cream that she whipped and whipped and whipped and whipped the cream until it was butter! She forgot that part of making whipped cream is knowing when to STOP whipping. A part of preaching is knowing when to stop!

Conclude the sermon:
- By giving a short summary of the Bible story;
- By connecting the life-lessons presented and their main applications to the story;
- With an invitation, appealing for the listeners to put into practice the will of God as presented in the sermon.

EXAMPLE: PREACHING PLAN: BIBLE STORYTELLING WITH PREACHING AFTER THE STORY

STORY: Joseph's Temptation

TEXT: Genesis 39:1-23

THE BIBLE STORY

Context:
Israel loved Joseph more than all his other sons. Joseph's brothers hated him. Joseph dreamed that his father, mother and brothers would bow down before him. Joseph's brothers sold him to slave merchants (Gen 37).

Sequence of events:
- Joseph was taken to Egypt and bought by Potiphar (39:1).
- The Lord was with Joseph (39:2).
- Joseph gained Potiphar's favor. Potiphar made Joseph the overseer of all he owned (39:4-6).
- Joseph was handsome. Potiphar's wife invited Joseph to go to bed with her (39:7).
- Joseph refused. He said his master had entrusted everything in the house, except his wife, to Joseph's care. Joseph asked how could he do such a wicked thing and sin against God? (39:8-9).
- Daily, she spoke to Joseph, but he refused to go to bed with her or even to be with her (39:10).
- One day when Joseph was alone in the house with her, she caught him by his garment. He left his garment in her hand and fled (39:11-12).
- The woman called her household servants and accused Joseph of trying to sleep with her. She said that when she screamed, he left his cloak and ran out of the house (39:13-19).
- When Potiphar returned home, she told him that Joseph tried to make sport of her. She said when she screamed, he left his cloak and ran out of the house (39:17-18).
- Potiphar burned with anger and put Joseph into the jail with the king's prisoners (39:19-20).
- In prison, the Lord was with Joseph (39:21).

DIVISIONS

1. God's servant is blessed, even when he is in undesirable circumstances

EXPLANATION:
God's servant may find himself living, working or studying in places that are undesirable to him. But even in those places, if he is faithful, God will bless him and make him a blessing to others.

Joseph was sold as a slave to Potiphar, an Egyptian who was one of Pharaoh's officials. Joseph wanted to be in Canaan enjoying the privileges of being his father's favorite son. He didn't want to be a slave in an Egyptian's home. The Lord was with Joseph and he prospered. The master saw that the Lord gave Joseph success in everything he did. Potiphar trusted Joseph and put him in charge of everything he owned. The Lord blessed the house of the Egyptian because of Joseph.

(Read Romans 8:28; Philippians 4:12.)

ILLUSTRATIONS:
Acts 16 records how God used Paul and Silas, when they were unjustly put into prison.

APPLICATION:
The Christian who finds himself in an undesirable situation may turn to complaining and miss an opportunity to be blessed and to become a blessing to others. God will not allow the faithful to be put in a situation where he cannot be a blessing. Those of you who are now experiencing undesirable situations need to trust that God can bless you and make you a blessing to others.

Bible Storytelling Tools © Jackson Day

2. The person who serves God is subject to strong temptation

EXPLANATION:

Being faithful to God does not free one from facing temptation. In fact, the opposite is true. The closer one gets to God, the more he comes under Satan's attacks and the stronger the temptations become.

Seventeen year old Joseph was tempted to have sex with his master's wife (39:7, 10-12).

ILLUSTRATION:

■Eve was tempted by Satan in the Garden of Eden (Gen 3:1-7).
■David was a man who loved and honored God, but he was tempted when he observed his neighbor's wife taking a bath (2 Sam 11:1-4).
■Jesus was tempted by Satan (Mt 4:1-11).
■Peter was tempted to deny Jesus (Mt 26:69-75).

APPLICATION:

Every Christian needs to be prepared at all times to face strong temptation. Every one of us is going to face temptation.

3. Belief in God gives a person reasons to resist temptation

ILLUSTRATION:

Jesus reacted to each temptation from Satan by quoting scripture saying: "It is written" (Mt 4:1-11).

A Christian man was at a convention when a woman suggested they spend the night together. He answered: "You are not my type." He did not establish the fact that his faith in God was the reason for resisting the temptation.

EXPLANATION

Joseph's belief in God gave him the conviction that betraying his master would be sin (39:9).

Belief in God gives the Christian reasons to resist temptation.

Belief in God results from believing the Bible is God's Word, and that the Bible gives one rules and principles for knowing what is right and wrong.

APPLICATION

Belief in God gives us reason to avoid alcoholic beverage, tobacco, and overeating because we do not wish to sin against God by damaging our bodies that the Bible describes as the Temple of the Holy Spirit.

Belief in God gives us reason to be honest, to respect others, to be kind, and to help others in need because God's Word teaches us to treat others as we desire to be treated.

Belief in God leads us to pray: "Lead us not into temptation," and then to watch and pray lest we give in to temptation.

4. Victory over temptation can be costly

ILLUSTRATIONS

■Daniel was cast into the lions' den when he refused to stop praying to God (Dan 6:1-28).
■Stephen was stoned for preaching about Jesus (Ac 7).
■An honest accountant was asked by his boss if he worked for the firm or for the government.

EXPLANATION

Joseph's seducer became his accuser, and he was cast into prison for resisting temptation.

Jesus taught his followers to watch and pray lest they enter into temptation. He also requires his disciples to take up their cross and follow him. It can be costly to resist temptation.

APPLICATION

If Jesus' faithfulness to God resulted in his crucifixion, don't be surprised if you must pay a high price to follow the Lord and resist temptation.

5. God seeks faithful servants, who resist temptation, to execute important tasks for him

EXPLANATION:

God's servants become stronger and better when they face temptation and resist it. See James 1:2-4.

The person who resists temptation becomes better qualified to serve God. To execute important tasks, God needs spiritual leaders who can and do resist temptation.

Joseph resisted strong temptations and became a person God could use to save the nation of Egypt and his own family.

ILLUSTRATION:

■Daniel resolved not to defile himself with the food and wine offered by King Nebuchadnezzar. Daniel became a spokesman for God (Dan 1:8).
■Jesus resisted temptation and was able to save us from our sins.

APPLICATION:

If you desire to be qualified to do important work for God, then you must seek to free yourself from sin's impurity and live a pure and holy life. You must fight and resist the temptations that come your way.

CONCLUSIONS:

Joseph was forced to live in Egypt when he wanted to be at home with his family. You also may be forced to adjust to undesirable situations. Seventeen-year-old Joseph faced a strong temptation, and so will you. God used Joseph to do a great task. Today God will use Christians who resist temptations to do a mighty work.

1. Determine to face up to unpleasant situations with God's help and be a blessing wherever you are.
2. You don't know when you will be tempted, but you do know that you will be tempted. Beware of the destruction that yielding to sin could have in your life. Be prepared and stay prepared to resist temptation.
3. Belief in God gives you reasons to resist temptation.
4. Decide to become a follower of Jesus and a faithful servant of God. It will not be an easy life. There will be unpleasant situations; there will be temptations; you may be betrayed, treated unjustly, and suffer for doing what is right. But God will bless you, make you a blessing and use you to advance his Kingdom.
5. Have as your goal to be someone God can use.

III. BIBLE STORYTELLING WITH PREACHING INSERTED

Bible Storytelling with Preaching After the Story is just one method of coupling Bible Storytelling with preaching. Bible Storytelling with Preaching Inserted is another method of Narrative Preaching. The storytelling preacher who uses this method inserts preaching applications during the telling of the story. He narrates the Bible story, but when he comes to an episode that reveals a life-lesson he wishes to explain, he stops storytelling, inserts his life-lesson, and develops it as a Preaching Cycle. Afterwards he continues storytelling until he reaches another episode that inspires a life-lesson he wishes to develop into a Preaching Cycle.

If the preacher emphasizes life-lessons more than the Bible story, listeners will consider the approach as interrupted storytelling. But I have found this method most helpful when Bible Storytelling a narrative that contains a cluster of stories. An example of storytelling a cluster of stories would be narrating the life of Abraham in one session.

Bible Storytelling with Preaching Inserted needs special attention when done with illiterate people who have little knowledge of the Bible. The listeners may not discern the difference between the Bible story and the preacher's interpretations. It is necessary that the listeners discern when the preacher is "Storytelling God's Word" and when he is explaining it. God's Word is infallible. The preacher's explanation does not have divine authority; but God's Word does.

Many storytelling missionaries do the following to help their listeners discern when they are Storying the Bible and when they are explaining it. The preacher keeps an open Bible in his hand while storytelling; he closes the Bible or sets it down when he gives his explanation.

1. How to prepare a sermon for Bible Storytelling with Preaching Inserted

1.1 Analyze the Bible story

The storyteller must become a story-analyst before he becomes a storytelling preacher. He should follow the steps in the chapter **HOW TO ANALYZE A BIBLE STORY**.

1.2 Select the most important life-lessons for the listeners

Practical suggestions on choosing life-lessons that will be developed into sermon divisions are found in the chapter: **Selecting Life-lessons from a Bible Story to Become the Divisions for a Sermon or Study**.

The storytelling preacher has a limited amount of time; therefore, he must select the life-lessons that are most needed for his listeners in their present circumstances.

If the sermon will be part of a Storying Track, the storytelling preacher will consider the following when selecting life-lessons for his listeners:
- The emphasis of the Storying Track;
- The life-lessons discovered in the story;
- The needs of the listeners and how they connect to the Storying Track emphasis;
- The life-lessons that most relate to the emphasis of the Storying Track and the needs of the listeners.

If the sermon will not be part of a Storying Track, the storytelling preacher will consider the following when selecting life-lessons for his listeners:
- The life-lessons discovered in the Bible story;
- The greatest need in the lives of the listeners;
- The life-lessons that best connect with the needs of the listeners.

2. Prepare the selected life-lessons, using the Preaching Cycle with each one

With each life-lesson that is chosen to become a division of the sermon, the storytelling preacher will develop the **Preaching Cycle**.

Each **Preaching Cycle** includes three activities:
- Explain the life-lesson;
- Illustrate the life-lesson;
- Apply the life-lesson to the lives of the listeners.

3. Prepare the Preaching Plan

The Preaching Plan is also called the sermon outline. The Preaching Plan will include the:
- **Story with Preaching Cycles Inserted**: Utilize the sequence of events with Preaching Cycles inserted where appropriate.

■**Conclusion**: Summarize the story, review life-lessons presented and appeal for change that would come from putting the life-lessons into practice.

In making his Preaching Plan, the storytelling preacher will:
■Copy or abbreviate the notes from the context and sequence of events;
■Make notes for the inserted sermon divisions with their Preaching Cycles.

The Preaching Plan for Bible Storytelling with Preaching Cycles Inserted

Sequence of Events in Chronological Order with Sermon Divisions Inserted

■**Sequence of events in chronological order**:
- <u>Consider the context</u>. Explain background information that will help listeners understand the historical circumstances surrounding the narrative, to understand the initial situation, and to identify key-characters in the story.
- <u>Follow the sequence of events</u>. Start at the beginning of the story. Follow the sequence of events until the end of the first episode that inspired a life-lesson that will be developed using the Preaching Cycle.

■**1st Division inserted.** (The first life-lesson selected to be inserted into the story becomes the first division of the sermon.) The **First Preaching Cycle**

■**Sequence of events in chronological order**: continue to copy or abbreviate the notes from the sequence of events.

■**2nd Division inserted.** (The second life-lesson selected to be inserted becomes the second division of the sermon.) The **Second Preaching Cycle**

■Continue the process of following the **sequence of events** and **inserting divisions** until the story is finished.

■**CONCLUSION**
Planning the sermon conclusion helps the storytelling preacher to stop talking when it is time to quit.
Conclude the sermon:
- By giving a short summary of the Bible story;
- By connecting the life-lessons presented and their main applications to the story;
- With an invitation, appealing for the listeners to put into practice the will of God as presented in the sermon.

EXAMPLE # 1: PREACHING PLAN: BIBLE STORYTELLING WITH PREACHING INSERTED

ABRAHAM
Genesis 11:27 - 25:11

Sequence of events
■Terah was one of the descendants of Noah. Terah was born several generations after the Tower of Babel.
■Terah became the father of Abram and Haran. Haran became the father of Lot. Haran died and Lot lived with his grandfather, Terah (11:27-28).
■Abram married Sarai who was barren and gave him no children (11:29-30).
■Terah left the city of Ur of the Chaldeans and settled in Haran. Terah took with him: Abram, Sara and Lot. Terah died in Haran (11:31-32).
■The Lord told Abram to leave his country, his people and his father's household and go to the land that the Lord would show him (12:1).

1. **God communicates with people**

EXPLANATION:
God told Abram to leave his country, his people and his father's household. God spoke directly to Abram and told him what to do.

God communicates with people. He has plans for everyone. God desires that each person understands what he should do and what he should not do.

ILLUSTRATIONS:
■God spoke to Adam and Eve in the Garden and told them not to eat fruit from one tree.
■God spoke to Noah and told him to build an ark in order to be saved from the flood.

APPLICATION:

God speaks to people today, but not by a voice that can be heard. He speaks to us through his Book, the Bible, and through prayer. Read the Bible, study it by yourself, study it with others, hear the Bible preached and spend time in prayer. Do this, and the Holy Spirit will communicate to you and help you to understand God's plan for your life. God is still a God who communicates to individual people. He desires to communicate to each person here.

Sequence of events

■ God made several promises to Abram. God promised that Abram would be a blessing, that he would be blessed and that all people on earth would be blessed through him (12:2-3).

2. God gives his servant tough tasks, but he promises to bless him and make him a blessing

EXPLANATION

God invites his servants to assume tough tasks, but God promises to bless those who take on the hard jobs, and to make them a blessing to others.

God gave Abram a tough job when he told him to leave his country, his people, his father's household and go to a land he did not even know. But God also promised to bless Abram and that all peoples on earth would be blessed through him.

ILLUSTRATION

■ God gave Noah a tough task, to build an ark, but Noah and his family were blessed by being saved during the flood.

APPLICATION

If you desire to be blessed by God and to be a blessing, then you must take on the tough jobs God has for you. You must leave your comfort zone.

I desire God's blessing, but I don't like tough jobs. I must take on the tough jobs if I am to receive God's blessing.

Sequence of events

■ Abram left Haran, setting out for Canaan, taking with him his wife Sarai, his nephew Lot, and all his possessions (12:4-5).

■ In a time of famine, the faith of Abram was transformed into fear, which resulted in his going down to Egypt without consulting God. Sarai, Abram's wife, was beautiful and Abram was afraid the Egyptians would kill him for her, so he told her to say she was his sister (12:10-20).

■ Abram left Egypt a wealthy man in livestock, silver and gold (13:1). He returned to Canaan and called on the Lord (13:4).

■ Lot, Abram's nephew, also had livestock and servants. Quarreling arose between the herdsmen of Abram and the herdsmen of Lot. Abram told Lot to choose the direction he would go and Abram would go in the other direction. Lot chose the fertile Jordan valley where there was the city of Sodom. Lot left Abram with the rocky hill country. After Lot left Abram, God promised Abram again that he would give him all of Canaan (13:1-17).

■ Sodom was captured and its residents, including Lot and his family, were taken prisoners. Abram took 318 of his men, and rescued Lot and his possessions, together with other people (14:1-16).

■ The Word of the Lord came to Abram in a vision. The Lord told him to count the stars. God promised Abram that his descendants would be as many as the stars and that he and his descendants would possess the land of Canaan (15:1-21). Abram believed God, and God credited it to him as righteousness (15:6).

3. A person needs faith in order to be considered righteous by God

EXPLANATION

Even though Abram had no children, God promised him that his descendants would be as many as the stars and that he and his descendants would possess the land of Canaan (Gen 15:1-21). Abram believed God and God credited it to him as righteousness (Gen 15:6). Abram believed God's promise when it appeared to be impossible.

In the same way, God will credit righteousness to those who believe that God raised Jesus from the dead (Rom 4:18-25).

Faith is believing that God keeps his promises. (Read Hebrews 11:1.)

The righteous live by faith (Rom 1:17). Daily they make decisions based upon the assurance that God does what he promises.

ILLUSTRATION

Hebrews chapter 11 contains a list of people who manifested faith in God.

■ Noah built an ark to save his family (Hb 11:7).

■ Moses chose to be mistreated along with God's people rather than enjoy the pleasures of sin (Hb 11:24-28).

APPLICATION

The only way you can please God is to believe God does what he promises. It is necessary to act in such a way as to prove that you believe God's promises.

Sequence of events

■ Abram and Sarai were advanced in years and had no children. Sarai suggested that Abram sleep with her Egyptian maidservant, Hagar. They would consider any child born as Sarai and Abram's. Although Ishmael was born to Hagar and Abram, this was not the son promised by God. Abram was 86 years old when Ishmael was born (16:1-15).

■ When Abram was 99 years old, the Lord appeared to Abram. He changed Abram's name to Abraham and Sarai's name to Sarah. God promised that nations and kings would come from Abraham. God established a covenant with Abraham, and a sign of the covenant was that Abraham and all of his male descendants were to be circumcised. God promised that Abraham and Sarah would have a child, and they were to name him Isaac (17:1-27).

4. **God is all powerful and is able to do whatever is necessary to accomplish his will**

ILLUSTRATION

During the creation, God had the power to speak and things were created as he ordered.

When he desired to destroy the human race that was disobedient to him, God had the power to send the flood.

EXPLANATION

God had the power to enable a 99-year-old man and his elderly wife to have a baby.

God has the power to accomplish his will.

APPLICATION

God has the power to bring about the reality of his will. He has the power to accomplish whatever he desires to do in your life and in the life of his church. Trust him to use his power in your life to enable you to accomplish his plans for your life.

Sequence of events

■ God informed Abraham that he would destroy the cities of Sodom and Gomorrah. Abraham prayed for the city of Sodom. He begged persistently in prayer until God agreed that if there were only ten just people in the city, the city would be spared divine judgment. God did not find ten just people in Sodom. The city was destroyed as an act of divine judgment (18:22-33).

■ Isaac was born to Abraham and Sarah (21:1-5).

■ When Sarah saw Ishmael mocking her son Isaac, she insisted that the slave woman Hagar and her son Ishmael be sent away (21:1-20).

■ Some years later, God tested Abraham, requiring that he offer his son Isaac as a burnt sacrifice. Abraham left with Isaac, certain that he and Isaac would return together, based on the promise that Isaac would be considered his descendant. When Abraham raised up his knife to slay his son, an angel called out, telling Abraham not to lay a hand on the boy. Abraham looked up and saw a ram caught by its horns in a thicket. God again promised Abraham to bless him and his descendants (22:1-19).

■ Sarah died when she was 127 years old. Abraham buried her in the land of Canaan (23:1-20).

■ Abraham sent a trusted servant to find a wife for Isaac. God led the servant to Rebekah who was a relative of Abraham. She had a brother named Laban (24:1-67).

■ Abraham died when he was 175 years old, and his sons Isaac and Ishmael buried him beside his wife Sarah (25:1-11).

CONCLUSIONS:

1. God is all-powerful and is able to do whatever is necessary to accomplish his will. He enabled Abraham and Sarah, an older couple, to have a child. Trust God to do whatever is necessary to bring about his plan for your life.
2. The one who has faith in God will be tested by the circumstances of life. During the testing time, one passes when he shows faith in God's promises by doing God's will. On the other hand, those who do not have faith and who disobey God, fail the test. Prove your faith in God during difficult times by doing his will.
3. The servant of God is called to attempt difficult tasks. But God promises that the faithful servant will be blessed and that he will be a blessing to others. When God called Abraham to leave his country and his father's household to go to a strange country, he also promised to bless him and that all people would be blessed through him. If you desire to be a blessing and to be blessed by God, you must be willing to take on tough jobs for God.

*EXAMPLE # 2: **PREACHING PLAN:***
BIBLE STORYTELLING WITH PREACHING INSERTED

JONAH: THE RELUCTANT PROPHET
Jonah 1 - 4

From 2 Kings 14:25, we learn that Jonah was a prophet in the Kingdom of Israel when Jeroboam II was king. Jeroboam II was the thirteenth king of Israel. His kingship was a time of prosperity and strong feelings of nationalism.

Assyria, Israel's great enemy, was famous for its cruelty toward conquered nations. The capital city of Assyria was Nineveh.

Sequence of events
■ The Lord told Jonah to go to the wicked city of Nineveh and preach against it (1:1-2).

1. God has a plan for each person.

Explanation
God told Jonah to go to Nineveh and proclaim his Word to that wicked city (1:1-2).

God wants all to be saved. God plans for each person to obey biblical commands and trust biblical promises. But he also has special plans for each person.

God's will is good for us (Rom 12:2).

Illustration
God planned for Noah to build an ark (Gen 6:14-21).

He planned for Abraham to leave his people and his country (Gen 12:1-4).

He planned for Gideon to free the Israelites from the Midianites (Jdg 6:14).

He planned for David to be king of Israel (1Sm 16:1-13).

He planned for Barnabas and Paul to be missionaries (Ac 13:1-3).

Application
God has plans for you. His plans are for your good. If you are committed to obeying God when he reveals his will to you, you will experience his plans.

Sequence of events
■ In Joppa, Jonah boarded a ship bound for Tarshish to get away from the Lord (1:3).
■ The Lord sent a storm. The terrified sailors cried out to their gods and threw the cargo overboard. The captain found Jonah asleep (1:4-5).
■ The sailors drew straws. Jonah got the short straw. They interrogated Jonah. He confessed his responsibility for the storm. Jonah told them to throw him overboard. When they threw him overboard, the sea grew calm (1:6-16).

2. Those who run from God cause others to suffer.

Explanation
Jonah tried to escape from God's plan (1:3). He became a curse for the sailors who were with him. They were terrified and lost their cargo because of him (1:4-14). If it were not for the intervention of God, Nineveh would have been destroyed because of Jonah's omission (3:1-10).

People who run from God often don't realize they are responsible for the suffering of others. Jonah was responsible for the storm that afflicted the sailors; yet he was asleep (1:5).

Illustration
The marriage partner who runs from God, but runs into the arms of a lover, brings suffering to his/her family.

The teenager who runs from God and experiments with drugs and sex brings suffering on his/her family.

Application
If you want to be a blessing to others, serve the Lord.

If you are running from God, you need to realize that you are responsible for others' suffering. Repent; change your actions.

Sequence of events
■ The Lord provided a large fish to swallow Jonah. Jonah was inside the fish for three days and nights (1:17).
■ Jonah prayed to the Lord God (2:1-9).
■ The Lord spoke to the fish, and it vomited Jonah onto dry land (2:10).
■ Again the Lord told Jonah to go to Nineveh and proclaim his message (3:1-2).

3. **God chases after the person who runs from him.**

Explanation
God used the storm, the fish and his words to chase after Jonah.

Illustration
Jesus compared God to the shepherd who would leave 99 sheep to go searching for one lost sheep (Lk 15:4-7).

When King David sinned, God sent his prophet to confront David (2 Sam 12:1-17).

Application
If you are running from God, he is chasing after you. Let him catch you.

If you are serving God, he wants you to help him chase after those who are running from him.

Sequence of events
- In Nineveh, Jonah proclaimed: "Forty more days and Nineveh will be destroyed!" The Ninevites believed God, declared a fast and put on sackcloth (3:3-5).
- The king dressed himself with sackcloth, decreed a fast, and called on the people to turn from their wicked ways (3:6-9).
- God saw what the people in Nineveh did. God changed his mind about destroying Nineveh (3:10).
- Jonah was furious and yelled at God. He told God why he ran off to Tarshish. He asked God to kill him. God questioned his right to be angry (4:1-4).
- Jonah built a shelter to the east of Nineveh. God provided a vine to give Jonah shade. Then he sent a worm to kill the vine. Jonah wished he were dead (4:5-8).
- God questioned Jonah's right to be angry (4:9).
- The Lord compared Jonah's concern for the vine to his own concern for Nineveh (4:10-11).

4. **God loves the people his servants hate.**

Explanation
Assyria was the enemy of Israel, Jonah's country. Nineveh was the capital city of Jonah's enemies. God wanted to save Jonah's enemies, and he wanted Jonah to help him by preaching to them (1:1-2; 4:2-11). The heart of God was willing to forgive wicked and violent pagans; in contrast Jonah wanted to see the people of Nineveh destroyed.

Illustration
My father died when I was 14, and some businessmen cheated my mother. I despise people who "con" widows. I despise those who sexually abuse children.

I have relatives who are prejudiced and despise people of other races.

Application
The person I hate, God loves, wants to save and wants me to help him. Whomever our friends, relatives, neighbors or co-workers hate, God loves; and he has the right to ask us to proclaim his message to them. That may involve personal ministry as well as helping send out missionaries.

CONCLUSION
1. Accept God's plan for your life, be it for salvation or to obey the Lord.
2. If you are running from God, turn around and return to him. He is seeking you as he sought Jonah.
3. If you have a problem with prejudice or hatred, you are making it difficult for God to use you to manifest his love. God loves those you don't like, and he wants to manifest his love to them through you.

PREACH THE SERMON; TEACH THE LESSON

> **OBSERVATION:**
> Some suggestions given in this chapter need to be adapted to the worldview of certain people groups.
> Examples:
> #1 Both in Brazil and in the United States of America, it is important for speakers to have eye contact with their listeners. However, most North American Indians and most tribal groups in South America avoid eye contact.
> #2 In Brazil, in Spanish speaking South America and in the United States, the leader stands in front of his listeners, raises his voice and speaks with authority. However, a people group called the Guarani live in South Brazil and in Paraguay. The Guarani leader sits in the middle of the multitude. He is reserved, calm, quiet and humble. A Guarani who attended a Brazilian school, stated he could never be a teacher because he could not stay angry all the time. Brazilians thought their teachers were expressing confidence and authority. The Guarani thought the same teachers were expressing anger.

1. **Prepare, but depend upon the inner confidence that one has in the Word of God and the Holy Spirit**

The preacher or teacher should always prepare. However, when it is time to make his presentation, he does not depend upon his preparation. He depends upon God to speak through the Bible story, and he depends upon the Holy Spirit to guide his students or listeners to understand what God wants to say to them.

The Bible Storytelling preacher or teacher can be certain that God's Word does not return empty and that the Holy Spirit communicates through the Bible story that is told and explained. The storyteller can know that the most powerful stories are those found in the Bible.

2. **Face the fear of speaking in public**

The one who preaches or teaches needs to understand that fear of public speaking is normal. Any speaker who takes seriously his responsibility has stage fright. Many pastors with years of experience may not show it, but every Sunday they face the enemy called fear. I, myself, have been preaching for more than forty years and constantly battle with fear before I preach. Fright gives the speaker an adrenalin rush that is useful. It gives him a heightened state of awareness, and that is good.

When one is approaching the time to speak, he should be careful not to inflame the fear that is within. Actions such as chewing the fingernails, constantly crossing and uncrossing the legs, and walking from one side to the other increase one's tenseness and make one more frightened. Seek to leave the body in a relaxed position. Let go of the arms and breathe deeply. Remember, the success of the Bible storyteller preacher or teacher is not dependant upon his own abilities and preparation. Any success will be the result of the Holy Spirit speaking through him; and divine power being active when the Bible story is told.

Fear that is channeled and controlled becomes energy that helps to communicate. Channel the fear within to give vibrations and emotions to the words spoken and to convince the listeners of truths expressed in the Bible. Nervousness will be transformed to energy when the preacher/teacher has conviction that the Bible is God's Word and he is confident that the Holy Spirit enables him to express God's truths.

3. **Dress appropriately for the audience**

The preacher or teacher makes an impression on his audience before he opens his mouth. The listeners will make a quick judgment about him based upon his clothing and appearance (hairstyle, use of cosmetics and jewelry for women; hairstyle, facial hair or lack of it for men; etc.). One should avoid clothes that distract the audience's attention from his words. The most important words for effective apparel are "be appropriate."

Women should be careful with the way they sit in front of an audience. They should avoid crossing their legs. They should avoid short dresses, tight clothes, or blouses that overemphasize their breasts. This vulgarizes a woman's image. Also, a lady should avoid jewelry that could reflect lights or make noise when she moves around.

Prior to appearing before an audience, one should always brush his hair and teeth, iron his clothes, fasten zippers and buttons and arrange his shirt (blouse) inside the pants (or the skirt). Always look in the mirror before going before one's listeners. Then check your fly, your zippers and your buttons.

There is not so much a right or wrong way to dress or groom, as an appropriate way for the occasion, location and listeners. Clothes that would be appropriate for preaching under a shade tree on a hot summer day could be inappropriate for a church accustomed to formal services. A good suggestion is to dress similarly or slightly better than the majority of the listeners present. It is better to be slightly overdressed than underdressed.

It is difficult to judge one's own appearance and the impression it makes on others. Therefore, a wise person will request advice from close friends about his image and seek suggestions on how to improve it.

4. Communicate with body language

OBSERVATION:
The person who is relating to a culture other than his own needs to be aware that appropriate gestures in one culture are inappropriate in others. The North American "OK" sign, with the thumb and forefinger touching in a circle, is considered vulgar in Brazil and many other places in the world. The "Thumbs up means "good" in the United States and South America, but it is considered rude in Australia. In Chile, slapping your right fist into your left open palm is considered obscene.

The entire body speaks when the preacher or teacher is talking. The position of the feet, the movement of the trunk, arms, hands and fingers, the position of the arms, the shaking of the head, the look in the eyes, and each gesture communicate and express messages and attitudes.

Some body expressions need to be avoided. For example: never speak with hands in the pocket or held together behind the back, neither with the arms crossed. Avoid leaning on the pulpit, a table or chair. Avoid the look of the self-conscious person with an inferiority complex whose head is bowed looking at his feet and the body curved forward. Also avoid the arrogant look of superiority, with the nose stuck up and eyes that look above the audience.

Certain gestures make the speaker look ridiculous. Some speakers unconsciously play with their watches or the microphone wires, pop their knuckles, rattle coins in their pocket, chew on their fingernails, pull up their shirts, twist the buttons on their coat or blouse, pass their hands through their hair or rub their heads. Some even pick their nose or scratch their rear end. Other negative actions are rocking from side to side, going back and forth on one's heels and toes, or pacing back and forth. A common adverse posture pattern is turning sideways to the audience and leaning back on one hip. The one who goes back on one hip is subconsciously saying: "I don't want to be here."

Poor body posture sends the message that one has low self-esteem. Therefore, stand tall or sit up strait!

An excellent posture position for the preacher is to use the "ready position" of an athlete who is poised to move in any direction. By leaning slightly forward with the legs slightly flexed, the preacher could bounce up and down on the balls of his feet or move in any direction. This position sends the message that the preacher is bursting with energy and ready to get into action.

Body language can be learned and improved with training. However, the speaker who plans his gestures runs the risk of becoming artificial and appearing to be an actor on stage. Most of the time, being natural leads to the proper gestures. Gestures obey a natural process. When the speaker thinks about what he is going to say, the mind tells the body the proper movement. It is natural for the body to begin expressing itself just before the words are spoken. Natural gestures occur just before the spoken words or at the same time as the words, but not afterwards.

Hand gestures should be expressive but never exaggerated. They should meet the needs of the message, flow naturally, and integrate with the spoken word. Usually the hand gestures need to be above the belt line in order to be visible by the audience. Hand gestures above the head need to be reserved for moments of exceptional emotions. A general rule to follow is the larger the auditorium, the larger and wider the gestures; the smaller the room, the smaller and more moderate the gestures.

Avoid faking. Falsehood doesn't work. Everybody has seen bad actors at work. While it is difficult to describe simulated gestures, everybody recognizes them when they are seen. The preacher or teacher who fakes with his gestures risks the danger of being known as a bad actor. One should not worry much about his gestures; he should be natural and concentrate on his message and his audience.

Considering the importance that the body has in communication, I recommend that the speaker avoid hiding behind a table or pulpit. He should move his position where he can be seen by all his listeners.

5. Communicate with the eyes

OBSERVATION:
The person who is relating to a culture other than his own needs to be aware that appropriate eye behavior in one culture may be inappropriate in others. In Northern Europe, North America and South America, it is expected for both the speaker and listener to sustain eye contact. In many African cultures, it is expected for the speaker to look into the faces of the listener, while the listener looks down. For the Maori people of New Zealand, it is the custom for both the speaker and the listener to avoid eye contact. My advice on eye contact relates to North America, South America and Europe.

The speaker communicates with his eyes. When he begins, he should survey all of his listeners, then begin eye communication with as many individuals as possible. He must remember to look at those at the far edges of the room, those sitting along the side of him, and even those sitting behind him. He should lock his eyes on individual listener's eyes for a few seconds at a time. Each listener should receive a look from the preacher or teacher. However, when addressing a large group, extended eye communication (five seconds or more) to people in different places in the congregation is essential. When he looks at one person, dozens of people around that person will think he is talking just to them. When the listener observes the speaker looking in his direction, he will feel that he is important. The one who never sees the speaker looking at him will feel left out and may become disinterested in the message or even reject the message of the communicator.

By looking in the eyes, the preacher or teacher will observe smiles and discern the happiness of some of his listeners. Other listeners' eyes express disagreement or confusion. The one who looks at his listeners' eyes receives feedback and knows when he needs to adapt his presentation in order to better communicate.

Eye movements can demonstrate that the storyteller is imagining the events and images of his story. If he looks up and to one side as he pauses, this usually suggests that he is searching his memory or thoughts. Looking straight down as he speaks suggests submission, embarrassment or absorption in his personal thoughts or feelings. When eye movements show that the storyteller is imagining the events and images of his story, they also help his listeners do the same.

Eye movements can be used as a dramatic tool to suggest the relationship between a character and the objects or people with whom the character interacts. The storyteller should face his listeners directly when he is speaking to them. However, when he is describing a dialogue, the direction he faces can show how a conversation passes from one character to another. Eye movements can be used as a dramatic tool to suggest the relationship between a superior character to an inferior character.

For example: In the Bible story found in Exodus chapters 1 - 12, God and Moses dialogue, and Moses and Pharaoh dialogue. While telling the story, when God is speaking to Moses, I look almost straight down. When Moses is speaking to God, I look almost straight up. When Moses is speaking to Pharaoh, I look toward my left, but looking up like a 5' 6" man would look up to a 6' 4" man. When Pharaoh speaks to Moses, I look toward my right, but looking down like a 6' 4" man looking down on a 5' 6" man. But when I am narrating the story where there is no dialogue, I look at my listeners.

6. Avoid speech addictions

Some speakers are addicted to speech habits. Words and phrases such as "unh-hum," "you know," "you understand," "ok," "well-ah," etc. and religious expressions such as "Glory to God," "amen," "my God," "O Lord," may be used in a redundant form. Speech addictions irritate the public, sacred expressions lose their value, and the communicator is subject to ridicule.

The one who teaches or preaches should ask someone to help him by calling attention to expressions used repeatedly and any other speech addictions. Recognizing speech addictions is the first step to eliminating them.

7. Speak at a volume which the public can hear

Speaking too loudly or too softly irritates the audience and interferes with their getting the message. Some speakers try to hold their listeners' attention by shouting. Others mumble and the listeners must strain to hear, while those with auditory difficulty don't understand anything. Some speakers have the habit of speaking softly. Often when listeners complain, the speaker increases the volume, but shortly he lowers it again. Even if listeners complain again, the speaker repeats the same mistake.

Success in transmission of a message is related to volume, rhythm and voice tone. The speaker needs to find a volume level that is comfortable for his audience.

8. Plan to follow an outline or plan, but adapt and use new ideas that occur during the worship service or class time

The speaker should follow the plan he prayerfully prepared while seeking the leadership of the Holy Spirit. However, while he is preaching or teaching, the Holy Spirit may remind him of a fact or illustration that helps him better communicate.

During the worship service, an event, a comment, a spoken prayer, an announcement, or special music can give the preacher thoughts for expressing God's message that he never would have considered otherwise. Happenings such as these are common. Often events during the worship service give the preacher opportunity to make remarks that tie in with his Preaching Plan. New thoughts may occur while the preacher is speaking; he may be able to incorporate them into his sermon. If new thoughts, that help communicate his message, occur during the worship service, marvelous! Use them!

Great ideas may come to the preacher during the worship service or the teacher during the class time. However, one should not neglect preparation and leave it entirely to God to give him something to say when it is time to talk. If new thoughts occur during the presentation, the speaker may use them. But the preacher or teacher who does not pray during the week seeking a word from God, who does not separate time to study the Bible, who does not prepare a plan to communicate God's message is unprepared. The unprepared person who expects God to give him a message when it is time to speak shows little consideration for his listeners and he challenges God. The unprepared preacher of teacher is taking a risk that no one should take!

The preacher/teacher who has the responsibility to communicate God's Word should prepare in advance. He should take time to analyze the chosen Bible story. He should choose life-lessons to communicate to his listeners. He should think through the story many times preparing to tell it. However, when it is time to talk, he does not depend upon his preparation, and neither does he depend upon God to inspire him with new ideas. He depends upon the conviction that the Bible is God's Word, that Bible stories communicate life life-lessons, and that the Holy Spirit guides the seeking listeners to understand God's truth.

9. Prepare, seek information about the audience and location, but adapt when faced with the unexpected

No matter how well prepared the preacher/teacher is, he may be required to adapt because of unexpected events. Sometimes Murphy's Law appears to function when one is communicating God's Word. Murphy's Law states: "If anything can go wrong, it will." His law also states: "If there is a possibility of several things going wrong, the one that will cause the most damage will be the one to go wrong."

The sound system may fail, lights may go out, the cutest baby may cry, children may get into a fight, a loud drunk may sit on the front seat, the wind may blow notes away, or dogs outside may start fighting. The speaker must

Bible Storytelling Tools © Jackson Day

resign himself to whatever problems arise. No matter what happens, just do one's best.

In Brazil, a Christian rancher invited a group of us to come to his ranch to preach. We were expecting a small crowd. But the rancher advised all his neighbors that he was going to kill three cows and prepare barbecue for all. We arrived expecting twenty or thirty people, but had an audience of several hundred. The preacher expected to preach in the living room or from the front porch, but the rancher had arranged for a truck with a large sound system to be present.

The preacher/teacher needs to be prepared to tell the Bible story and to make his presentation, but he should be able to adapt to unexpected circumstances. Unexpected events can either bring great frustrations or be transformed into opportunities to transmit God's message in an unexpected manner.

The preacher/teacher must also adapt to his own mistakes. The Bible storyteller will make mistakes. He's going to leave out a plot element, he may call a character by the wrong name. It happens to everyone. He needs to discern whether to make a correction or whether the listeners know he made a mistake, but they are still with him anyway. When he makes a mistake that needs correction, he should admit his error, correct it, and continue.

The only place that perfect people exist are in fictional books and movies. That's because errors were edited out. The preacher or teacher must struggle through his presentation without dress rehearsals or editors. As a result, he will make mistakes at times. One must be willing to experience failure if he is to improve. The best way to improve one's skills is to: keep on trying, and keep on trying to improve. The one who practices and attempts to improve will never become perfect, but he will constantly get better.

NARRATIVE TEACHING
BIBLE STORYTELLING WITH TEACHING

OBSERVATION:
Some of the suggestions given in this chapter need to be adapted to fit the worldview of people culture groups.
For Example:
How questions are used is a cultural matter. The Munduruku are a tribal people group who live in the State of Pará, Brazil. The Mundurukus do not use questions for teaching. They ask questions to find out if someone transgressed the cultural norms (like a police interview) or to obtain information concerning an event witnessed by the individual being questioned. The Munduruku would never ask a question if he knew the answer.

Bible Storytelling With Teaching is also called **Narrative Teaching**. The storyteller tells the story and then uses the story as a basis for teaching. The story is the text for the study. The Bible story is the main emphasis, but it is framed with a Bible study and discussion. Two basic methods for teaching with Bible stories are presented:

■ **Bible Storytelling Combined with Using Questions**
The storytelling teacher tells the Bible story and then leads discussions by asking questions related to the story.

■ **Bible Storytelling Combined with Using Teaching Cycles**
The teacher prepares an Outlined Lesson Plan. The storytelling teacher narrates the Bible story, mentions and explains life-lessons discovered in the story, asks questions about the story and life-lessons, and leads discussions with the students. The process of explaining a life-lesson and asking questions continues until the Bible study is finished. The teacher will use the **Teaching Cycle** with each life-lesson taught.

I. BIBLE STORYTELLING COMBINED WITH QUESTIONS

Jesus knew how to create group dynamics by asking questions. Many times he told stories (parables) and then asked questions to help his listeners discover and apply lessons. Examples of Jesus using questions when teaching:
■ After telling the story of the two sons sent to work in their father's vineyard, Jesus asked: "Which one did the will of his father?" (Mt 21:28-31).
■ After telling the parable of the landowner who rented his vineyard to evil men, Jesus asked: "When the landowner returns, what will he do with those evil renters?" (Mt 21:33-40).
■ Other examples of Jesus teaching using questions are found in Mt 22:15-21; Lk 7:40-47 (47); 10:25-37 (26,36); 17:11-19 (17-18); 18:18-19 (19).

Advantages of teaching by using questions:
■ Everybody likes to participate in a good discussion.
■ People learn better when they themselves discover truths and apply them to their own lives.
■ By means of asking questions, the teacher can evaluate himself and determine if the students really understood the life-lessons and if they know how to apply them to their own lives.
■ The teacher who asks good questions takes advantage of the wisdom and experiences of his students.
■ If all questions are related to the Bible Story just told, everybody can participate. Even those who don't know others in the group or those with limited biblical knowledge can participate.

Using the method of **Bible Storytelling with Questions**, the storytelling teacher tells the Bible story and then leads a discussion by asking questions related to it. Through the asking of questions, the storytelling teacher leads his students to pay attention to the story and its characters in order to learn the life-lessons that God has for them.

If the story is well known to the students, the questions may also be inserted while telling the story. While narrating an episode of the story, the storyteller stops and inserts an appropriate question that leads the students to think about a life-lesson from the episode.

When the storytelling teacher is narrating in chronological order, questions asked before telling a new story help to recapture previous told stories. It is necessary to keep reviewing stories already told in order for the students to understand what is happening in chronological order.

GENERIC QUESTIONS THAT MAY BE USED WITH ANY BIBLE STORY

Here are some examples of generic questions that may be used with any Bible story:
1. What catches your attention in the story?
2. Is there anything in the story that is hard to understand?
3. Who are the main characters in the story?
4. What problems did the characters face?
5. How did the characters face their problems?
6. How have you faced similar problems?
7. Is there someone in the story who is similar to you or who is different from you?
8. What does the story tell about God?

How to Prepare a Bible Study Using Bible Storytelling with Questions

1. **Analyze the Bible story**

The Bible teacher must first be a Bible student. The teacher should follow the steps in the chapter **HOW TO ANALYZE A BIBLE STORY**.

2. **Select the most important life-lessons for the students**

When analyzing a Bible story, many life-lessons are discovered. The teacher must choose the life-lessons most appropriate for the needs of his students. Practical suggestions on choosing life-lessons are found in the chapter: (6) **Selecting Life-lessons from a Bible Story to Become the Divisions for a Sermon or Study**.

The storytelling teacher has a limited amount of time. Therefore, he must select the life-lessons that are most needed for his students in their present circumstances and transform them into questions.

If the Bible Storytelling with Questions will be part of a Storying Track, consider the following when selecting the life-lessons for the students:
- The emphasis of the Storying Track;
- The life-lessons discovered in the story;
- The needs of the students and how they connect to the Storying Track emphasis;
- The life-lessons that most relate to the emphasis of the Storying Track and the needs of the students.

If the Bible Storytelling with Questions will not be part of a Storying Track, consider the following when selecting the life-lessons for the students:
- The life-lessons discovered in the Bible story;
- The greatest need in the lives of the students;
- The life-lessons that connect with the needs of the students.

3. **Prepare the selected life-lessons, transforming each one into one or more questions**

The life-lessons discovered from the Bible story and selected to be taught must be transformed into good questions. Learning takes place when the teacher asks questions and the students discover the answers. The teacher needs the following conviction: If the students don't discover the life-lesson, the flaw belongs to the teacher who did not ask good questions.

The teacher limits his speaking to asking questions, to guiding the students to discover answers, and to applying those answers to their own lives. The teacher does not mention the life-lesson he wishes to teach. The teacher speaks less than the students.

Group dynamics and lively discussion are created by good questions. Poor questions either don't generate participation, or they liberate the students to escape from the subject. For example: after telling the story of Joseph's temptation in Genesis 39, a teacher could ask: "Does anyone wish to speak?" Sometimes the teacher receives a blank stare from the students; at other times a student could answer: "Yes, I want someone to explain to me the dragon with seven heads in Revelation!"

I want to emphasize: if the students don't participate, if they do not discover life-lessons from the Bible story, if they don't know how to apply discovered life-lessons to their own lives, or if they escape from the subject, the blame doesn't belong on them, it belongs on the teacher! It is the teacher's responsibility to generate group dynamics by transforming selected life-lessons into good questions.

A teacher's questions can be compared to a city sign post. If signs are insufficient, or if some point to the wrong direction, the drivers can not be accused of being incompetent. The city hall is to blame for the drivers' mistakes. If students don't discover truths from the Bible story, the teacher needs to improve his questions.

The teacher should transform each life-lesson he wishes to teach into simple questions. The teacher should limit questions to the Bible story being emphasized and to life-lessons from the story that he wishes to teach.

DIFFERENT KINDS OF QUESTIONS

KIND OF QUESTION	EXAMPLE
OPEN: the question doesn't have a correct answer; it opens discussions.	■What was your opinion on the story of Joseph's temptation? ■What most impressed you about Joseph's story?
CLOSED: the question is very specific and it should be answered with a "yes," "no" or with appropriate details.	■What was the name of the man who bought Joseph in Egypt? ■Was Joseph being tempted when Potiphar's wife asked him to go to bed with her?
DISCOVER: the objective of the question is to help the students discover information or facts mentioned in the story or life-lesson taught by it.	■How was Joseph tempted? ■How did Joseph react to his temptation?
FOLLOW THE SEQUENCE: the intention is to obtain information on chain of events, or to obtain opinions of others about a subject in progress.	■List the different times when Joseph suffered injustice.
APPLICATION: the objective of the question is to help the students to apply truths taught in the Bible story to their own lives.	■Today, what types of temptations do Christians suffer? ■What types of injustices do Christians suffer today when they do what is right?

With each life-lesson selected to be taught, the teacher should at least use two main types of questions to help the students:
1) QUESTIONS TO *HELP THE STUDENTS DISCOVER* the life-lessons found in the Bible story and selected by the teacher. Usually, the teacher begins asking questions that verify that the students understood the details of the story from which the life-lesson is extracted.
2) QUESTIONS TO HELP THE STUDENTS *APPLY* the discovered life-lessons to their lives. Verify that the students can apply the life-lesson to their own lives. Ask questions that lead them to relate the story to themselves. All Bible studies should have a common goal: to get the students to change. The teacher wants his students to:
■Believe a truth they didn't believe;
■Trust a promise they haven't trusted;
■Understand a truth they hadn't known;
■Obey a commandment or biblical teaching;
■Become something they have not been;
■Do something they have not been doing.

DISCOVERY QUESTIONS	APPLICATION QUESTIONS
Past tense: Biblical times	Present tense: Today
Refers to names, people and locations mentioned in the Bible story	Refers to people, places, and events that are presently current
Pronouns: him/her, them, they, their	Pronouns: you, us, yours, our, me, mine

Words that help to transform life-lessons into good questions:

- Who?
- What?
- When?
- Where?
- Why?
- How?

EXAMPLE OF LIFE-LESSONS TRANSFORMED INTO QUESTIONS

STORY: Joseph's Temptation
TEXT: Gen 39:1-23

LIFE-LESSON #1 Those who are faithful to God are subject to temptation (39:7, 10-12).

1) How did God manifest his approval and his presence with Joseph?

2) What temptation did Joseph face?

3) When Joseph was tempted, how did he manifest his belief in God?

4) Today, how are those who serve God subject to similar temptations?

LIFE-LESSON #2 Knowing the will of God helps to resist temptation (39:9).

1) How did Joseph react to temptation?

2) What reasons did Joseph give for resisting temptation?

3) How could understanding biblical truths help you resist strong temptations?

LIFE-LESSON #3 The faithfulness of God's servant in a world corrupted by sin may result in his suffering injustice (39:20).

1) What was the woman's reaction when Joseph resisted her invitation to have sex?

2) Why did Joseph suffer for doing what was right?

3) What kinds of situations may result in a faithful Christian suffering injustice for doing right?

4. **Organize the Teaching Plan for Bible Storytelling with Questions**

Those who know how to write should make notes on a sheet of paper. The notes become the Teaching Plan. The Teaching Plan should include the following:

- **BIBLE STORY**: the telling of the Bible story, utilizing the sequence of events;
- **QUESTIONS**: selected life-lessons from the story that are transformed into questions;
- **CONCLUSION**: summarize the story, review the questions asked and the students' contributions, and appeal for change that would come from putting the life-lessons into practice.

BIBLE STORY

Bible Storytelling with Questions begins by telling the Bible story. This is a good time to review the chapter: **Telling the Bible Story**. Each telling of the story must be true to the biblical facts, even when complementary facts are included in order to help today's listeners understand the Bible story. The teacher should follow **the sequence of events**, telling the story in chronological order:

- Consider the context. Explain background information that would help the listeners to understand the historical circumstances surrounding the narrative, to understand the initial situation, and to identify characters in the story.
- Follow the sequence of events. Start at the beginning of the story, making sure to include the facts that will enable the listeners to identify the initial-problem. Continue following the sequence of events until the final-situation of the story has been told.

In making the Teaching Plan, the storytelling teacher will include the notes made when analyzing the story about the context and the sequence of events. He will copy or abbreviate the notes from the context and sequence of events.

QUESTIONS

Prepare a list of questions to be asked. However, the teacher needs to know that the questions on the list will not be sufficient. He will need to craft new questions while teaching. When the students' answers are incomplete, more questions need to be asked. Students' answers may indicate a need for a new line of questioning. During the Bible study, the teacher should ask questions until he is satisfied the students understand the Bible story, comprehend life-lessons taught by the story and know how to apply those life-lessons to their own lives.

CONCLUSION

Summarize the story, review the questions asked, recall the students' contributions and appeal for the change that would come from putting the life-lessons into practice. The conclusion should associate the discussions with the content of the Bible story.

All Bible Storytelling with Teaching has a common goal: to get the students to change. The change may be emotional, intellectual, behavioral, physical or a combination of all four, but change must occur for teaching to be successful. The teacher wants his students to change in one or more of the following:
- Believe a truth they haven't believed;
- Trust a promise they haven't trusted;
- Understand something they haven't understood;
- Obey a command or law they haven't been obeying;
- Become something they haven't been;
- Do something they haven't been doing.

The conclusion should consume about ten percent of the total Bible study. A fifty-minute Bible study should not have more than a five-minute conclusion.

Conclude the Bible study:
- By giving a short summary of the Bible story;
- By connecting the questions asked, the students' contributions and the events of the story;
- With an appeal for the students to put into practice the will of God as discovered in the discussion time.

EXAMPLE: TEACHING PLAN FOR BIBLE STORYTELLING COMBINED WITH QUESTIONS

BIBLE STORY: Joseph in Potiphar's House
TEXT: Genesis 39:1-23

Context:
Israel loved Joseph more than all his other sons. Joseph's brothers hated him. Joseph dreamed that his father, mother and brothers would bow down before him. Joseph's brothers sold him to slave merchants (Gen 37).

Sequence of events:
- Joseph was taken to Egypt and bought by Potiphar (39:1).
- The Lord was with Joseph (39:2).
- Joseph gained Potiphar's favor. Potiphar made Joseph the overseer of all he owned (39:4-6).
- Joseph was handsome. His master's wife invited Joseph to go to bed with her (39:7).
- Joseph refused. He said his master had entrusted everything in the house, except his wife, to Joseph's care. Joseph asked how could he do such a wicked thing and sin against God? (39:8-9).
- Daily, she spoke to Joseph, but he refused to go to bed with her or even to be with her (39:10).
- One day when Joseph was alone in the house with her, she caught him by his garment. He left his garment in her hand and fled (39:11-12).
- The woman called her household servants and accused Joseph of trying to sleep with her. She said that when she screamed, he left his cloak and ran out of the house (39:13-19).
- When Potiphar returned home she told him that Joseph tried to make sport of her. When she screamed, he left his cloak and ran out of the house (39:17-18).
- Potiphar burned with anger and put Joseph into the jail with the king's prisoners (39:19-20).
- In prison, the Lord was with Joseph (39:21).

QUESTIONS:

1. Where was God when Joseph was sold into slavery?
2. How did God show his presence with Joseph?
3. What temptation did Joseph face?
4. How do Christians today suffer temptations similar to Joseph's?
5. How did Joseph react to his temptation?
6. What were the reasons Joseph gave for resisting his temptation?
7. How did the fact that wrong against a fellow person is sin against God help Joseph resist temptation?
8. How can knowing God help you to resist your temptation?
9. What were the woman's reactions when Joseph refused to go to bed with her?
10. How did Joseph suffer for doing what was right?
11. Today, how may faithful Christians suffer injustice for doing what is right?

CONCLUSION:

Be prepared to mention the following conclusions and seek to refer to the contributions made by the students during the discussion time.

1. Faithful Christians will be tempted. Be prepared to face temptations (39:7, 10-12).
2. Know that God will help you resist your own temptation (39:9). Study the Bible and spend time with God in prayer so you will know him better and be able to resist your temptations.
3. The faithful Christian may suffer injustice when he resists temptation (39:20). Don't be surprised if you suffer when you do what is right.

SUGGESTIONS FOR USING QUESTIONS WHEN TEACHING

1. Have confidence in the students' abilities. Teach with the expectation that the Holy Spirit will guide the students to new truths.

2. When it is possible to organize the seating arrangements, arrange the room in a way that helps all present feel comfortable to participate. The best arrangement is to place the chairs in the form of a circle or semicircle. Thus, each person can see everyone else. The teacher should sit down in order to be on the same level with everyone else. When the teacher is sitting down with the others, the group feels more freedom to share and also presumes that others' contributions can be as important as the teacher's.

3. Be sure to allow your students to answer your questions. Don't ask a question and then answer it yourself.

4. After asking the question, give time for the students to think and discuss the issues that are important to them.

5. When a student asks a question, permit another student to respond.

6. Respect the answers given by paying attention to what your students say.

7. In order to involve all students, some questions should be directed to the group at large and others to specific individuals.

8. Involve all the students by asking the same question to more than one person, neither agreeing nor disagreeing with any answer given. The teacher may ask if others agree or disagree with an answer given.

9. Never push a student to answer a question. Questioning time should not become a time to embarrass or constrain anyone present.

10. If the students were unable to respond or if they gave an incorrect answer, it would be wise to:
    ■ Offer another question that would help the students recall the correct answer, or
    ■ Explain the answer, giving more details when necessary.

11. When the answers are incorrect, explain with caution, showing consideration for a part of the answer if possible.

12. It is wise to avoid questions where the answer is a "YES" or a "NO"! Such questions don't require the students to reflect. Usually, the way the questions are asked telegraphs the answer.

Bible Storytelling Tools © Jackson Day

13. When a student asks a question and the teacher doesn't know the answer, the teacher should be sincere with his students. He may say he doesn't know but will seek the answer; or, he may say he needs to think about the question and request that the student ask the same question later. When the teacher doesn't know the facts, it is better to admit it immediately instead of guessing and possibly giving wrong information.

14. Once in a while a student asks a vicious question, seeking to provoke an argument, to discredit the teacher, or to interfere with teaching. Jesus always answered honest questions; however, he avoided answering malicious ones. Try to have some prepared answers, such as: "I didn't intend to cover this subject today"; or "This is a subject we do not have time to discuss today"; or "Perhaps the two of us can discuss this later." The teacher must avoid becoming angry or irritable. When a malicious question is asked, the teacher needs to react with politeness, yet firmness. The teacher who explodes in anger, loses control of his class. While it is not easy to deal with hateful questions, the teacher should be mature enough to avoid allowing malicious questions to disrupt the class.

II. BIBLE STORYTELLING COMBINED WITH USING TEACHING CYCLES

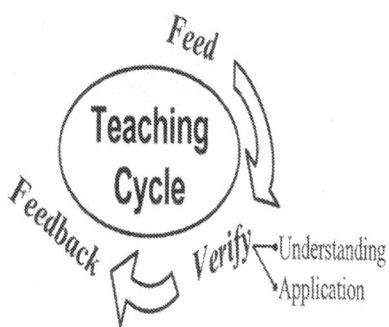

To use teaching cycles, the storytelling teacher narrates the Bible story, explains life-lessons discovered in the story, asks questions, and leads discussions with the students. There are two basic plans for Bible Storytelling Combined with Using Teaching Cycles.

■**Bible Storytelling Combined with Using Teaching Cycles After the Story**
The normal method for Bible Storytelling with lessons and discussions is to tell all the story, explain a life-lesson discovered in the story and then lead discussion by asking questions. The **Teaching Cycle** is used with each life-lesson taught. The process of explaining a life-lesson and asking questions continues until the Bible study is finished.

■**Storytelling Combined with Inserting Teaching Cycles while Narrating the Story**
The storytelling teacher starts narrating the story. When he comes to an episode that inspires a life-lesson, he stops storytelling, inserts his life-lesson, and leads a discussion utilizing the **Teaching Cycle**. He continues storytelling until he reaches another episode that inspires a life-lesson he wishes to develop. He continues storytelling and inserting life-lessons until the end of the story. This method should only be used with a group that already knows the story.

In this chapter, only the plan for using **Bible Storytelling Combined with Using Teaching Cycles After the Story** will be presented.

1. Use the Teaching Cycle with each life-lesson selected

The storytelling teacher begins preparing for the Bible study by analyzing the Bible story. He will discover many life-lessons taught by the story. He will then select some of the life-lessons he wishes to use. Each life-lesson selected will become a division of the Teaching Plan. With each division of the Bible study, the storytelling teacher will develop the **Teaching Cycle**.

The principal difference between a Bible study and a sermon is that all may participate in a discussion during the study. During the sermon only one person talks. Therefore, in order to have the participation of the students, it is necessary to plan to use questions. The **TEACHING CYCLE** is an effective approach to guarantee the participation of students during the Bible study.

To use the **Teaching Cycle**, three activities must be done with each selected life-lesson:

■<u>Feed the students the life-lesson</u>. Transmit the life-lesson to the students by explaining the life-lesson and giving them information about it.

■<u>Verify with questions</u> that the students understand the life-lesson and know how to apply it to their own lives.

■<u>Give feedback to the students</u>. Feedback is given by responding to the students' answers. Respond according to the students' answers in order to recall for them facts about the life-lesson, confirm a right answer, remove a doubt, clear up a misunderstanding, or correct an error.

1.1 Feed the students the life-lesson
(transmit the life-lesson and explain it)

Make notes for plans to explain the life-lesson. Some of the things done while explaining the life-lesson are:
- Make the life-lesson clear or understandable;
- Present facts that may not be known to the students;
- Shed light on the life-lesson by offering details or motives previously unclear or only implicit;
- Define or clarify words that might be better understood;
- Show the logical development of the life-lesson;
- Use other Bible texts that help explain and reinforce the life-lesson.

Illustrations may be included in communicating the life-lesson to the students. To illustrate the life-lesson, the storytelling teacher will tell a story, anecdote, joke or describe an instance or event that serves as an example to clarify the life-lesson. The life-lesson may be explained with events from the story that is the text to the Bible study, or the storytelling teacher may seek illustrations from outside that story.

Explanations, stories, jokes and anecdotes are selected only for the purpose of transmitting the life-lesson to the students.

1.2 Verify with questions

Make notes for questions to be asked that will verify whether the students understand the story and the life-lesson. The questions should be simple so the student who is participating for the first time will be able to answer them. Questions should be limited to Bible stories told to the group and the life-lesson being taught. Ask questions that verify that the students:
- Understand the life-lesson explained;
- Know how to apply it to their own lives.

Verify that the students understand the life-lesson by asking questions about the episode in the story that relates to the life-lesson as well as the life-lesson itself.

Verify that the students are able to apply the life-lesson to their own lives by asking questions that require them to relate the life-lesson to their individual lives. All Bible studies should have a common goal: get the students to change. The teacher wants his students to change in one or more of the following:
- Believe a truth they haven't believed;
- Trust a promise they haven't trusted;
- Understand something they haven't understood;
- Obey a command or law they haven't obeyed:
- Become something they haven't been;
- Do something they haven't been doing.

The teacher needs to ask questions that will help students discover for themselves the changes they need to make in order to apply the life-lesson to their own lives.

SUGGESTIONS FOR VERIFYING WITH QUESTIONS

1) Questions should relate to both the Bible story told and the life-lesson explained by the teacher.
2) Always be sure to include at least two types of questions that verify that students:
   - Understand the life-lesson explained;
   - Know how to apply it to their own lives.
3) Be sure to allow your students to answer your questions. Don't ask a question and then answer it yourself.
4) When a student asks a question, permit another student to respond.
5) In order to involve all the students, ask the same question to more than one person, neither agreeing nor disagreeing with any answer given. The teacher may ask if others agree or disagree with an answer given.
6) Never push a student to answer a question. Questioning time should not become a time to embarrass or constrain anyone present.

7) If the students were unable to respond or gave an incorrect answer:
   - Offer another question that would help the students recall the correct answer, or
   - Explain the answer, giving more details when necessary.
8) When the answers are incorrect, correct with caution, showing consideration for a part of the answer if possible.
9) It is wise to avoid questions where the answer is a "YES" or a "NO"! Such questions don't require the students to reflect. Usually the way the questions are asked telegraphs the answer.
10) Words that help make good questions are: who? what? when? where? why? how?

1.3 Give feedback to the students

The teacher's feedback will be in response to the students' participation. The teacher can not prepare notes ahead of time for the feedback. Only after hearing the students' answers does the teacher decide how to respond.

Before giving feedback, the teacher needs to hear the students' answers. The capacity to listen and understand one's students is essential to good teaching. To hear, it is necessary to be silent and pay attention to the student! When the teacher doesn't understand the students, he should ask questions until he does. When a student is speaking, the teacher should avoid being anxious to resume speaking. When a student is speaking, some teachers have the bad habit of planning what they will say next instead of paying attention to the student.

Some of the things accomplished during feedback are:
- Correct answers are confirmed;
- Incorrect answers are corrected;
- Life-lessons are fixed in the memory of the students;
- Facts about the life-lesson are recalled;
- Facts about the Bible story are recalled;
- Doubts are removed;
- Misunderstandings are cleared up.

The teacher needs to cultivate certain good habits and avoid certain bad ones when using the Teaching Cycle. For example:

1) Cultivate the students' participation. Avoid being a motor-mouth teacher who talks, talks, talks during the entire class time. The motor-mouth teacher does not verify with questions and never interacts with the students. The motor-mouth teacher makes it difficult for students to learn.
2) Stimulate the participation of all the students. Avoid a private chat with just a few students. Ask questions to stimulate the participation of everybody.
3) Pay attention to the students' answers and respond to their questions with respect.
4) After asking a question, give the students the opportunity to answer it. Cutting off a student's participation interferes with learning. Don't begin feedback before the student finishes talking. When the teacher interrupts the students' answers or avoids responding to their questions, it gives the students the impression that the teacher considers them as foolish or ignorant.
5) Stick with the Bible story and life-lesson being emphasized. Avoid chasing rabbits. Avoid leaving the story and the life-lesson being treated.
6) Avoid belittling a student. Teachers, who belittle the student who has different opinions from theirs, give the impression that they consider themselves superior to the students. They also make their students feel miserable.
7) Show respect to students who have convictions different from the teacher. Avoid attacking non-biblical beliefs or any specific religion. During the discussion students may express beliefs from their worldview that differ from biblical teachings. Be alert but don't attack the students nor their convictions. When a student expresses a non-biblical belief, the teacher has an opportunity to gain information about his student's beliefs, prepare himself to teach the biblical truth when the moment in the life-lesson is adapted, or prepare another life-lesson with a narrative or text that deals with the non-biblical viewpoint.
8) Maintain self-control at all times. The teacher who loses self-control gives the impression that he is a spoiled child in an adult's body. To lose one's patience, scream at the students, or get on the defensive, provokes the students' hostility and will sabotage the class. If the teacher does lose self-control, he should apologize to his students.

EXAMPLE: TEACHING CYCLE

Story: The Temptation of Jesus (Matthew 4:1-11)

Life-lesson converted into a division of a Bible study using the Teaching Cycle: Satan is the one who schedules the temptation.

FEED (Explain the life-lesson):
Satan is the one who schedules the temptations that each person must face. He schedules the time, the place and the kind of temptation without informing the person to be tempted.

After Jesus had fasted forty days, Satan came to tempt him.

VERIFICATION QUESTIONS:
Verify understanding:
- When did Satan tempt Jesus?
- Where was Jesus tempted?
- What temptations did Satan schedule for Jesus?

Verify application:
- What temptations has Satan scheduled for you?
- Since Satan does not advise you ahead of time when you will be tempted, how can you prepare for your temptations?

FEEDBACK
The teacher can not plan ahead of time for feedback since it is done in response to the students' answers.

2. **Organize Plans for Bible Storytelling Combined with Using Teaching Cycles After the Story**

   2.1 **Analyze the Bible story**

   The teacher should begin preparation by analyzing the Bible story. He should follow the steps in the chapter **HOW TO ANALYZE A BIBLE STORY**.

   2.2 **Select the most important life-lessons for the students**

   The storytelling teacher needs to select appropriate life-lessons to be transformed into the Teaching Cycle. Suggestions on choosing life-lessons are found in the chapter: **Selecting Life-lessons from a Bible Story to Become the Divisions for a Sermon or Study**.

If the Bible study will be part of a Storying Track, the storytelling teacher will consider the following when selecting life-lessons for his students:
- Emphasis of the Storying Track;
- Life-lessons discovered in the story;
- Needs of the students and how they connect to the Storying Track emphasis;
- The life-lessons that most relate to the emphasis of the Storying Track and the needs of the students.

If the Bible Study will not be part of a Storying Track, the storytelling teacher will consider the following when selecting the life-lessons for his study:
- The life-lessons discovered in the Bible story;
- The greatest needs of the students;
- Select the life-lessons that connect with the needs of the students.

   2.3 **Prepare the selected life-lessons, using the Teaching Cycle with each one**

   With each life-lesson chosen to become a division of the Bible study, the storytelling teacher will develop the **Teaching Cycle**. Three activities must be done with each selected life-lesson:
- Feed the students the life-lesson;
- Verify with questions that the students understand and know how to apply the life-lesson;
- give feedback to the students.

   2.4 **Prepare the Teaching Plan for Bible Storytelling Combined with Using Teaching Cycles After the Story**

   The Teaching Plan is often called the Bible study outline. Those who know how to write should make notes on paper concerning their Teaching Plan.

   The Teaching Plan will include:
- <u>Bible story</u>: the telling of the Bible story utilizing the sequence of events;
- <u>Bible study divisions</u>: life-lessons chosen from the story and developed following the Teaching Cycle;
- <u>Conclusion</u>: summarize the story, review life-lessons presented and appeal for changes that would come from putting the life-lessons into practice.

THE BIBLE STORY

Bible Storytelling with Teaching begins by telling the Bible story. Each telling of the story must be true to the biblical facts. Complementary facts may be included in order to help today's listeners understand the Bible story. The storyteller should economize his words by staying close to the words used in a first-rate contemporary translation. This is a good time to review the chapter **Telling a Bible Story**.

The storyteller should follow **the sequence of events** when telling the story:
- <u>Consider the context</u>. Explain background information that would help the listeners to understand the historical circumstances surrounding the narrative, to understand the initial situation, and to identify characters in the story;
- <u>Follow the sequence of events</u>. Continue following the sequence of events until the final-situation of the story has been told.

In making his Teaching Plan, the storytelling teacher will include the notes made when analyzing the story about the context and the sequence of events. He will copy or abbreviate those notes.

DIVISIONS: Selected Life-Lessons from the Story are Transformed into Teaching Cycles

Life-lessons selected to be communicated become the divisions of the Bible study. Each division will be developed using the Teaching Cycle. For each division, prepare notes for:
- Feeding the life-lesson;
- Verifying the life-lesson using questions. (<u>Observation</u>: *The teacher can only make plans to feed the life-lesson and verify with questions since feedback is determined by the students' answers.*)

1ˢᵗ DIVISION (*The first life-lesson selected to be presented becomes the first division of the Bible Study.*) The **First Teaching Cycle**
- Feed;
- Verify:
  - Verify the students understand the life-lesson;
  - Verify the students can apply the life-lesson to their own lives;
- Give feedback (*The teacher can not plan ahead of time and make notes for the feedback since it is done in response to the students' answers*).

2ⁿᵈ DIVISION: (*The life-lesson selected to be the second one presented becomes the second division of the sermon.*) The **Second Teaching Cycle**

Continue until each life-lesson selected is developed using the Teaching Cycle.

CONCLUSION

Prepare to conclude the Bible study. Summarize the story, review the life-lessons taught, recall the students' contributions, and appeal for change that would come from putting the life-lessons into practice.

The conclusion should be short. It should consume about ten percent of the total Bible study. A fifty-minute Bible study should not have more than a five-minute conclusion.

EXAMPLE: TEACHING PLAN: BIBLE STORYTELLING COMBINED WITH USING TEACHING CYCLES

BIBLE STORY: Joseph in Potiphar's House
TEXT: Genesis 39:1-23

Context:
Israel loved Joseph more than all his other sons. Joseph's brothers hated him. Joseph dreamed that his father, mother and brothers would bow down before him. Joseph's brothers sold him to slave merchants (Gen 37).

Sequence of events:
- Joseph was taken to Egypt and bought by Potiphar (39:1).
- The Lord was with Joseph (39:2).
- Joseph gained Potiphar's favor. Potiphar made Joseph the overseer of all he owned (39:4-6).
- Joseph was handsome. His master's wife invited Joseph to go to bed with her (39:7).
- Joseph refused. He said his master had entrusted everything in the house, except his wife, to Joseph's care. Joseph asked how could he do such a wicked thing and sin against God? (39:8-9).
- Daily Joseph refused to go to bed with her or even to be with her (39:10).

- One day when Joseph was alone in the house with her, she caught him by his garment. He left his garment with her and fled (39:11-12).
- The woman called her household servants and accused Joseph of trying to rape her (39:13-19).
- She told Potiphar that Joseph tried to make sport of her, when she screamed, Joseph left his cloak and ran out of the house (39:17-18).
- Potiphar burned with anger and put Joseph into the jail with the king's prisoners (39:19-20).
- In prison, the Lord was with Joseph (39:21).

DIVISIONS

1. God's servant is blessed, even when he is in undesirable circumstances

FEED:

God's servant may find himself in circumstances that are undesirable to him. But even in those places, if he is faithful, God will bless him and make him a blessing to others.
(Read Rom 8:28; Ph 4:12.)
Joseph wanted to be in Canaan enjoying the privileges of being his father's favorite son. He didn't want to be a slave in an Egyptian's home. The Lord was with Joseph and he prospered. The master saw that the Lord gave Joseph success in everything he did. The master trusted Joseph, and put him in charge of everything he owned. The Lord blessed the house of the Egyptian because of Joseph.

VERIFICATION:
Understanding
- Joseph was put in what kind of undesirable circumstances?
- How did God manifest his blessing to Joseph when he was a slave in Egypt?

Application
- Give examples of Christians who find themselves in undesirable circumstances.
- Why does a Christian who finds himself in an undesirable circumstance have reason to have hope to be blessed by God?
- What reactions would prevent a Christian caught in undesirable circumstances from being blessed by God?

2. The person who serves God is subject to strong temptation

FEED
- Being faithful to God does not free a person from facing temptation. In fact, the opposite is true. The closer one gets to God, the more he will come under Satan's attacks, and the stronger the temptations will become.
- Seventeen-year-old Joseph was tempted to have sex with his master's wife (39:7, 10-12).
- Eve was tempted by Satan in the Garden of Eden (Gen 3:1-7).

VERIFICATION:
Understanding
- How was Joseph tempted?
- Why was Joseph's temptation a difficult one?

Application
- Today, what strong temptations do God's servants face?
- What temptations are most common to you and to your friends?

3. Belief in God gives a person reason to resist temptation

FEED:
- Joseph's belief in God gave him the conviction that betraying his master would be sin (39:9).
- Belief in God results in believing the Bible tells us what is right and wrong.

VERIFICATION:
Understanding
- How did Joseph answer the woman's request to go to bed with her?
- In his answer, how did Joseph express his belief in God?

Application
- How should your belief in God help you to resist your temptations?

4. Victory over temptation can be costly
FEED:
- When Joseph resisted temptation, his seducer became his accuser and he was cast into prison.
- Daniel was cast into the lions' den when he refused to stop praying to God (Dan 6:1-28)
- Stephen was stoned for preaching about Jesus (Ac 7).
- An honest accountant was asked by his boss if he worked for the firm or for the government.
- Jesus tells his followers to watch and pray lest they enter into temptation. Jesus seeks disciples who will take up a cross and follow him. It can be costly to resist temptation.
- If Jesus' faithfulness to God resulted in his crucifixion, do not be surprised if you must pay a high price to follow the Lord and resist temptation.

VERIFICATION:
Understanding
■ How did Joseph pay a high price for saying no to the woman's invitation?

Application
■ Do you know of Christians who have paid a high price for resisting temptation?
■ How can you be prepared to do what is right even if it costs you?

5. **Faithful servants who resist temptations are the ones God seeks to execute important tasks**

FEED:
God's servants become stronger and better when they face and resist temptation. (See James 1:2-4.)

Joseph resisted strong temptations and became a person God could use to save the nation of Egypt and his own family.

VERIFICATION:
Understanding
■ How did resisting temptation help Joseph become someone God could use to become a leader in Egypt?

Application
■ If you desire to be qualified to do important work for God, what will be your reaction to the temptations that come your way?

CONCLUSIONS:
Joseph was forced to live in Egypt when he wanted to be at home with his family. You also may be forced to adjust to undesirable situations. Seventeen-year-old Joseph faced a strong temptation and so will you. God used Joseph to do a great task. Today, Christians who resist temptations will be the ones God uses to do a mighty work.

1. Determine that you are going to face up to unpleasant situations with God's help and be a blessing wherever you are.
2. You never know when you will be tempted, but you can know you will be tempted. Beware of the destruction that yielding to sin could have in your life. Be prepared and stay prepared to resist temptation.
3. Have as your goal to be someone God can use.

THREE METHODS USEFUL FOR COMMUNICATING SELECTED LIFE-LESSONS FROM BIBLE STORIES

METHOD	PREACH	TEACH	
	PREACHING CYCLE	QUESTIONS	TEACHING CYCLE
1ST STEP	**Analyze the Bible Story** Discover the maximum number of life-lessons taught by the story.	**Analyze the Bible Story** Discover the maximum number of life-lessons taught by the story.	**Analyze the Bible Story** Discover the maximum number of life-lessons taught by the story.
2ND STEP	**Select the most important life-lessons for the listeners.**	**Select the most important life-lessons for the students.**	**Select the most important life-lessons for the students.**
3RD STEP	**Use Preaching Cycle to develop each selected life-lesson.** With each selected life-lesson: **Explain** **Illustrate** **Apply**	**Transform selected life-lessons into questions.** Use two types of questions with each selected life-lesson: 1ST **Discovery questions** 2ND **Application questions**	**Use Teaching Cycle to develop each selected life-lesson.** ■**Feed the students.** Explain and give information about the life-lesson. ■**Verify with questions** that the students understand the life-lesson and know how to apply it to their own lives; ■**Give feedback** to the students.
4TH STEP	**Organize the sermon outline:** **BIBLE STORY** **PREACHING CYCLES** 1. Division #1 1ST Preaching Cycle *(Explain, Illustrate, Apply)* 2. Division #2 2ND Preaching Cycle *(Explain, Illustrate, Apply)* **CONCLUSION**	**Organize the Bible study plan:** **BIBLE STORY** **QUESTIONS** 1. Life-lesson #1 transformed into questions 2. Life-lesson #2 transformed into questions **CONCLUSION**	**Organize the Bible study plan:** **BIBLE STORY** **TEACHING CYCLES** 1. Life-lesson #1 1ST Teaching Cycle *(Feed, Verify, Give feedback)* 2. Life-lesson # 2 2ND Teaching Cycle *(Feed, Verify, Give feedback)* **CONCLUSION**
5TH STEP	**PREACH** the sermon.	**TEACH** the Bible study.	**TEACH** the Bible study.

Bible Storytelling Tools © Jackson Day

MIRACLES

OBSERVATION: A list of miracles is in the Chapter: Lists of Bible Stories with References.

DEFINITION

A miracle is an event in which God intervenes and transcends ordinary laws of nature. Nature was created by God, and he can intervene and change its power. When God manipulates, alters or inverts a law of nature, a miracle happens.

BIBLICAL WORDS FOR MIRACLES

Some terms used in the Old Testament to identify miracles are: miracles, signs, wonders, works, great terrors, and miraculous signs.

Words used in the New Testament to identify miracles are: signs, prodigies and wonders.

HISTORICAL TIMES WHEN MIRACLES WERE COMMON

1. Old Testament

In the Old Testament, miracles always point toward God. They are revelations of his power and glory. The purpose of a miracle is the glorification of God's divine name. Therefore, when a person witnessed a miracle and still disbelieved God or disobeyed him, he was judged guilty of having hardness of heart.

There are four biblical periods of miraculous signs. Three of them occurred during Old Testament times. The three historical times when it was common for miraculous signs to occur during the Old Testament times are:

1st When God was delivering the Israelites from slavery in Egypt and establishing them in Canaan.
2nd When the Kingdom of Israel was divided, there was a conflict between pagan religion and the worship of the God of Israel. God used the prophets Elijah and Elisha to battle against the pagan religion.
3rd During the exile period, God's supremacy over other gods was demonstrated when God used miraculous signs to protect Daniel and his companions.

Each historical time when it was common for God to perform miracles was marked by the following common characteristics: God's people faced a conflict between life or death; God assisted his people with abnormal events that were of themselves saving acts and also an indication of a greater salvation.

2. New Testament

The fourth biblical period of miraculous signs happened during the life of Jesus and the establishment of the church. These events are recorded in the Gospels and in Acts.

The miracles reveal Jesus' divine credentials. They authenticate that Jesus is the Son of God (Jn 5:36; 15:24; 20:30-31).

Miracles reveal spiritual truths about Jesus. For example:
- The multiplication of bread (Jn 6:1-14, 25-59) reveals that Jesus is the bread of heaven, he is spiritual food.
- The healing of the blind man (Jn 9) reveals that Jesus is the cure for spiritual blindness.
- Miracles reveal Jesus' power over disease, over defects of the body (healing the paralyzed and blind), over nature (walking on water), over substances (transforming water into wine and multiplying bread and fish), over demons (casting out demons) and over death (raising Lazarus from the dead).

Miracles also attracted listeners and made some attentive to hear Jesus' words (Jn 12:9).

Another characteristic of Jesus' miracles can be observed in the combination of proclamation with the healing work.

During his earthly ministry, Jesus sent his disciples to preach and to perform miracles (Mt 10:7-8; Mk 3:14-15; Lk 9:1-2; 10:9). After his resurrection, he again sent the disciples out to preach and perform miracles (Mk 16:9-20).

Miracles were legitimate evidence of divine authority and apostolic work (2 Cor 12:12 with Rom 15:18-19). Several times the Book of Acts mentions the correlation between apostolic proclamation and performance of miracles (2:2-3; 4:16, 22, 29-30; 6:8; 8:6-8; 9:32-42; 15:12; 20:7-12).

The Holy Spirit also transmits miraculous powers to those who listen to preaching (Gal 3:5). The gifts of proclamation, together with charismatic gifts of healing and miracle working, are included in the spiritual gifts given to the Church (1 Cor 12:8-11; Jas 5:14-15).

The Book of Hebrews testifies that God confirms the preaching of salvation by means of signs, wonders and miracles (Heb 2:3-4).

Through miracles, Jesus proves that he is a living Lord and is present in his Church by means of the Holy Spirit.

OBSERVATION: Miracles are also operated by the enemy. The Old and the New Testaments emphasize the fact that signs and wonders operated by false prophets and messiahs (Mk 13:22; Mt 24:24; Rev 13:11-15; 16:14; 19:20) will seduce people into falling away from God.

HOW TO ANALYZE A BIBLE STORY ABOUT A MIRACLE

The basic guidelines for analyzing any story also applies to analyzing miracles. But miracles need special attention, and require some additional guidelines. When studying a miracle, pay attention to the following:

1. **Identify the structure of the story that describes the miracle**

   Consider the context:
   The context of the miracle is an important key to its interpretation. The scripture before the text that contains the miracle establishes the initial situation and the reason for the miracle. The scripture that follows the miracle story reveals the reaction of those involved in the miracle. From the context, try to find answers for the following questions:
   1) What was the historical occasion when the miracle occurred?
   2) What was God's servant doing or teaching when God performed the miracle?
   3) What was the need that provoked the miracle?
   4) Who were the people or groups involved in the miracle? What was the involvement of each one?
   5) What was the cultural and religious context of the time when the miracle occurred? (Were pagan religions in conflict with God's servants? Were pharisees or Samaritans involved? etc.)
   6) What were the results of the miracle?
   7) Do Scripture texts before or after the miracle interpret it? How do the teachings or reactions of the miracle worker explain the miracle?

   Determine the key persons:
   - The performer of the miracle;
   - The one benefitted by the miracle;
   - Other people or groups involved.

   Determine the key location (The location where the events took place.)

   Determine key-repetitions (Words, themes, facts or ideas that are repeated either exactly or with minor variations.)

   Determine key attitudes expressed in the story (Be sure to include attitudes expressed in the context.)

   Determine the key problem (The incident that describes the problem or need that provoked the miracle.)

   Identify the sequence of events in their chronological order

   Identify the final-situation of the story (The episode that establishes the state of affairs at the end of the story.)

2. **Discover life-lessons taught by the miracle story**

   Seek to discover life-lessons taught by the miracle that relate to the following:
   - The character of God;
   - The power of God;
   - The credentials of the miracle worker;
   - Truths revealed by the miracle worker.

Bible Storytelling Tools © Jackson Day

ANALYSIS OF A BIBLE STORY THAT DESCRIBES A MIRACLE

TITLE OF THE MIRACLE:

TEXT:

STRUCTURE

    Context: (historical circumstances when the miracle was performed, the need or purpose for the miracle, and the initial situation when the miracle story begins):

    Key-people (the performer of the miracle, the beneficiary of it and those who observed it):

    Key-location (the place where the miracle occurred):

    Key-repetitions (words, themes, facts or ideas that are repeated with the same words or with small variation):

    Key-attitudes (feelings, emotions, moods, sentiments and sensations expressed in the story):

    Key-problem (problem or need that provoked the miracle):

    Sequence of events in their chronological order:

    Final-situation (culminating event, final state of affairs, effects of the miracle):

LIFE-LESSONS TAUGHT BY THE MIRACLE STORY: (When other scripture teaches the same truth, use the symbol for parallel text "//" and note its address.)

    ■Life-lessons related to the situation, occasion or need that provoked the miracle.

    ■Life-lessons related to each person or group involved with the miracle, especially the miracle worker, the beneficiary, and the observers.

    ■Life-lessons which the miracle story teaches about God: his character, his power, and his relationship with the miracle worker.

    ■Other life-lessons taught by the miracle story.

EXAMPLE: ANALYSIS OF A MIRACLE STORY

STORY: MIRACULOUS CATCH OF FISH

TEXT: Luke 5:1-11

STRUCTURE

Context:
Jesus was beginning the second year of his public ministry. King Herod had imprisoned John the Baptist. Jesus was becoming popular, and large crowds were beginning to follow him. His main message was the Gospel of the Kingdom of God (Lk 4:43).

Jesus wanted to give priority to preaching about the Kingdom of God, but the main reason the multitudes followed him was that he cured the sick and expelled demons (Lk 4:38-44).

Key-people:
- The performer of the miracle: Jesus
- The beneficiaries of the miracle: Simon Peter, James and John

Key-repetition:
- The words: boats, nets and fish.
- The great quantity of fish caught by the fishermen.

Key-attitudes:
- The crowd's anxiety to hear Jesus.
- The fishermen's exhaustion after fishing all night without catching anything.
- Peter felt it was useless to obey Jesus, but reluctantly followed his orders.
- Peter was shocked after the supernatural catch of fish.
- The fishermen's disposition to follow Jesus after the supernatural catch of fish.

Key-problem:
The multitude pressed around Jesus in order to hear the Word of God (5:1).

Sequence of events in their chronological order:
- Jesus was standing by the lake, and the multitude pressed in to hear him (5:1).
- Jesus saw two boats that fishermen had left at the edge of the lake (5:2).
- Jesus entered into Simon's boat, asked him to put out a little way from land, sat down and taught from the boat (5:3).
- Jesus finished speaking and ordered Simon to take the boat to deep water and let down their nets to fish (5:4).
- Simon answered that they had worked all night without catching anything, yet they would obey Jesus (5:5).
- They caught a great quantity of fish, their nets began to break, they signaled for their partners in another boat to come help them, and they filled both boats (5:6-8).
- Simon fell down at Jesus' feet and said: "Depart from me, for I am a sinful man!" (5:8).
- Simon, James and John were amazed at the quantity of fish caught (5:9-10).
- Simon, James and John left everything and followed Jesus (5:11)

Final-situation: After the miraculous catch of fish, Simon, James and John brought their boats to land, left everything and followed Jesus (5:11).

LIFE-LESSONS TAUGHT BY THE MIRACLE STORY

Life-lessons related to the situation, occasion or need that provoked the miracle:

Jesus was teaching the multitude by the side of a lake. Fishermen who had worked all night without catching anything were on the lakeshore.

1. Teaching is an important activity. The fact that Jesus dedicated himself to teaching reveals the importance God gives to teaching.

2. One some occasions, hard work does not produce the desired rewards. The fishermen worked all night without catching anything.

Life-lessons related to people or groups involved in the miracle:

<u>Jesus: the performer of the miracle</u>

3. A spiritual leader should use available resources to do his ministry. Jesus used available resources to achieve his ministry. He saw two boats by the lake and used one to sit in and teach the multitude (Lk 5:2-3). // To feed five thousand he used a boy's lunch with five pieces of bread and two fish (Jn 6:9-12).

4. Jesus is concerned about the practical problem of people having results from their work. Jesus made it possible for the fishermen to catch fish (Lk 5:6).

Simon Peter: beneficiary of the miracle. Even though he doubted, Simon Peter obeyed Jesus. Simon was a fisherman, Jesus was a carpenter, and Simon had worked all night without success (Lk 5:5).

5. A person should always humble himself and recognize Jesus' right to command.

6. A person should obey Jesus, even when rational reason questions the wisdom of doing so.

7. Even when one is experiencing depression and disbelief, Jesus should be obeyed.

The fishermen: beneficiaries of the miracle. They were filled with amazement (Lk 5:9-11).

8. The person who recognizes Jesus' sovereignty and holiness will be horrified at his own sinfulness.

9. The one who recognizes Jesus' sovereignty will place him above all other interest. The fishermen left everything to follow Jesus (Lk 5:11 // Mt 4:20, 22; Lk 5:28).

10. Those who follow Jesus will experience changes in their lives. The fishermen changed from catching fish to catching people (Lk 5:10 // Mt 4:19).

Observers of the miracle: the multitude.

11. Jesus attracts the attention of people.

Life-lessons the miracle story teaches about God: his character, his power, and his relationship with the miracle worker:

12. Jesus is Lord of creation and has power over nature (// Mt 28:18).

13. Sometimes, Jesus acts in ways that exceed all expectations. There was a great quantity of fish (Lk 5:6). // He transformed more than 125 gallons of water into wine (Jn 2:1-11). // After multiplying five pieces of bread, five thousand ate and 12 baskets were filled with leftovers (Jn 6:12-13).

14. Sometimes, Jesus the creator of nature will miraculously manipulate nature to achieve his objectives (// Col 1:15-18).

15. Jesus does not desire to provoke terror and fear when he demonstrates his power, but to have followers whose lives are transformed (Lk 5:10-11).

Other life-lessons taught by the miracle story:

PREPARING A SERMON ABOUT A MIRACLE

The plan for preparing a sermon for a Bible story about a miracle is the same as for other Bible stories.

1. Analyze the miracle Bible story

The storyteller should follow the steps given in HOW TO ANALYZE A BIBLE STORY ABOUT A MIRACLE.

2. Select the most important life-lessons for the listeners

The storytelling preacher has a limited amount of time; therefore, he must select the life-lessons that are most needed for his listeners in their present circumstances. Life-lessons selected become the division of the sermon.

When selecting life-lessons to become sermon divisions, be sure to consider:
- Life-lessons related to the situation, occasion or need that led up to the miracle.
- Life-lessons related to each person or group involved with the miracle, especially the miracle worker, the beneficiary, and the observers.
- Life-lessons the miracle story teaches about God: his character, his power, and his relationship with the miracle worker.
- Other life-lessons taught by the miracle story.

If the sermon will be part of a Storying Track, consider the life-lessons that most relate to the emphasis of the Storying Track and the needs of the listeners.

3. **Prepare the selected life-lessons, using the Preaching Cycle with each one**

Each division will be developed using the Preaching Cycle. For each division prepare notes for:
- Explanation;
- Illustration;
- Application.

4. **Prepare the Preaching Plan**

The Preaching Plan will include:
- The Bible story: the telling of the miracle Bible story, utilizing the sequence of events;
- Sermon divisions: life-lessons chosen from the story and developed, following the Preaching Cycle;
- Conclusion: a summary of the story, life-lessons presented, and appeal for change that would come from putting the life-lessons into practice.

THE BIBLE STORY

Begin by telling the Bible story about the miracle.
- Consider the context. Explain the background information about historical circumstances when the miracle was performed, the need or purpose for the miracle, the initial situation when the miracle story begins. Also, identify the characters in the story.
- Follow the sequence of events. Start at the beginning of the story, continue following the sequence of events until the final-situation of the story has been told.

The storytelling preacher should copy or abbreviate the notes from the context and sequence of events.

DIVISIONS: Selected Life-Lessons from the Story are Transformed into Preaching Cycles

Life-lessons selected to be communicated become the division of the sermon. Each division will be developed using the Preaching Cycle. For each division prepare notes for:
- Explanation;
- Illustration;
- Application.

It does not matter whether explanation or illustration comes first. However, application always comes last.

CONCLUSION:

The conclusion should review the main aspects treated in the sermon and call for action on the part of the listeners.

The conclusion should invite the listeners to change by putting the truths and applications presented into action.

PREPARING A BIBLE STUDY ABOUT A MIRACLE

The plan for preparing a Bible study for a story about a miracle is the same as for other Bible stories.

This chapter presents only the plan for narrative teaching using **Bible Storytelling Combined with Using Teaching Cycles After the Story.**

1. **Organize Plans for Bible Storytelling Combined with Using Teaching Cycles After the Story**

Analyze the Bible story. The teacher who couples Bible Storytelling with teaching should begin preparation by analyzing the Bible story about the miracle.

Select the most important life-lessons for the students. When selecting life-lessons to teach, be sure to consider:
- Life-lessons related to the situation, occasion or need that led up to the miracle.
- Life-lessons related to each person or group involved with the miracle, especially the miracle worker, the beneficiary, and the observers.
- Life-lessons the miracle story teaches about God: his character, his power, and his relationship with the miracle worker.
- Other life-lessons taught by the miracle story.

If the Bible study will be part of a Storying Track, consider the life-lessons that most relate to the emphasis of the Storying Track and the needs of the students.

Prepare the selected life-lessons, using the Teaching Cycle with each one. To use the **Teaching Cycle** for each division of the Bible study, three activities must be done with each selected life-lesson:
- Feed the students the life-lesson;
- Verify with questions that the students understand the life-lesson and know how to apply it to their own lives;
- Give feedback to the students.

2. **Prepare the Teaching Plan for Bible Storytelling Combined with Using Teaching Cycles After the Story.**

The Teaching Plan will include:
- **Bible story about the miracle**: the telling of the Bible story utilizing the sequence of events;
- **Bible study divisions**: life-lessons chosen from the story and developed following the Teaching Cycle;
- **Conclusion**: summarizes the story, reviews the life-lessons presented and appeals for changes that would come from putting the life-lessons into practice.

THE BIBLE STORY

Bible Storytelling with Teaching begins by telling the Bible story. The storyteller should follow **the sequence of events** when telling the story:
- <u>Consider the context</u>. Explain the background information about historical circumstances when the miracle was performed, the need or purpose for the miracle, and the initial situation when the miracle story begins, identify characters in the story.
- <u>Follow the sequence of events</u>. Start at the beginning of the story, continue following the sequence of events until the final-situation of the story has been told.

DIVISIONS: Selected Life-Lessons from the Story are Transformed into Teaching Cycles

Life-lessons selected to be communicated become the divisions of the Bible study. Each division will be developed using the Teaching Cycle.

1st DIVISION *(The first life-lesson selected to be presented becomes the first division of the Bible Study.)* The **First Teaching Cycle**
- Feed;
- Verify:
  - Verify that the students understand the life-lesson;
  - Verify that the students can apply the life-lesson to their own lives;
- Give feedback. *(The teacher cannot plan ahead of time for the feedback since it is done in response to the students' answers.)*

2nd DIVISION: The **Second Teaching Cycle**

Continue until each life-lesson selected is developed using the Teaching Cycle.

CONCLUSION

Summarize the story, review the life-lessons taught, recall the students' contributions, and appeal for change that would come from putting the life-lessons into practice.

PARABLES

DEFINITION

A parable is a story about events common to daily life that illustrate spiritual truths.

Two things are combined in a parable:
- The story;
- The spiritual truth exemplified by the story.

PURPOSE OF PARABLES

A Jewish Teaching Story has been told and retold since the eleventh century.

Lady Truth was naked and cold. She had been turned away from every door in the village. People were frighten by her nakedness. Parable found Lady Truth huddled in a corner, shivering and hungry. Parable took pity on her, gathered her up and took her home. Parable clothed her in a story, warmed her and sent her out into the village again. Lady Truth knocked again at the villagers' doors and was welcomed into the people's homes. They invited her to eat at their table and to warm herself by their fire.

Jesus narrated parables to the crowds which followed him. He never spoke to them without telling a parable. (See Mark 4:33-34.)

Jesus always used parables when teaching people who did not believe that he was sent by God. Matthew 13:10-17 indicates that Jesus had two purposes when using parables with the skeptics:
- To teach basic truths and to generate interest so that the listeners would want to hear more;
- To hide truths from skeptics who were out to get him, while revealing those same truths to his followers.

LITERARY ASPECTS OF THE PARABLES

1. **Jesus' parables spoke about things common to daily life**

   Examples of parables speaking about things common to daily life:
   - <u>Trade</u>: fishermen, builder, merchant, money, interest, debts, treasure, boss, servants, creditor, debtor, tax collector, taxes, traveler, administrator.
   - <u>Agriculture</u>: farmer, shepherd, sheep, soil, seeds, trees, birds, thorns, crops, barns, fig trees and vineyard.
   - <u>Domestic things</u>: houses, cooking, sewing, sweeping, sleeping, eating and children playing.
   - <u>Social events</u>: a wedding, a banquet, and a friend who arrives at midnight.
   - <u>Religious people</u>: priest, Levite and Pharisee.
   - <u>Civil events</u>: soldier, judge, king and war.

2. **Jesus' parables contained suspense**

   Jesus used simple plots, conflict, strong contrasts and, in some parables, exaggerations to create the suspense.

   Examples of parables that created suspense:
   - How will the merciful master treat his cruel servant? (Mt 18:21-35).
   - What will happen to the tenants who killed the master's servants and his son? (Mt 21:33-46).
   - What will happen to the prodigal son who left home? (Lk 15:11-32).

3. **Jesus' parables contained surprises that increase the impact**

   Jesus' parables contained exaggerations, the opposite of what is expected and unusual situations that increase the impact.

   Examples of parables with atypical situations:
   - Men who worked one hour received the same wage as those who worked all day (Mt 20:1-16).
   - A Samaritan demonstrated more compassion than priests (Lk 10:25-37).

4. Jesus' parables contained an abundance of contrasts

Examples of contrasts in parables:
- House built on the rock versus house built on the sand (Mt 7:24-29).
- New clothes versus old clothes (Mt 9:17).
- Good fish versus bad fish (Mt 13:47-50).
- The sower sowed wheat versus the enemy who sowed weeds (Mt 13:24-30; 36-43).
- The rich man acquired more wealth versus he lost his soul (Lk 12:13-21).

5. Jesus' parables contained a lot of conflict

Examples of conflicts in parables:
- The men who worked all day were angry when those who worked one hour received the same wages (Mt 20:1-16).
- The careful virgins refused to supply olive oil to the foolish ones (Mt 20:1-16).
- The older brother had conflict with his father over the party for the prodigal son (Lk 15:11-32).

6. Many parables contain three main characters or groups of characters

Examples of parables containing three characters:
- The Unforgiving Creditor (Mt 18:23-35): the king, the forgiven servant, the unforgiven servant.
- The Two Sons (Mt 21:28-32): the father, the first son, the second son.
- The Ten Virgins (Mt 25:1-13): the groom, five wise virgins, and five foolish virgins.
- The Prodigal Son (Lk 15:11-32): the father, the prodigal son, the firstborn.

7. Many parables include the spoken words or thoughts of characters in the story

Examples of characters speaking in the parables:
- The prodigal son's monologue (Lk 15:17-19).
- The monologue of the rich fool (Lk 12:17-19).
- The evil servant spoke to himself (Mt 24:48).

8. Many of Jesus' parables contain questions

Some of the parables ask rhetorical questions that encourage the listener to respond in his mind. Other times Jesus asked questions when he expected his listeners to respond.

Examples of parables with rhetorical questions:
- "Suppose one of you has a hundred sheep and loses one of them. Does he not leave the ninety-nine in the open country and go after the lost sheep until he finds it?" (Lk 15:4).
- The landowner asked one of his employees: "Didn't you agree to work for a daily wage? Take your pay and go. I want to give the man who was hired last the same as I gave you. Don't I have the right to do what I want with my own money? Or are you envious because I am generous?" (Mt 20:15).
- Jesus asked a question about his critics: "To what, then, can I compare the people of this generation? What are they like?" (Lk 7:31).

Examples of parables where Jesus asked questions where he expected his listeners to respond:
- After telling Simon the Pharisee the parable of the two debtors, Jesus asked him: "Now which of them will love him more?" (Lk 7:42).
- After telling the parable of the good Samaritan, Jesus asked: "Which of these three do you think was a neighbor to the man who fell into the hands of robbers?" (Lk 10:36).
- After telling the parable of the two sons, Jesus asked the priest and Jewish leaders: "Which of the two did what his father wanted?" (Mt 21:31).

PRINCIPLES FOR INTERPRETING PARABLES

The basic guidelines for analyzing any Bible story applies to parables. But parables need special attention, and require some additional guidelines. Here are some basic principles that will help the storyteller analyze any parable.

1. A parable teaches only one main truth

Parables are similar to most sermon illustrations in that they only illustrate one truth. Since a parable teaches only one main truth, determine the main truth and stick with it.

Examples of parables teaching one main truth:
- The Lost Sheep: there is rejoicing in heaven when one sinner repents (Lk 15:7).
- The Unjust Judge: God will bring about justice for those who persistently pray to him (Lk 18:7).
- The Ten Virgins: Jesus' followers need to keep watch for his return.
- The Two Foundations: hearing and obeying God's Word should be the foundation of life (Mt 7:21-29).

1.1 The correct interpretation of a parable emphasizes the main truth and not the subordinate details

Since a parable teaches only one main truth, don't go beyond the intended emphasis of it. Don't make the parable say more than it was intended to say. Determine the main truth and stick with it. To search for meaning in every detail of the parable turns it into an allegory.

1.2 The main details of the parable illustrate and explain the main truth

The main details of the parable are in harmony with the main truth. Consider only the details that illustrate the main truth.

To determine that a detail is subordinate means that it is secondary to the main truth of the parable. Subordinate details have spiritual meaning when they reinforce the main truth.

1.3 Not all the details in the parable have spiritual meaning

Don't try to interpret details that don't explain the main truth. Mistakes will be made by the person who tries to interpret each detail found in the parable. He will turn it into an allegory. He will read into the parable something that Jesus was not teaching.

Examples of parables having details that do not illustrate the main truth:
- In the Parable of the Lost Sheep, it is obvious that the shepherd represents Jesus, that the sheep symbolizes a lost sinner, and that the 99 sheep represent those who do not need to repent. However, some details, such as the open country, the shepherd's shoulders, his friends and neighbors, do not have spiritual meaning (Lk 15:3-7).
- In the Parable of the Good Samaritan, Jesus did not give spiritual meaning for the details about the robbers, the victim's clothes, his wounds, olive oil, wine, donkey, the inn, the innkeeper, or the two coins (Lk 10:30-37). These details put the story in its cultural setting but do not have spiritual meaning.

2. The correct interpretation of a parable is in harmony with its context

The context includes the verses that come before or after the parable, that deal with the same matter as the parable.

The context helps to understand why Jesus told certain parables. The <u>verses before</u> help to understand the occasions when Jesus told it. The <u>verses before and after</u> help to understand the analogy between the parable and the spiritual truth that Jesus was transmitting. The <u>context after</u> the parable often reveals the reaction of the listeners; this gives clues for discovering the parable's meaning.

Questions that help establish the context of the parable:
- What was the occasion when Jesus told the parable?
- To whom was the parable told?
- What was the listeners' reaction to the parable?
- If Jesus interpreted the parable, what was his interpretation?

Parables also need to be understood within their cultural context of first century Palestine when Jesus told them. Understanding the common-to-life incidents of the in its cultural setting, guides one to understand the main truth of the parable. Learn what impact these details had in the lives of ordinary people in first century Palestine.

Examples of details related to the cultural context of first-century Palestine that one needs to understand in order to understand Jesus' parables:

- A lost sheep;
- A lost coin to a woman;
- A talent of money;
- A wedding banquet;
- Oil lamps;
- A fig tree barren after three years;
- Jews' contempt for tax collectors;
- Building a house on a foundation of rock or sand.

3. The correct interpretation of a parable is in harmony with the whole Bible

Each parable is in agreement with the teaching of all the other parts of the Bible. The main truth of the parable is in agreement with other texts that talk about the same subject.

However, some details in the parables do not have the same meaning in other parts of the Bible. For example yeast represents evil in Ex 12:15; Lev 2:11; Mt 16:6; 1 Cor 5:7-8. But in the parable in Matthew 13:33, yeast represents the process of leavening and implies that those who belong to the kingdom would grow in numbers, and they would keep on growing.

4. Parables illustrate doctrine, but they do not establish doctrine

The storyteller should not extract doctrinal conclusions from the parables, unless the context gives an interpretation that teaches a doctrine. Parables illustrate doctrines and should be interpreted in light of doctrinal passages. The conclusions made from the parables must walk in harmony and not in discord with doctrines taught in didactic texts. Didactic texts are teaching texts, such as those found in Paul's epistles. One should validate the main truth of the parable with teachings from other scripture.

ANALYSIS OF A PARABLE

TITLE FOR PARABLE:

TEXT:

STRUCTURE

    Context: (The context of the parable includes the occasion when Jesus told it, the listeners, the culture, the listeners' reactions and interpretation if given.):

    Key-person:

    Key-location (This includes Jesus' location when he told the parable, and the location of the events mentioned in the parable):

    Key-repetitions:

    Key-attitudes:

    Initial-problems (The problem that provoked Jesus to tell the parable, and the problem presented at the beginning of the parable):

    Sequence of events:

    Final-situations (The final-situation of the parable and the main effect produced by the parable):

LIFE-LESSONS TAUGHT BY THE PARABLE (When other scripture teaches the same truth, use the symbol for parallel text "//" and note its address.)

    1) **The main truth taught by the parable:**

    2) **Life-lessons from subordinate details that reinforce the main truth:**

EXAMPLE: ANALYSIS OF A PARABLE

TITLE: The Wheat and the Weeds

TEXT: Matthew 13:24-30; 36-43

STRUCTURE

Context:
Jesus was using stories to teach. He told the story about the sower and the seeds. He used illustrations of the earth, the farmer and the seed to illustrate spiritual truths.

Key-persons: The landowner who sowed good seed, his enemy who sowed the weeds in the wheat field, and servants to the landowner.

Key-location: Jesus was sitting in a boat close to the shore while a crowd was onshore listening. The location for the events in the parable was an agricultural setting.

Key-repetitions:
- In the context, Jesus used several parables to teach truths about the Kingdom of God: The Sower (Mt 13:1-9); The Wheat and the Weeds (13:18-23); The Mustard Seed (13:31-32); The Yeast (13:33); The Hidden Treasure (13:44); The Pearl of Great Value (13:45-46); The Fishing Net (13:47-50); The Owner of a House with New Things and Old Things (13:52).
- Repeated words in the parable are: wheat, weeds, good seed and enemy.

Key-attitudes:
- The intelligence and cruelty of the enemy who sowed the weeds.
- The devotion of the servants to their master.
- The impatience of the servants who wanted an immediate solution.
- The wisdom and patience of the landowner.

Initial-problems:
The problem that led Jesus to tell the parable was that the disciples needed to understand more about the Kingdom of God (Mt 13:10-11).

The initial-problem in the parable: an enemy planted weeds in a landowner's wheat field.

Sequence of events:
The parable
- The man sowed good seed in his field (13:24).
- While he slept, an enemy sowed weeds in the wheat field (13:25).
- The wheat and the weeds grew together (13:26).
- The servants wanted to know if they should pull the weeds (13:28).
- The owner answers no, because in doing so they could also pull the wheat (13:29). At harvest time, they can separated them, burn the weeds and collect the wheat in the barn (13:30).

Jesus explained the parable (Mt 13:36-43).
- The disciples asked Jesus: What does the parable of the weeds mean? (13:36).
- Jesus answered: the sower of the good seed is the Son of Man; the land is the world; the good seed are God's children; and the weeds are people who belong to Satan (13:37-38).
- The enemy is the devil (13:39).
- The harvest is the end of the world; the harvesters are God's angels (13:39).
- At the end of time, angels will gather out of God's kingdom those who cause sin and do evil and throw them into the fire (13:40-42); then God's people will shine (13:43).

Final-situations:
- In the parable: At harvest time the wheat and the weeds will be separated, the weeds burned and the wheat collected in the barn (13:30).
- In Jesus' explanation: At the end of time, the angels will gather out of his kingdom those who cause sin and do evil, and throw them into the fire (13:40-42); then God's people will shine (13:43).

LIFE-LESSONS TAUGHT BY THE PARABLE

The main truth:

1. Until the day of final judgment, God's children and children of the evil one will be side by side in the church.

Life-lessons from subordinate details that reinforce the main truth:

Detail: Everyone was asleep (13:25).

2. When God's children are not paying attention, they give opportunity for Satan to do his work and to bring confusion to God's children.

> Detail: An enemy puts bad seed in the wheat field (13:25).

3. Satan is an enemy who causes problems for God's children; he influences them negatively and harms the life of the Church.

4. Satan brings into the church people who pretend to belong to God's Kingdom with the intention of harming the church. // There are false Christians and false prophets (Mt 24:24). // Satan can pretend to be an angel of light in order to deceive people (2 Cor 11:14).

> Detail: The weeds and the wheat at times are similar. It is only when they are fully grown and ready for harvest that the difference is obvious (13:29).

5. Those who are evil can disguise themselves, imitate the children of God and deceive many people. // False apostles and servants of Satan disguise themselves to look like God's people (2 Cor 11:12-15).

6. Two types of people are found Inside the church: true believers and imitators.

> Detail: The servants wanted to pull the weeds out of the wheat field (13:28).

7. God's children are often impatient in wanting to purify the church.

> Detail: The landowner ordered to let the wheat and weeds grow together until the harvest time (13:30).

8. The desire to immediately get the hypocrites out of the church is a sign of impatience and can harm many who are God's children.

9. God allows some of Satan's people to remain in the church for the time being; however, a day is coming when they will be separated from the church and destined to destruction. // Separation of the goats from the sheep (Mt 25:33).

> Detail: Wheat will be gathered into the barn (13:30).

10. God has a safe place prepared for his children. // When Jesus returns, he will gather his people from every part of the world (Mt 24:31). // Many rooms are in the Father's house, where Jesus is preparing a place for his followers (Jn 14:2-3).

PREPARING A SERMON ABOUT A PARABLE

The plan for preparing a sermon whose text is a parable is similar to that used with other Bible stories, except that the sermon gives primary emphasis to the parable's main truth.

> *If the sermon will be part of a Storying Track, consider the life-lessons that most relate to the emphasis of the Storying Track and the needs of the listeners.*

1. **Analyze the parable Bible story**

   One must become the story-analyst before he becomes the storytelling preacher. Analyze the parable using the plan presented in this chapter.

2. **Select life-lessons to become the divisions of the sermon**

   The first life-lesson selected to be a division of the sermon is the main truth. Then select other life-lessons from subordinate details that reinforce the main truth. Choose the life-lessons that are most needed for the listeners in their present circumstances. Life-lessons selected become the divisions of the sermon.

3. **Prepare the selected life-lessons, using the Preaching Cycle with each one**

   Each division will be developed using the Preaching Cycle which includes:
   - Explanation;
   - Illustration;
   - Application.

4. **Prepare the Preaching Plan**

   The Preaching Plan will include:
   - Bible story;
   - Sermon divisions;
   - Conclusion.

THE BIBLE STORY

1st Tell the Bible story about the parable.
- <u>Consider the context that preceded the telling of the parable</u>. The context of the parable includes the occasion when Jesus told it, the listeners, and the culture.
- <u>Follow the sequence of events</u>. Start at the beginning of the story. Include facts that enable the listeners to identify the initial-problem or need for the parable. Narrate the parable. Include the listeners' reactions and interpretation if given. Continue following the sequence of events until the final-situation has been told.

2nd Mention the main truth.

3rd Explain how the context relates to the main truth.

DIVISIONS: Selected Life-Lessons from the Story are Transformed into Preaching Cycles

1st **Division:** the first division will be the main truth of the parable. Develop the main truth using the Preaching Cycle:
- Explanation;
- Illustration;
- Application.

Other Divisions: Other life-lessons selected from subordinate details that reinforce the main truth will be developed. Each one will follow the Preaching Cycle.

CONCLUSION:

The conclusion should review the main aspects treated in the sermon and invite the listeners to change by putting the truths and applications presented into action.

EXAMPLE: SERMON OUTLINE WHOSE TEXT IS A PARABLE

TEXT: Matthew 13:24-30

TITLE: Wheat and Weeds in the Same Church

BIBLE STORY

1st Bible Story

Jesus was using stories to teach. He told the story about the sower and the seeds. He continues using the agricultural life to illustrate spiritual truth in the parable of the Wheat and Weeds.
- The problem that led Jesus to tell the parable was the disciples needed to understand more about the Kingdom of God (Mt 13:10-11).

<u>The parable</u> (Mt 13:24-30):
- The man sowed good seed in his field (13:24).
- While he slept, an enemy sowed weeds in the wheat field (13:25).
- The wheat and the weeds grew together (13:26).
- The servants wanted to know if they should pull the weeds (13:28).
- The owner answered no, because in so doing, they could also pull the wheat (13:29). At harvest time, they could separate them, burn the weeds and collect the wheat into the barn (13:30).

<u>Jesus explained the parable</u> (Mt 13:36-43):
- The disciples asked Jesus: What does the parable of the weeds mean? (13:36).
- Jesus answered: the sower of the good seed is the Son of Man; the land is the world; the good seed are God's children; and the weeds are people who belong to Satan (13:37-38).
- The enemy is the devil (13:39).
- The harvest is the end of the world, the harvesters are God's angels (13:39).
- At the end of time, angels will gather out those who cause sin and do evil and throw them into the fire (13:40-42); then God's people will shine (13:43).

2nd Main Truth:

Until the day of final judgment, God's children and children of the evil one will be side by side in the church.

3rd How context relates to the main truth:

Jesus was using stories to teach. The problem that led Jesus to tell the parable was that the disciples needed to understand more about the Kingdom of God (Mt 13:10-11).

Jesus told the parable of The Sower (Mt 13:13-23), which teaches that when God's Word is sowed, children of the Kingdom of God will sprout up. The parable of the Wheat and Weeds shows that with Kingdom growth, some children of the evil one will enter the church and create confusion.

THE DIVISIONS:

(The main truth of the parable).
1. Until the day of final judgment, God's children and children of the evil one will be side by side in the church.

EXPLANATION:
The weeds represent the children of the evil one. Some of Satan's children are in the church.

The wheat represents the children of God.

The wheat and the weeds look similar (Mt 13: 29). The children of the evil one can disguise themselves by pretending to be children of God.

False prophets and false Christians, who fool many are found in the church. (See Matthew 24:24 and 1 John 2:19.)

ILLUSTRATION:
Judas was one of the 12 disciples.

Demas, Paul's co-worker, abandoned Paul because of his love for the world (2 Tim 4:10).

Paul warned Timothy about false teachers inside the church (2 Tim. 3:5).

APPLICATION:
Our churches have members who are not followers of Jesus Christ. They are children of the evil one. They disguise themselves as children of God, deceiving many.

Not all church member are converted. You need to verify that you are a believer in Jesus.

The church member who is not converted is planted in the church by Satan to confuse and harm the church.

(Other life-lessons selected from subordinate details that reinforce the main truth).

2. The church needs caution when judging its members to determine who is a child of God and who belongs to the evil one.

EXPLANATION:
The servants of the landowner wanted to pull up the weeds immediately. But the landowner knew they would pull up some wheat with the weeds.

ILLUSTRATION:
In Brazil, a certain church calls the soccer ball "the devil's egg." That church believes that a person can not be a Christian and play ball. Youth who play soccer have their names removed from the list of church members.

When Jesus healed on the Sabbath, he did not follow the traditions of the Pharisees. The Pharisees argued that Jesus could not be from God since he healed on the Sabbath (Jn 9:16).

APPLICATION:
When we try to determine if someone is a true Christian, we usually judge the person by the traditions of our church instead of using biblical guidelines. We risk rejecting and expelling from the church those who are really God's children. We also risk children of the evil one deceiving us into thinking they are true Christians, and they could influence us to follow guidelines inspired by the evil one.

We need to recognize that except when a church member disobeys clearly stated biblical commands, we are unqualified to determine who is faithfully serving God.

3. On judgment day, the children of the evil one will be exposed and destroyed.

EXPLANATION:
At the time of the harvest, the weeds are exposed and thrown into the fire.

God allows the children of the evil one to remain in the church with his children for the time being. However, on judgment day, they will be separated. The weeds, children of the evil one, will be destined for destruction by fire. God's children will be gathered to a safe place with the Father.

ILLUSTRATION:
In Mt 25:33, Jesus speaks of separating sheep from the goats.

APPLICATION:
The church today has children of the evil one who disguise themselves as true believers. We may not know who they are, but God knows. On judgment day he will separate his children from the children of the evil one.

CONCLUSIONS:
1. The church should use caution when judging its members to determine who is a child of God and who belongs to the evil one.
2. On judgment day God will correct the present situation in the church, separating the children of the evil one from the children of the Kingdom. The church can make a mistake in judging, but God does not.
3. Make sure that you are a child of God who has Jesus as your Lord and Savior.

PREPARING A BIBLE STUDY ABOUT A PARABLE

The plan for preparing a Bible study whose text is a parable is similar to that used with other Bible stories, except that the study gives primary emphasis to the parable's main truth.

In this chapter, only the plan for narrative teaching using the **Bible Storytelling Combined with Using Teaching Cycles After the Story** will be presented.

1. **Analyze the Bible story**

   Begin preparation by analyzing the Bible text that includes the parable.

2. **Select life-lessons to be taught to the students**

   The first life-lesson selected is the main truth.
   Then select other life-lessons from subordinate details that reinforce the main truth and meet the needs of the students in their present circumstances.

   > If the study will be part of a Storying Track, consider the life-lessons that most relate to the emphasis of the Storying Track and the needs of the students.

3. **Prepare the selected life-lessons, using the Teaching Cycle with each one**

   The use of the **Teaching Cycle** includes three activities:
   - Feed the students the life-lesson;
   - Verify with questions that the students understand the life-lesson;
   - Give feedback to the students.

4. **Prepare the Teaching Plan**

   The Teaching Plan will include:
   - Bible story;
   - Bible study divisions which use the Teaching Cycle;
   - Conclusion.

THE BIBLE STORY

1st Tell the Bible story about the parable.
- <u>Consider the context that preceded the telling of the parable</u>. The context of the parable includes the occasion when Jesus told it, the listeners, and the culture.
- <u>Follow the sequence of events</u>. Start at the beginning of the story. Include facts that enable the listeners to identify the initial-problem or need for the parable. Narrate the parable. Include the listeners' reactions and interpretation if given. Continue following the sequence of events until the final-situation has been told.

2nd Mention the main truth.

3rd Explain how the context relates to the main truth.

DIVISIONS: Selected Life-Lessons Transformed into Teaching Cycles

1st **Division:** The main truth becomes the first division of the Bible Study. The **First Teaching Cycle**
- Feed;
- Verify: 1) that the students understand the life-lesson and 2) that they can apply the life-lesson to their own lives;
- Give feedback. (Feedback is done in response to the students' answers.)

Other Divisions: Life-lessons selected from subordinate details that reinforce the main truth will be developed.

CONCLUSION

Summarize the story, review the life-lessons taught, recall the students' contributions, and appeal for change that would come from putting the life-lessons into practice.

EXAMPLE: TEACHING PLAN FOR A PARABLE USING TEACHING CYCLES

TITLE: Wheat and Weeds in the Same Church

TEXT: Matthew 13:24-30

BIBLE STORY

Jesus was basically using stories to teach. He told the story about the sower and the seeds. He continued using agricultural life to illustrate spiritual truth in the parable of the Wheat and Weeds.

The problem that led Jesus to tell the parable was that the disciples needed to understand more about the Kingdom of God (Mt 13:10-11).

<u>The parable</u> (Mt 13:24-30):
- The man sowed good seed in his field (13:24).
- While he slept, an enemy sowed weeds in the wheat field (13:25).
- The wheat and the weeds grew together (13:26).
- The servants wanted to know if they should pull the weeds (13:28).
- The owner answered no, because in so doing they could also pull the wheat (13:29). At harvest time, they could separated them, burn the weeds and collect the wheat in the barn (13:30).

<u>Jesus explained the parable</u> (Mt 13:36-43):
- The disciples asked Jesus: What does the parable of the weeds mean? (13:36).
- Jesus answered: the sower of the good seed is the Son of Man; the land is the world; the good seed are God's children; and the weeds are people who belong to Satan (13:37-38).
- The enemy is the devil (13:39).
- The harvest is the end of the world; the harvesters are God's angels (13:39).
- At the end of time, angels will gather out those who cause sin and do evil and throw them into the fire (13:40-42); then God's people will shine (13:43).

2ⁿᵈ Main Truth:

Until the day of final judgment, God's children and children of the evil one will be side by side in the church.

3ʳᵈ How context relates to the main truth:

Jesus was using stories to teach. The problem that led Jesus to tell the parable was that the disciples needed to understand more about the Kingdom of God (Mt 13:10-11).

Jesus told the parable of The Sower (Mt. 13:13-23) which teaches that when God's Word is sowed, children of the Kingdom of God will sprout up. The parable of the Wheat and Weeds shows that with Kingdom growth, some children of the evil one will enter the church and create confusion.

THE DIVISIONS:

<u>(The main truth of the parable)</u>.

1. Until the day of final judgment, God's children and children of the evil one will be side by side in the church.

FEED:

The weeds represent the children of the evil one. The Devil places some of his children in the church.

The wheat represents the children of God, those who heard God's Word and accepted Jesus as Lord and Savior.

The wheat and the weeds look similar (Mt 13:29). The children of the evil one can disguise themselves by pretending to be children of God.

There are false prophets and false Christians in the church who fool many. (See Matthew 24:24 and 1 John 2:19.)

Judas was one of the 12 disciples.

Paul warned Timothy about false teachers inside the church (2 Tim. 3:5).

VERIFICATION:

- *Understanding*
  - What does the wheat represent?
  - What do the weeds represent?
  - Who sows each one of these seeds?
  - How did the enemy plant weeds in the landowner's wheat field?

- *Application*
  - What do the two kinds of seed have to do with our church?
  - Why would the devil plant some of his people as members of the church?
  - How does a person become a child of God?

(<u>Other life-lessons selected from subordinate details that reinforce the main truth</u>).

2. The church should use caution when judging its members to determine who is a child of God and who belongs to the evil one.

FEED

The servants of the landowner wanted to pull up the weeds immediately. But the landowner knew they would pull up some wheat with the weeds.

VERIFICATION:

■*Understanding*
- What did the servants want to do with the weeds?
- Why did the land owner not want them to pull out the weeds?

■*Application*
- Why is it hard for us to determine who is really a child of God and who is only pretending to be one?
- Why is it dangerous for the church to judge the spiritual condition of its members?

3. On judgment day, the children of the evil one will be exposed and destroyed.

FEED

At the time of the harvest, the weeds are exposed and thrown into the fire.

God allows the children of the evil one to remain in the church with his children for the time being. However, on judgment day, they will be separated. The weeds, children of the evil one, will be destined for destruction by fire. God's children will be gathered to a safe place with the Father.

VERIFICATION:

■*Understanding*
- In the parable, what does the harvest represent?
- On judgment day, what happens to the church members, both those who are children of God and to the pretenders?

■*Application*
- Why is God qualified to make the separation between his children and the pretenders?
- Do you know where you will be going to spend eternity after the Judgment Day?

CONCLUSIONS:

1. The church should use caution when judging its members to determine who is a child of God and who belongs to the evil one.
2. On judgment day, God will correct the present situation in the church, separating the children of the evil one from the children of the Kingdom. The church can make a mistake in judging, but God does not.
3. Make sure that you are a child of God who has Jesus as your Lord and Savior.

Bible Storytelling Tools © Jackson Day

BIOGRAPHICAL ANALYSIS USING BIBLE STORIES

The analysis that seeks to know and describe the life of a person is called biographical. A biblical biography is the history of a person as registered in the Bible. A biographical analysis consists of the study of the life, work, circumstances of life, and character of a person mentioned in the Bible.

The most common type of literature in the Bible is the story or narrative. Bible stories narrate historical happenings and are treasures for biographical studies. The Bible mentions about three thousand people.

The majority of biographical studies hide the worst and exalt the best about their subjects. In contrast, the Bible stories describe the individuals as they actually were. Many demonstrated character and dignity while others revealed all kinds of faults and imperfections. In some stories, the same person who is presented as a model of faith and virtue becomes guilty of hideous actions.

HOW TO DO A BIOGRAPHICAL ANALYSIS

1. Note the name of the person being analyzed

Caution is needed when seeking texts that contain the name of the person being studied. One person may be mentioned with more than one name; the same name may be used by more than one person; and some stories that are similar may, in fact, be about different people.

1.1 An individual may be mentioned by more than one name

Examples of a person having more than one name:
- Abram and Abraham are names used for the same person.
- Moses' father-in-law is called both Reuel and Jethro (Ex 2:18, 3:1, 4:18; 18:1,12; Num 10:29);
- Matthew and Levi are the same person (Mt 9:9-11 ; Lk 5:27-29);
- Simon and Peter are names used for the same person.
- Saul and Paul are names used for the same person.

1.2 The same name may refer to more than one person

Examples of the same name referring to more than one person:
- The name Judas may refer to the disciple who betrayed Jesus (Mt 10:4; 26:14; Jn 12:4; At 1:16); another disciple, Judas son of James (Lk 6:16; Jn 14:22; At 1:13); one of the brothers of Jesus (Mt 13:55); Judas, the Galilean (Ac 5:37); Judas from Damascus (Ac 9:10-11); or Judas Barsabbas (Ac 15:22).
- The New Testament mentions five different women named Mary;
- Twenty different people are named Nathan in the Bible;
- The names John, Herod, and James also may refer to different people.

1.3 Stories that are similar may involve completely different people

Examples of similar stories involving different people:
- The story of the woman anointing the feet of Jesus in Luke (7:36-50) is similar to the story of Mary the sister of Lazarus anointing the feet of Jesus (Mk 14:3-9; Jn 12:1-8), but the story in Luke is not about Mary, the sister of Lazarus.

2. Unite all the texts that mention the person being studied

Begin the biographical analysis by noting all biblical passages that mention the name of the person being analyzed. When analyzing an Old Testament personality, pay attention to any reference to that person in the New Testament. Consulting a Bible concordance, a Bible dictionary or the reference of a Study Bible will help discover all the references to the person being analyzed.

3. **Arrange the texts in chronological order and make notes of what each one says about the person being analyzed**

Chronological order is the historical sequence in which the events happened. Seek to arrange all texts that mention the person being analyzed in historical, chronological order. At the same time make notes about the context that surrounds each text.

The Bible student must always consider the context or background of every text being considered. After considering the context, make notes about every fact registered in the text that has a connection to the person being analyzed. If the text contains a Bible story, note the sequence of events that have a connection to the individual being studied. Do not note all the events in the story, only mention those related to the person. Be sure to note all sequence of events connected to the person. All details are important. If it is registered in the Bible, it is there for a reason, and the student should note it.

It is important to pay attention to details such as:
- Events in the person's life;
- Responsibilities;
- Opportunities given to the person;
- Reactions to the opportunities;
- Reactions to other people;
- Problems and difficulties faced;
- Successes or failures experienced;
- Strengths and weaknesses of the character;
- Relationship with God;
- Relationship to others;
- Good and bad influence exercised over others.

When preparing a biographical study, it is important to consider other people connected to the individual being studied. Certain individuals are intertwined with another to the extent that it is impossible to consider one without the other. Such a person could not be disassociated from the other.

Examples:
- Boaz is intertwined with Ruth and could not be considered disassociated from her;
- Jonathan is intertwined with David and could not be disassociated from him;
- Delilah is intertwined with Samson and could not be disassociated from him;
- Martha is intertwined with her sister Mary and she could not be disassociated from her.

After one has made his own observation and analysis of each text related to the individual being analyzed, he may take advantage of the observations of others, consulting commentaries or other books.

4. **Analyze the character of the person being studied**

   4.1 Analyze the character of the person

   Things to consider when analyzing the character of a person:
   - Actions, both good and bad;
   - The accomplishments of the person;
   - Qualities that dominated his life;
   - Weaknesses and failures;
   - Difficulties overcome and victory obtained;
   - Methods used to overcome difficulties;
   - Privileges that were taken advantage of or those that were wasted;
   - Opportunities that were taken advantage of and those that were wasted;
   - Dangers that were faced or avoided;
   - Influences that determined character traits;
   - Spiritual development or decline.

   4.2 How to determine if behavior narrated is right or wrong

   4.2.1 The text that narrates the story may explain if a certain action is approved or condemned

   Example:
   - Peter visited the church at Antioch, Syria, and ate with the Gentiles. However, when Jewish Christians from Jerusalem arrived, Peter segregated himself from the Gentiles. One may know Peter's actions were wrong because the text tells that Paul reprimanded Peter and explained why his actions were wrong (Gal 2:11-14).

4.2.2 When the text that narrates the story does not manifest either approval or disapproval for certain behavior, that action needs to be judged by what the rest of the Bible says about such behavior

Examples:

#1 ■ Abraham and Sarah go to Egypt because of the famine in Canaan. Abraham was afraid that Pharaoh would kill him in order to obtain beautiful Sarah. Abraham told Sarah: "Say you are my sister, so that I will be treated well for your sake and my life will be spared because of you" (Gen 12:10-20). Even though the biblical text does not express either approval or condemnation, Abraham's behavior may be judged by what the rest of the Bible teaches about being honest or lying, and a man's responsibilities for his wife.

#2 ■ When God destroyed Sodom, Lot lost his wife. Lot and his two daughters went to live in a cave close to Zoar. The two girls were afraid they would never marry, and Lot would be without descendants. The girls took things into their own hands. For two nights in a row they helped their father get drunk, and both had intercourse with him. Both conceived a child with their father (Gen 19:30-38). The Genesis account does not manifest either approval or disapproval for either Lot or his two daughters' behavior in the cave. However, the Bible has much to say about incest and drunkenness. Lot's and his daughters' behavior may be judged on the basis of those numerous texts that speak about incest and drunkenness.

5. Discover life-lessons from the life of the person being studied

It is essential to remember that the Bible is, first and foremost, the biography of God. The Bible was not written to teach us about Abraham, Isaac, Jacob, David, Elijah, Mary, Peter or Paul. It was written to reveal the involvement of God in their lives. It is not a revelation of David, Mary, John, Peter and Paul, but a revelation of the Lord and Savior of them. Discover life-lessons about God from his involvement in the person's life being studied.

Write down the life-lessons discovered from the life of the biblical character being studied, his life, the circumstances of his life, and his character. Pay attention to God's working and his redemptive plan as expressed through the person's life.

The Bible narrates stories about individuals in order to teach people today by their examples (1 Cor 10:6). The narrating of those lives reveals life-lessons about human nature. They reveal mistakes to avoid, weaknesses that haunt humans, and successes that can be obtained by the grace of God. The virtues of the heroes are presented to edify and to inspire hope. The stories of wrong actions and sinful people warn not to fall into the same temptations. The stories of those who were models of faith, yet committed shocking wrongs, warn the faithful of the danger that anyone could fall into temptation.

BIOGRAPHICAL ANALYSIS

1. Name:

    Other names that refer to the same person:

2. All texts that mention the person:

3. The texts in chronological order, with a summary of the facts and sequence of events related to the person:

TEXT:

   Context:

   Facts or sequence of events related to the person:

TEXT:

   Context:

   Facts or sequence of events related to the person:

4. Analysis of the person's character:

5. Life-lessons discovered from the person's life:

EXAMPLE #1: *BIOGRAPHICAL ANALYSIS*

1. **Name:** Andrew

   Other names that refer to the same person: None

2. **All texts that mention the person:**

   Matthew 4:18-20; Mark 1:29; 13:3; John 1:35-42; 6:8-9; 12:21-22; Acts 1:13

3. **The texts in chronological order with a summary of the facts and sequence of events related to the person**

TEXT: Jn 1:35-42

Context:
   Jesus was beginning his ministry and was unknown outside the city of Nazareth. John the Baptist was well known, and the multitudes were going to hear and be baptized by John. Jesus began his ministry by being baptized; then he went to the desert where he conquered Satan's temptation.

Facts or sequence of events related to the person:
■Andrew was a disciple of John the Baptist (Jn 1:35, 40).
■John the Baptist said that Jesus was the "Lamb of God." Andrew followed Jesus and spent the rest of the day with him (Jn 1:35-40).
■Andrew testified to his brother Simon that he had found the Messiah (Jn 1:41).
■Andrew brought Simon to Jesus (Jn 1:42).

TEXT: Mt 4:18-20

Context:
   Jesus was beginning his second year of public ministry. During the first year, some men began to follow him and make some trips with him. However, he did not have disciples who constantly stayed with him.

Facts or sequence of events related to the person:
■Andrew and his brother Simon, called Peter, were fishermen (4:18).
■Andrew and his brother Simon Peter were casting a net into the Lake of Galilee when Jesus walked up to them (4:18).
■Jesus said: "Come follow me, and I will make you fishers of men" (4:19).
■Andrew and Peter left their nets and followed Jesus (4:19-20).

TEXT: Mk 1:29

Context:
   Jesus was beginning his second year of ministry. He had invited the four fishermen, Andrew, Peter, John and James, to leave fishing for fish to become fishers of men.

Facts or sequence of events related to the person:
■Jesus, with his disciples, went to the home of Simon and Andrew (Mk 1:29).

TEXT: Jn 6:8-9

Context:
   Jesus was popular with the multitudes during his second year of ministry. After hearing about John the Baptist's death, Jesus left Capernaum in a boat to be alone with his disciples, but the multitude followed by walking on the shore around the lake (Mt 14:13; Mk 6:32-33). When Jesus arrived on the other side of the lake and saw the multitude, he had pity on the people, taught them (Mk 6:34) and cured the sick (Mt 14:14; Lk 9:11). The disciples wanted to send the people away so they could go to the surrounding countryside and villages and buy themselves something to eat (Mk 6:35-36).

Facts or sequence of events related to the person:
■Jesus asked the disciples: "Where shall we buy bread for these people to eat?" (Jn 6:5).
■Philip answered him, "Eight months' wages would not buy enough bread for each one to have a bite!" (Jn 6:7).
■Andrew spoke up: "Here is a boy with five small barley loaves and two small fish, but how far will they go among so many?" (Jn 6:9).
■Jesus multiplied the bread and fish to feed about five thousand men (Jn 6:10-13).

TEXT: Jn 12:21-22

Context:
   Jesus is in the last week of his public ministry. The week is often called "Holy Week." It is the week that the Jews celebrate the Passover. On Sunday, Jesus had his Triumphal Entry into the city of Jerusalem.

Facts or sequence of events related to the person:
■There were some Greeks among the people who went to worship God at the Passover Feast (12:20).
■The Greeks went to Philip with a request:

"Sir, we would like to see Jesus" (12:21).
- Philip went to tell Andrew (12:22).
- Andrew and Philip together told Jesus that the Greeks wanted to see him (12:22).

TEXT: Mk 13:3

Context:
On Monday of "Holy Week," Jesus cleansed the Temple. On Tuesday, the Jewish leaders challenged Jesus in the Temple, wanting to know what authority he had. When they were leaving the Temple, one of the disciples admired the massive stones and magnificent buildings. Jesus then prophesied the total destruction of the Temple (Mk 13:2).

Facts or sequence of events related to the person:
- Jesus was sitting on the Mount of Olives opposite the Temple (13:3).
- Peter, James, John and Andrew asked Jesus privately, "Tell us, when will these things happen? And what will be the sign that they are all about to be fulfilled?" (13:4).

TEXT: At 1:13

Context:
After Jesus was taken up to heaven, his disciples returned to Jerusalem (Ac 1:12-13).

Facts or sequence of events related to the person:
- Andrew was part of a group who went to an upstairs room where they all joined together constantly in prayer (Ac 1:13).

4. Analysis of Andrew's character

Accomplishments:
- He was one of the disciples and had a close relationship with Jesus (Mk 13:3; Jn 12:21-22).
- He was responsible for introducing others to Jesus (Jn 1:41-42; 6:8-9; 12:21-22).

Weakness and failures:
- He expressed unbelief that five pieces of bread and two fish could help feed a multitude. He had walked with Jesus, yet he was unaware of Jesus' greatness (Jn 6:8-9).

Difficulties overcome:
- He expressed unbelief that five pieces of bread and two fish could help feed a multitude, but he brought the lad with the lunch to Jesus (Jn 6:8-9).
- He felt difficulty in knowing what to do with the Greeks who wanted to see Jesus, but he took them to Jesus (Jn 12:21-22).

Privileges and opportunities that were taken advantage of:
- He became the disciple of a great man, John the Baptist (Jn 1:35-40).
- He spend a day with Jesus and discovered that he was the Messiah (Jn 1:35-40).
- He testified to his brother Simon Peter that he had discovered the Messiah (Jn 1:41-42).
- He followed Jesus as a disciple as soon as Jesus invited him (Mt 4:19-20).
- He took his doubts to Jesus (Jn 6:8-9).

Spiritual development:
- He began as a disciple of John the Baptist.
- He took advantage of the opportunity to spend a day with Jesus.
- He recognized that Jesus was the Messiah.
- He testified of his knowledge that Jesus was the Messiah to Simon Peter.
- He accepted Jesus' invitation and left his fishing nets to become a fisherman of men.
- He became one of the twelve disciples.
- He took advantage of opportunities to take others to Jesus.
- He persevered in prayer and fellowship with other followers of Jesus.

5. Life-lessons from Andrew's life

1) The believer in Jesus should give priority to evangelizing his own family (Jn 1:41-42).

2) The new believer in Jesus should begin immediately to tell others about who he has discovered Jesus to be (Jn 1:41-42).

3) The person who brings others to Jesus is making a great contribution to the Kingdom of God (Jn 1:41-42; 6:8-9; 12:20-22).

4) God is able to use things and people, who appear to be inadequate, to accomplish great results for his glory (Jn 6:8-9).

5) Little things, when turned over to Jesus, may be used as instruments to achieve marvelous realizations (Jn 6:8-9).

6) When the servant of Jesus has doubts about the power of Jesus to resolve certain problems, he should remain faithful to Jesus and turn over to him all that he has available (Jn 6:8-9).

7) The Christian should be honest about his doubts and take them directly to Jesus (Jn 6:9; Mk 13:3-4).

8) The follower of Jesus should take advantage of opportunities to introduce others to Jesus (Jn 6:9; 12:20-22).

9) The Christian should persevere in both prayer and fellowship with other followers of Jesus (Ac 1:13).

EXAMPLE #2: *BIOGRAPHICAL ANALYSIS*

1. **Name:** Miriam, Moses' sister

   Other names that refer to the same person: None

2. **All texts that mention Miriam:**

   Exodus 2:4; 15:20-21; Numbers 12:1-15; 20:1; Micah 6:4

3. **The texts in chronological order with a summary of the facts and sequence of events related to the person:**

TEXT: Num 26:59

Context:
Numbers 26:59 is within the context of the second numbering of the people after the exodus. The Israelites have wandered in the wilderness for forty years and are at the edge of the Jordan River in front of Jericho. The people are preparing to enter the Promised Land. While the historical time of the text is after the death of Miriam, the text mentions her beginnings. The text mentions the origin of the Levites.

Facts or sequence of events related to the person:
■Miriam is the daughter of Amram and Jochebed and the sister of Aaron and Moses (Num 26:59).

TEXT: Ex 2:4-8

Context:
Pharaoh, the king of Egypt, was afraid of the Israelites and sought to destroy them (Ex 1:8-10) by:
1) oppressing them with forced labor (Ex 1:11-12);
2) making them slaves and using them ruthlessly (Ex 1:13-14);
3) instructing the midwives to kill the baby boys who were born (Ex 1:17-21);
4) ordering that every boy that was born be thrown into the Nile River (Ex 1:22).

Facts or sequence of events related to the person:
■A baby boy was born and his parents hid him for three months. Then they placed him in a basket among the reeds along the banks of the Nile River (2:2-3).
■The baby's sister stood at a distance to see what would happen to the baby (2:4). (The name of the sister is not mentioned, but Num 26:59 mentions Miriam as Moses' only sister).
■When Pharaoh's daughter found the baby, Miriam asked her: "Shall I go and get one of the Hebrew women to nurse the baby for you?" (2:7).
■Pharaoh's daughter answered: "Yes, go" (2:8).
■Miriam went and got the baby's mother (2:8).
■Pharaoh's daughter named the baby Moses (2:9).

TEXT: Ex 15:20-21

Context:
God freed the Israelites from slavery in Egypt and began to guide them to return to the land of Canaan. When they left Egypt, God went in front of them: during the day, in a pillar of cloud; during the night; in a pillar of fire. God guided the Israelites until the Red Sea (14:1-3). Pharaoh decided to recapture them. When the Israelites saw the king of Egypt and his army marching against them, they were terrified (14:12). The army of Egypt was behind them and the sea in front.
Moses extended his hand over the sea, and God drove the sea back with a strong wind, and he turned it into dry land. The waters were divided, and the Israelites went through the sea on dry ground, with a wall of water on either side (14:21-22). When the Egyptian army pursued them, Moses stretched out his hand, the water flowed back and covered the chariots, horsemen and the entire army of Pharaoh (14:23-28). God drowned the Egyptian army in the sea, but he saved all the Israelites.
Moses and the Israelites sang a song to the Lord, celebrating his giving them victory over the Egyptians.

Facts or sequence of events related to the person:
■Aaron's sister is called "Miriam, the prophetess" (15:20). This is the first time she is called by her name.
■Miriam took a tambourine in her hand, and

all the women followed her, with tambourines and dancing. Miriam sang to them: "Sing to the Lord, for he is highly exalted. The horse and its riders he has hurled into the sea" (15:20-21).

TEXT: Num 12:1-15

Context:
God had freed the Israelites from slavery in Egypt and was leading them toward the land of Canaan. After the Israelites received the Ten Commandments from God, they built the Tabernacle, and God continued to lead them toward the entrance of Canaan, the land he had promised them.

Facts or sequence of events related to the person:
- Miriam, together with Aaron, criticized Moses because he married a Cushite (12:1).
- Miriam and Aaron asked: "Has the Lord spoken only through Moses? Hasn't he also spoken through us?" (12:2).
- At once the Lord ordered Moses, Aaron and Miriam to go to the Tabernacle (12:4).
- The Lord came down in a pillar of cloud and reprimanded Aaron and Miriam. God's anger burned against them (12:5-9).
- When the cloud, with the Lord in it, lifted from above the Tabernacle, Miriam stood sick with leprosy. She was as white as snow (12:10).
- Aaron pleaded with Moses for Miriam (12:11-12).
- Moses cried out to the Lord: "O God, please heal her!" (12:13).
- God healed Miriam but required that she remain outside the camp for seven days, and the people did not move on until she returned (12:15-16).

TEXT: Dt 24:9

Context:
God led the Israelites to the border of the land of Canaan. Twelve spies traveled into the land. When the spies returned, ten gave their report that the people in the land were giants and the Israelites could not conquer them. The Israelites murmured against God. Because they lacked faith in him, God required them to wander in the wilderness for forty years. When forty years were coming to an end, Moses spoke to the Israelites.

Facts or sequence of events related to the person:
- In his speech, Moses mentions the leprosy of Miriam (Dt 24:9).

TEXT: Num 20:1

Context:
The Israelites wandered in the wilderness for forty years because they did not have faith that God would enable them to enter and conquer the land of Canaan.

Facts or sequence of events related to the person:
- Before entering the land of Canaan, the Israelites were in the Zin Desert at Kadesh. There Miriam died and was buried (20:1).

TEXT: Mic 6:4

Context:
Micah was a prophet about seven centuries after Miriam and eight centuries before Jesus. He lived during the same time as Isaiah. He prophesied for the kingdom of Judah.

Facts or sequence of events related to the person:
- The Prophet Micah states that God brought the Israelites out of Egypt and redeemed them from slavery. The Lord sent Moses with Aaron and Miriam to lead them (6:4).

4. **Analysis of Miriam's character**

- When she was a girl, Miriam looked after her baby brother (Ex 2:4-8).
- She had incentive and was creative. This was revealed in her dialogue with Pharaoh's daughter (Ex 2:4-8).
- As an older woman, she expressed joy and knew how to celebrate. She sang and danced to celebrate the crossing of the Red Sea (Ex 15:20-21).
- Miriam was a prophetess; she was one who spoke for God (Ex 15:20).
- Miriam was a leader. After crossing the Red Sea, she led the women to celebrate. The prophet Micah states that Miriam was a leader, together with Moses and Aaron (Ex 15:20-21; Mic 6:4).
- Miriam did not know how to distinguish between her responsibility and the responsibility of Moses. Because she was a leader and a prophetess, she thought that she was equal with Moses. She became presumptuous (Num 12:1-2).
- She was critical when she disagreed with her brother's action. She criticized Moses when he married a Cushite (Num 12:1-2).
- She lacked humility when she disagreed with Moses (Num 12:1-10).
- She had a good beginning (Ex 2:4-8; 15:20-21), made a serious mistake when she was an adult

(Num 12:1-10), but deserves to be respected as a leader (Mic 6:4).

5. Life-lessons discovered from Miriam's life

1) Young people need courage to manifest their faith by their actions. The incentive and courage of Miriam were revealed in her dialogue with the princess (Ex 2:4-8).

2) A good beginning does not protect a person from making serious mistakes later in life. Miriam had a good beginning (Ex 2:4-8; 15:20-21), but she made a serious mistake when she was older (Num 12:1-10).

3) The people of God need to celebrate the manifestations of God. Miriam sang and danced, leading the women to celebrate the crossing of the Red Sea (Ex 15:20-21).

4) The person who begins serving God as a youth and becomes a recognized spiritual leader is not protected from making serious mistakes. Miriam made a serious mistake when she was older (Num 12:1-10).

5) The spiritual leader is subject to pride and becoming presumptuous. Therefore, it is necessary for the leader to be on guard to remain humble before God and others. Miriam thought that because she was a leader and a prophetess, she was equal with Moses. She became presumptuous (Num 12:1-2). // "If you think you are standing firm, be careful that you don't fall!" (1 Cor 10:12).

6) Each spiritual leader needs to know and remain within the limits of responsibilities God has given him in order to be of service to God. Each spiritual leader is gifted by God to realize a ministry that he alone can do, and he is not capable of accomplishing the ministry that God has given to another. Miriam did not know how to distinguish between her responsibility and that of Moses (Num 12:1-2).

7) The spiritual leader who goes beyond the limits established by God will contribute to disharmony within the community of God's people. Miriam criticized Moses when he married a Cushite (Num 12:1-2).

8) One is benefitted by the prayers of a faithful servant of God. When Miriam became sick with leprosy, Moses cried out: "O God, please heal her!" The Lord healed Miriam (Num 12:10-16).

9) The spiritual leader's influence will continue beyond his life on earth. The prophet Micah states that God brought the Israelites out of Egypt and redeemed them from slavery. The Lord sent Moses with Aaron and Miriam to lead them (Mic 6:4).

10) Spiritual leaders are gifts from God to his people. The prophet Micah states that the Lord sent Moses with Aaron and Miriam to lead the Israelites (Mic 6:4).

BIOGRAPHICAL SERMON
Biographical Bible Storytelling with Preaching

A biblical biography is the history of a person as recorded in the Bible. A biographical analysis consists of the study of the life, work, circumstances of life and character of a person mentioned in the Bible. The text for a biographical sermon consists of all the Bible passages together that refer to that person. A biographical sermon consists of telling the story of the person as recorded in the Bible and then making preaching applications. To preach a biographical sermon, the storytelling preacher narrates the story of the selected person. Then he develops life-lessons discovered from that person's life as the divisions of his sermon.

HOW TO PREPARE A BIOGRAPHICAL SERMON

1. **Do a biographical analysis of the person being considered**

   Before one can preach a biographical sermon, he needs to study the life of the person being considered. Follow the method presented in the chapter **Biographical Analysis Using Bible Stories**.

2. **Select the life-lessons most important for the listeners**

   During the biographical analysis, many life-lessons discovered from the life of the person being considered were noted. Some of the life-lessons noted were taken from the life of the person, others from the circumstances of his life, others were from conclusions about his character. Still others were taken from God's involvement and his redemptive plan, as expressed through the biblical character's life. From the life-lessons noted, select those that are most important for the listeners who will hear the sermon. The preacher will not have time to communicate all the great life-lessons that are discovered from the life of one person. He must choose the life-lessons that are most important for the listeners.

   From the life-lessons selected, choose those that will only be mentioned and the ones that will receive emphasis. Some of the life-lessons can be mentioned without further comment. The ones that are most important for the listeners will be developed using the **Preaching Cycle**.

3. **Prepare each life-lesson selected to be emphasized using the Preaching Cycle**

   The life-lessons selected become the divisions of the sermon. Some of the life-lessons may be mentioned without further comment. The most important will be developed by utilizing the **Preaching Cycle**. Three activities must be done with each life-lesson selected:
   - ■<u>Explain</u> the life-lesson;
   - ■<u>Illustrate</u> the life-lesson;
   - ■<u>Apply</u> the life-lesson to the lives of your listeners.

4. **The Preaching Plan for the biographical sermon may follow either the plan for "Bible Storytelling with Preaching after the Story" or the plan for "Bible Storytelling with Preaching Inserted"**

   ### 4.1 Biographical Bible Storytelling with Preaching after the Story

   The storytelling preacher tells the story of the person's life who is the text for his sermon. After narrating the person's life, he develops the life-lessons discovered from that life as the points of his sermon. The preaching application is delayed until after the biographical story is told.

   ### 4.2 Biographical Bible Storytelling with Preaching Inserted

   The storyteller inserts preaching applications during the telling of the story. He starts narrating the biographical story. When he comes to an episode that inspires a life-lesson, he stops storytelling, inserts the life-lesson and develops it as a sermon point, utilizing the Preaching Cycle. Then he continues narrating the person's life until he reaches another episode that inspires a life-lesson he wishes to develop. He continues storytelling and inserting life-lessons until the end of the biographical story.

BIOGRAPHICAL BIBLE STORYTELLING WITH PREACHING AFTER THE STORY

The Preaching Plan for the biographical sermon with preaching after the character's story will include:
- Narration of the person's story.
- Sermon divisions.
- Conclusion.

NARRATION OF BIBLE CHARACTER'S STORY

Tell the person's life story in chronological order. Include notes made from the biographical analysis. Copy or abbreviate the notes from the sequence of events. When moving from one episode to another, there may be changes in the historical circumstances. If needed, include notes helpful to understand the historical circumstances surrounding each new episode.

DIVISIONS: Selected Life-Lessons are Transformed into Preaching Cycles

OBSERVATION: Some of the life-lessons may be mentioned without further comment. The most important will be developed by utilizing the **Preaching Cycle**.

Selected life-lessons become the divisions of the sermon. Each division will be developed using the **Preaching Cycle**.

1st DIVISION (The first life-lesson selected to be presented becomes the first division of the sermon.)
First Preaching Cycle

Explain; illustrate and apply the life-lesson to the lives of the listeners.

2nd DIVISION: (The second life-lesson selected to be presented becomes the second division of the sermon.)
Second Preaching Cycle

Explain; illustrate and apply the life-lesson to the lives of the listeners.

Continue until each life-lesson selected is developed using the Preaching Cycle.

CONCLUSION:

Conclude the sermon:
- By giving a short summary of the biographical story;
- By connecting the life-lessons presented and their main applications to the story;
- With an invitation, appealing for the listeners to put into practice the will of God as presented in the sermon.

BIOGRAPHICAL BIBLE STORYTELLING WITH PREACHING INSERTED

To do Biographical Bible Storytelling with Preaching Inserted, the storyteller inserts preaching applications during the telling of the story. He starts narrating the biographical story. When he comes to an episode that inspires a life-lesson, he stops storytelling, inserts the life-lesson and develops it utilizing the Preaching Cycle. Then he continues narrating the person's life until he reaches another episode that inspires a life-lesson he wishes to develop. He continues storytelling and inserting sermon divisions until the end of the biographical story.

1. **Prepare the Preaching Plan for the biographical story with preaching inserted**

- **Sequence of events in chronological order**:
Begin copying or abbreviating the notes from the historical context and the sequence of events. When moving from one episode to another, include notes helpful to understand the historical circumstances surrounding each new episode. When concluding an episode that teaches a life-lesson that is to be emphasized, insert the life-lesson and its Preaching Cycle.

Bible Storytelling Tools © Jackson Day

OBSERVATION: Some of the life-lessons may be mentioned without further comment. The most important ones will be developed by utilizing the **Preaching Cycle**.

1st DIVISION (The first life-lesson selected to be presented becomes the first division of the sermon.) The **First Preaching Cycle**: Explain, illustrate and apply

■**Sequence of events in chronological order**: Continue to copy or abbreviate the notes from the sequence of events. If needed, include notes helpful to understand the historical circumstances surrounding each new episode.

2nd DIVISION: (The second life-lesson selected becomes the second division of the sermon.)

The **Second Preaching Cycle**: Explain, illustrate and apply

Continue with the sequence of events and inserting the Preaching Cycle until the story of the person's life is finished.

CONCLUSION

Conclude the sermon:
■By giving a short summary of the biographical story;
■By connecting the life-lessons presented and their main applications to the story;
■With an invitation, appealing for the listeners to put into practice the will of God as presented in the sermon.

EXAMPLE # 1: *BIOGRAPHICAL BIBLE STORYTELLING WITH PREACHING AFTER THE STORY*

STORY: Andrew

NARRATION OF ANDREW'S LIFE

TEXT: Jn 1:35-42
Context:
Jesus was beginning his ministry and was unknown outside the village of Nazareth. John the Baptist was well known, and the multitudes were going to hear and be baptized by John. Jesus began his ministry by being baptized; then he went to the desert where he conquered Satan's temptation.

Sequence of events:
■Andrew was a disciple of John the Baptist (Jn 1:35, 40).
■When John said that Jesus was the Lamb of God, Andrew quickly followed Jesus and spent the rest of the day with Jesus (Jn 1:35-40).
■Andrew found his brother Simon and testified that he had found the Messiah (Jn 1:41).
■Andrew brought Simon to Jesus (Jn 1:42).

TEXT: Mt 4:18-20
Context:
Jesus was beginning his second year of public ministry. During the first year, some people began to follow him and make some trips with him. However, he did not have disciples who constantly stayed with him.

Sequence of events:
■Andrew was the brother of Simon called Peter (4:18).
■Andrew and Simon Peter were fishermen. They were casting a net into the Lake of Galilee when Jesus walked up to them (4:18).
■Jesus said: "Come follow me, and I will make you fishers of men" (4:19).
■Andrew and Peter left their nets and followed Jesus (4:20).

TEXT: Mk 1:29
Context:
The four fishermen, Andrew, Peter, John and James, left fishing for fish to follow Jesus and become fishers of men.

Sequence of events:
■Jesus, with his disciples, went to the home of Simon and Andrew (Mk 1:29).

TEXT: Jn 6:8-9
Context:
Jesus experienced popularity during his second year of ministry. After hearing about John the Baptist's death, Jesus left Capernaum in a boat to be alone with his disciples, but the multitude followed by going around the shore of the lake (Mt 14:13; Mk 6:32-33). When Jesus arrived on the other side of the lake and saw the multitude, he had pity on the people, taught them (Mk 6:34) and cured the sick (Mt 14:14; Lk 9:11). The disciples wanted to send the people away, so they could go to the surrounding countryside and villages and buy themselves something to eat (Mk 6:35-36).

Sequence of events:
- Jesus asked the disciples: "Where shall we buy bread for these people to eat?" (Jn 6:5).
- Philip answered him, " Eight months' wages would not buy enough bread for each one to have a bite!" (Jn 6:7).
- Andrew spoke up: "Here is a boy with five small barley loaves and two small fish, but how far will they go among so many?" (Jn 6:9).
- Jesus multiplied the bread and fish to feed about five thousand men (Jn 6:10-13).

TEXT: Jn 12:21-22
Context:
Jesus was in the last week of his public ministry. The week is often called "Holy Week." It is the week that the Jews celebrate the Passover. On Sunday Jesus had his Triumphal Entry into the city of Jerusalem.

Sequence of events:
- There were some Greeks among the people who went to worship God at the Passover Feast (12:20).
- The Greeks went to Philip with a request: "Sir, we would like to see Jesus" (12:21).
- Philip went to tell Andrew (12:22).
- Andrew and Philip together told Jesus that the Greeks wanted to see him (Jn 12:22).

TEXT: Mk 13:3
Context:
On Monday of "Holy Week," Jesus cleansed the Temple. On Tuesday, the Jewish leaders challenged Jesus in the Temple, wanting to know what authority he had. When they were leaving the Temple, one of the disciples admired the massive stones and magnificent buildings. Jesus then prophesied the total destruction of the Temple (Mk 13:2).

Sequence of events:
- Jesus was sitting on the Mount of Olives, opposite the Temple (13:3).
- Peter, James, John and Andrew asked Jesus privately: "Tell us, when will these things happen? And what will be the sign that they are all about to be fulfilled?" (13:4).

TEXT: At 1:13
Context:
After Jesus was taken up to heaven, his disciples returned to Jerusalem (Ac 1:12-13).

Sequence of events:
- Andrew was part of a group which went to an upstairs room where they all joined together constantly in prayer (Ac 1:13).

DIVISIONS:

1. **The new believer in Jesus should have as a priority to evangelize his own family** (Jn 1:41-42). As soon as Andrew discovered who Jesus was, he found his brother Simon and brought him to Jesus. (*Mention the life-lesson without further comment. Don't utilize the* **Preaching Cycle**.)

2. **The person who brings others to Jesus is making a great contribution to the Kingdom of God** (Jn 1:41-42; 6:8-9; 12:21-22).

EXPLAIN
To lead other people to come to Jesus is one of the greatest contributions one can make in advancing the Kingdom of God. The Kingdom spreads with new converts. Satan loses a battle every time a person becomes a follower of Jesus by repenting of his sins, and believing that Jesus is the Son of God who died for man's sin and then rose from the grave.

Jesus commands his followers to make disciples (Mt 28:19-20).

Three times the Bible shows Andrew taking others to Jesus: (1) Simon Peter (Jn 1:41-42); (2) the boy with the bread and fish (Jn 6:8-9); (3) the Greeks (Jn 12:21-22).

ILLUSTRATE
- On the day of Pentecost, Peter preached and three thousand believed and became followers of Jesus (Ac 2). Peter also was the first disciple to go to the home of a non-Jew named Cornelius and lead non-Jews to become followers of Jesus.
- The deacon Philip helped Samaritans become followers of Jesus (Ac 8).

APPLY
As believers in Jesus, we need to take advantage of normal opportunities through our daily lives to introduce others to Jesus.

We need the conviction that one of the greatest contributions we can make for the Kingdom of God is to evangelize and lead others to follow Jesus.

Our church should have evangelism as a priority.

3. **Little things when turned over to Jesus may be used as instruments to achieve marvelous accomplishments** (Jn 6:8-9).

EXPLAIN

Things and people which appear to be insignificant and of little value, when turned over to Jesus, can be used by him to achieve great results.

Jesus used a small boy's lunch of five pieces of bread and two fish to feed 5,000 people (Jn 6:8-9). Andrew was the one who brought the boy with his small lunch to Jesus.

(Read 1 Cor 1:26-29.)

ILLUSTRATE

Examples of God using insignificant things or weak people:
- In the book of Judges, God used things and people considered to be insignificant and weak: Deborah, a woman (Jdg 4:4 - 5:2); Gideon and his 300 men (Jdg 7:6-8); the jawbone of a donkey used by Samson (Jdg 15:15).
- God used the boy David to defeat the giant Goliath (1 Sam 17:1-54).
- Jesus transformed water into wine (Jn 2:1-11).
- Jesus considered the widow's mite to be of great value (Lk 21:1-4).

APPLY

You may consider yourself a weak, insignificant person, but God can use you to achieve great things in his Kingdom.

The poor weak person or the small weak church that offers its all to Jesus will realize that God uses weak instruments to achieve great results.

4. **Even when the servant of Jesus has doubts about the power of Jesus to resolve certain problems, he should still remain faithful to Jesus and offer him all that he has available** (Jn 6:8-9).

EXPLAIN

God demands faithfulness, even when his servants doubt his ability to use them.

Andrew thought that five pieces of bread and two fish were too little to help feed five thousand men (Jn 6:8-9). Andrew expressed doubt that Jesus could use so little to feed so many people. However, he still brought the little boy with his lunch to Jesus.

ILLUSTRATE
- When the disciples received the "Great Commission," some doubted Jesus (Mt 28:17).
- When God spoke to Moses from the burning bush, Moses doubted his ability to free the Israelites from slavery in Egypt (Ex 3-4).
- Gideon doubted that he had the strength to free Israel out of Midian's hand (Js 6:14-15).
- Jeremiah doubted his ability to be a prophet, claiming: "I do not know how to speak; I am only a child" (Jer 1:6).

APPLY

We need to be faithful to God, even when we doubt he could use us. We need to be faithful, even when we doubt it is worth the effort to serve God. God demands faithfulness at all times from us, even when we doubt that he is able to use us.

5. **The person who begins to follow Jesus should persist in being faithful to him** (Ac 1:13).

EXPLAIN

After Jesus returned to heaven, Andrew was part of the group of followers of Jesus who joined with others, constantly in prayer (Ac 1:13-14).

It is important to begin to follow Jesus and to begin to be faithful to him. However, it is not sufficient only to begin well. The Christian needs to continue to be faithful to Jesus.

ILLUSTRATE

Examples of people who began to follow God but did not continue being faithful to him:
- King Saul;
- Solomon;
- Demas, Paul's co-worker;
- A basketball team may finish the first half with 15 points in front. However, they can still lose the game in the second half.

APPLY

The fact that many begin to follow God as faithful servants but do not persist and thus fall into sin, alerts each Christian to the necessity to watch and pray in order not to fall into sin and backslide.

CONCLUSIONS

1. Andrew is seldom mentioned in the Bible. A dominant characteristic of Andrew is that he took individuals to Jesus: (1) his brother, Simon Peter (Jn 1:41-42); (2) the little boy with his lunch of bread and fish (Jn 6:8-9); (3) the Greeks (Jn 12:21-22). We need to

imitate Andrew in introducing others to Jesus.
2. Andrew and his friend Philip were the first followers of Jesus. Andrew also was part of the group which remained united in prayer after Jesus returned to Heaven (Ac 1:13-14). It is important to begin to follow Jesus; however, we need to remain being faithful to Jesus.

- Some of you need to decide to begin to follow Jesus, recognizing him as the Son of God, the Lord and Savior, who was crucified and conquered death.
- Some of you Christians have relaxed in their commitment to follow Jesus. You need to reconfirm your commitment to Jesus and re-establish your relationship to Jesus with a determination to remain faithful to him.

EXAMPLE # 2: *BIOGRAPHICAL BIBLE STORYTELLING WITH PREACHING INSERTED*

STORY: Miriam, Moses' Sister

NARRATION OF MIRIAM'S LIFE

TEXT: Num 26:59

Context:
The members of Miriam's family are named.

Sequence of events:
- Miriam is the daughter of Amram and Jochebed and the sister of Aaron and Moses (Num 26:59).

TEXT: Ex 2:4-8
Context:
Pharaoh, the king of Egypt, was afraid of the Israelites and sought to destroy them by (Ex 1:8-10):
1) Oppressing them with forced hard labor (Ex 1:11-12).
2) Making them slaves and using them ruthlessly (Ex 1:13-14).
3) Instructing the midwives to kill the baby boys who were born (Ex 1:17-21).
4) Ordering that every baby boy be thrown into the Nile River (Ex 1:22).

Sequence of events:
- A baby boy was born and his parents hid him for three months. Then they placed him in a basket among the reeds along the banks of the Nile River (2:2-3).
- The baby's sister stood at a distance to see what would happen to the baby (2:4). (The name of the sister is not mentioned, but Num 26:59 mentions Miriam as Moses' only sister).
- When Pharaoh's daughter found the baby, Miriam asked her: "Shall I go and get one of the Hebrew women to nurse the baby for you?" (2:7).
- Pharaoh's daughter answered: "Yes, go" (2:8).
- Miriam went and got the baby's mother (2:8).
- The baby was named Moses (2:9).

1. Youth need to have courage to manifest their faith by their actions.

EXPLAIN
When she was a youth, Miriam helped care for her brother, the baby Moses. She showed creativity and courage when she offered to help Pharaoh's daughter find an Israelite woman to give milk to baby Moses. Miriam's courage was an act of faith.

Ec 12:1 gives the youth the counsel to: "Remember your Creator in the days of your youth."

Youth must have courage to manifest their faith by doing the will of God.

ILLUSTRATE
Other examples of youth being faithful to God:
- Joseph (Gen 39:1-19).
- Daniel (Dan 1:3-17).

APPLY
Youth, be courageous and manifest your faith in God by the way you live.

TEXT: Ex 15:20-21
Context:
God freed the Israelites from slavery in Egypt and began to guide them to return to the land of Canaan. When they left Egypt, God went in front of them: during the day, in a pillar of cloud and during the night in a pillar of fire. God guided the Israelites to the Red Sea (14:1-3). Pharaoh decided to recapture them. When the Israelites saw the king of Egypt and his army marching against them, they were terrified (14:12). The army of Egypt was behind them and the sea in front.

Bible Storytelling Tools © Jackson Day

Moses extended his hand over the sea, and God drove the sea back with a strong wind and turned the sea into dry land. The waters were divided, and the Israelites went through the sea on dry ground, with a wall of water on either side (14:21-22). When the Egyptian army pursued them, Moses stretched out his hand. The water flowed back and covered the chariots, horsemen and the entire army of Pharaoh (14:23-28). God drowned the Egyptian army in the sea, but he saved all the Israelites.

Moses and the Israelites sang a song to the Lord, celebrating his giving them victory over the Egyptians.

Sequence of events:
- Aaron's sister is called: "Miriam the prophetess" (15:20).
- Miriam took a tambourine in her hand, and all the women followed her with tambourines and dancing. Miriam sang to them: "Sing to the Lord, for he is highly exalted. The horse and its rider he has hurled into the sea" (15:20-21).

2. **The people of God need to celebrate when God reveals himself through his actions** (Ex 15:20-21).

EXPLAIN
Celebration is an important part of man's worship to God. The people of God need to celebrate the great acts of God that are recorded in the Bible. They also need to celebrate the things God is doing in their midst in the present day and age.

Miriam sang and danced, leading the Israelite women to celebrate the crossing of the Red Sea (Ex 15:20-21).

ILLUSTRATE
- Noah celebrated his leaving the ark (Gen 8:20).
- The completion of a work for God is a motive for celebration. Solomon constructed the Temple for God (1 Kg. 6:1-14), and there was celebration when it was dedicated (1 Kg. 8:1-9:9).
- After the Israelites returned from captivity in Babylonia, they started rebuilding the Temple that had been destroyed. They celebrated when they finished rebuilding the foundation (Ezr 3:10-13), and they celebrated again when they finished the reconstruction (Ezr 6:13-16).
- When Nehemiah led the Israelites to rebuild the wall of the city of Jerusalem, there was a great celebration (Ne 12:27-43).
- Martha and Mary were grateful for the resurrection of their brother Lazarus; to celebrate, they offered Jesus a dinner (Jn 12:1-7).

APPLY
We, the followers of Jesus, need to celebrate the acts of God in the past and in the present. Our worship services should celebrate what God is doing in our midst. When God blesses us, we need to celebrate.

TEXT: Num 12:1-15
Context:
God had freed the Israelites from slavery in Egypt and was leading them toward the land of Canaan. After the Israelites received the Ten Commandments, they built the Tabernacle, and God continued to lead them toward the entrance of Canaan, the land he had promised them.

Sequence of events:
- Miriam, together with Aaron, criticized Moses because he married a Cushite (12:1).
- Miriam and Aaron asked: "Has the Lord spoken only through Moses? Hasn't he also spoken through us?" (12:2).
- At once the Lord ordered Moses, Aaron and Miriam to go to the Tabernacle (12:4).
- The Lord came down in a pillar of cloud and reprimanded Aaron and Miriam. God's anger burned against them (12:5-9).
- When the cloud, with the Lord in it, lifted from above the Tabernacle, Miriam stood sick with leprosy. She was as white as snow (12:10).
- Aaron pleaded with Moses for Miriam (12:11-12).
- Moses cried out to the Lord: "O God, please heal her!" (12:13).
- God healed Miriam but required that she remain outside the camp for seven days, and the people did not move on until she was brought back (12:15-16).

3. **The spiritual leader needs to be on the lookout because he is subject to the temptation to be proud and to feel self-sufficient.** The Bible warns all of us, too: "If you think you are standing firm, be careful that you don't fall" (1 Cor 10:12). *(Mention, without developing the Preaching Cycle.)*

4. **Many years of faithfully serving God is not a guarantee against falling into sin.**

EXPLAIN
The spiritual leader is a visual target for Satan's temptation. Many years of faithfulness

does not protect one from today's temptation.

Miriam was a prophetess, a spiritual leader for the Israelites. However, Miriam, together with Aaron, criticized Moses because he married a Cushite (Num 12:1). Then they questioned Moses' leadership saying: "Has the Lord spoken only through Moses? Hasn't he also spoken through us?" (Num 12:2).

ILLUSTRATE
■David was a man after God's own heart and had faithfully served God from the time he was a boy. However, when he was a middle aged man, he was tempted by seeing his neighbor's wife, Bathsheba, taking a bath.

APPLY
As a spiritual leader, I need to be careful that I do not lose my credibility by falling into sin.

The leadership you exercise over others may feed your pride and serve to make you open to temptations.

Those who have been following our Lord Jesus for many years need to be careful, because the faithfulness of years past does not protect you from yielding to today's temptation. The church has been embarrassed when those who were respected for their service to God fell into sin. What happened to others, can happen to us.

TEXT: Num 20:1
Context:
The Israelites had wandered in the wilderness for forty years because they did not have faith that God would enable them to enter and conquer the land of Canaan.

Sequence of events:
■Before entering the land of Canaan, the Israelites were in the Zin Desert at Kadesh. There Miriam died and was buried (20:1).

TEXT: Mic 6:4
Context:
Micah was a prophet seven centuries after the time of Miriam and Moses and eight centuries before Jesus.

Sequence of events:
■The prophet Micah states that God brought the Israelites out of Egypt and redeemed them from slavery. The Lord sent Moses with Aaron and Miriam to lead them (6:4).

CONCLUSIONS:

1. Miriam had a good beginning (Ex 2:4-8), was faithful in serving God for many years before she was defeated by the sin of jealousy and pride (Num 12:1-10), but she recovered and finished her life as a faithful servant (Mic 6:4). The life of Miriam should challenge children, youth and adults to begin early doing the will of God and to continue serving him.

2. Miriam helps the church to understand that an important element of worship is celebration. Let us celebrate God's great acts in history and what he is doing in our midst today.

3. Miriam helps the follower of Jesus to realize that one who has served Jesus faithfully for a long time still runs the risk of falling into sin. Miriam was a prophetess, a spiritual leader for the Israelites. However, Miriam, together with Aaron, sinned when they criticized Moses and questioned his leadership (Num 12:1). We who are the leaders of the church need to watch and pray lest we fall into temptation.

4. Miriam's life is proof that one who failed does not need to remain a failure. Miriam sinned, but after she was punished by God, she recovered and remained a faithful servant of God. She deserves to be imitated. As a church, let us seek to restore Christians who have fallen into sin. If you, a Christian, have fallen into sin, you do not need to remain in your sin. Repent, confess your sin, renew your relationship to God and begin again to serve him.

DOCTRINAL ANALYSIS USING BIBLE STORIES IN CHRONOLOGICAL ORDER

1. **A doctrinal analysis using Bible stories**

The analysis that draws together and summarizes all that the Bible says on a given subject is called doctrinal or thematic. A doctrinal analysis using Bible stories consists in traveling through the Bible stories in chronological order and stopping to visit those that connect to the selected doctrine. Each time one stops to visit a story, life-lessons are discovered that relate to the topic being studied.

The most common type of literature in the Bible is the story or narrative. Bible stories narrate historical happenings and are treasures for doctrinal studies.

The method of doctrinal analysis may be used to study the great subjects repeated through the Bible.
Examples:
- The attributes of God;
- The nature of man;
- Justification;
- The church;
- Forgiveness: giving and receiving forgiveness;
- Satan's strategies.

To do a doctrinal study using Bible stories, the student will:
- Determine the topic to be studied;
- Discover all the Bible stories that relate to the topic;
- Place all the stories in chronological order;
- For each separate story:
  - Consider its context;
  - Make notes of the sequence of events that relate to the doctrine;
  - Discover life-lessons taught by the story that relate to the doctrine.
- Develop a summary of the doctrine by condensing, rearranging and combining all the life-lessons in order to make a composite statement or outline.

Examples of doctrines that can be taught using Bible stories:

#1 To do a doctrinal study on "FAITH," discover all the Bible stories that relate to the topic. For each separate story, discover the sequence of events and life-lessons that relate to "FAITH." The following stories might be included:
- Noah;
- The call of Abram;
- Abraham and Isaac;
- Joseph;
- Moses;
- The lack of faith of the Israelites who murmured in the wilderness;
- Joshua;
- Rahab;
- Samuel;
- David;
- The faith of the Centurion;
- The sinful woman who anointed Jesus in Simon's house;
- The resurrection of Lazarus;
- Jesus and Thomas;
- The first converts;
- Paul.

#2 To do a doctrinal study about "TEMPTATION," discover all the Bible stories that relate to the topic. For each separate story discover the sequence of events and life-lessons that relate to the subject. The following stories might be included:
- Adam and Eve;
- Cain and Abel;
- Abram in Egypt;
- Joseph and Potiphar's wife;
- David and Bathsheba;
- Jesus' temptations;
- Peter's denial of Jesus;
- Ananias and Sapphira;
- Peter separates himself from the Gentiles at Antioch.

2. **Using Bible stories to analyze a doctrine is a biblical method**

The Bible has many examples of teaching doctrines by using stories.

Examples of explaining doctrines with stories:

#1 Moses in the book of Deuteronomy

The book of Deuteronomy contains the five speeches Moses made to the Israelites after they had wandered forty years in the wilderness. They were getting ready to cross the Jordan River and conquer Canaan. In his discourses, Moses retold the stories of God's dealing with the Israelites. He narrated things that God had done to free the Israelites from slavery, how he had guided them through the desert, and how he had brought them to the promised land. Moses used those stories to teach the Israelites doctrines about God and about their inability to obey God's laws.

#2 Joshua (Js 24:1-15).

In his good-bye speech, Joshua retold the stories: of Abraham and how the descendants of Abraham went down to Egypt; of Moses and Aaron; of the exodus from Egypt; of the conquering of Jericho and the land of Cannan. Joshua used those stories to teach them doctrines about their inability to serve God, the necessity to fear the Lord and to serve him with faithfulness, and the consequences of abandoning God in order to serve foreign gods.

#3 Samuel (1 Sam 12:6-16)

In his good-bye speech, Samuel told stories to summarize the history of Israel and to teach the doctrine that, if the Israelites did not hear God and obey his orders, God would be against them and against their king.

#4 Stephen (Ac 6-7)

Stephen preached about Jesus Christ. Opponents attacked his preaching, but they could not stand up against his wisdom given by the Holy Spirit. False witnesses claimed that Stephen was blaspheming against Moses and against God (6:8-15). Stephen was arrested and taken before the Sanhedrin, the Jewish high court. In his defense, Stephen used stories from the history of the Israelites to explain the fact that the Israelites had always rejected the servants sent by God. After reviewing the story of Abraham, Isaac and Jacob, Stephen told how the children of Jacob rejected their brother Joseph. Yet Joseph was the one God used to save Jacob's family during a time of famine (7:1-16).

Stephen told how the Israelites became slaves in Egypt. When Moses tried to help the Israelites, he was rejected, yet Moses was the one who God used to free the Israelites from slavery in Egypt (7:17-38). The Israelites refused to obey Moses when he was leading them through the wilderness; they wanted to return to Egypt. They even requested Aaron to make an idol in the form of a calf to worship (7:39-41).

When God brought them to the promised land, they worshiped the heavenly bodies and the gods of the surrounding nations (7:42-43).

Stephen terminated his speech: "You stiff-necked people! You are like your fathers: You always resist the Holy Spirit! Was there ever a prophet your fathers did not persecute? They even killed those who predicted the coming of the Righteous One. And now you have betrayed and murdered him" (7:51-53).

#5 Faith in God's promises sustains his servants (Hb 11).

The author of Hebrews used stories from the Old Testament to teach that faith in God's promises sustains his servants and results in perseverance. He gave the following examples: Abel (11:4), Enoch (11:5), Noah (11:7), Abraham (11:8-19), Isaac (11:20), Jacob (11:21), Joseph (11:22), Moses (11:23-28), the Israelites (11:28-30), Rahab (11:31), and others (Gideon, Barak, Samson, Jephthah, David, Samuel and the prophets) (11:32-40).

These are just a few of the examples to show that the analysis of a doctrine by using stories is a biblical method. The great men of the Bible taught the great doctrines through stories. Today's teachers and preachers should use storytelling to teach the great doctrines.

3. **How to analyze a doctrine using Bible stories**

To do a doctrinal study using Bible stories, the student will:
- Identify the doctrine to be analyzed;
- Discover all the Bible stories that relate to the doctrine;
- Place the stories in their historical, chronological order;
- For each separate story:
  - Consider its context;
  - Make notes of the sequence of events that relate to the doctrine;
  - Discover life-lessons from the story that relate to the doctrine;
- Develop a summary of the doctrine by condensing, rearranging and combining all the life-lessons in order to make a composite statement or outline.

3.1 Identify the doctrine to be analyzed

There are different kinds of doctrinal studies. A doctrinal study may be done on certain words or phrases found in the Bible. For example: eternal life, faith, death, and justification. A doctrinal study may be done on a subject whose idea is expressed in the Bible even if the exact words are not found anywhere in the Bible. For example: the responsibilities of a disciple of Jesus; discipline within the church; foundations for character; secrets for the victorious life; the attributes of God; and the nature of man.

The doctrine to be studied needs to be identified. Summarize with a few words an explanation of the doctrine to be studied.

3.2 Discover all the Bible stories that relate to the doctrine being analyzed

Begin the analysis by discovering and writing down all the Bible stories that have a connection to the doctrine being studied. Two charts in this book may be helpful: **List of Bible Stories with References** and **Chart of Bible Stories and Doctrinal Objectives**.

3.3 Place the Bible stories in their historical, chronological order

The historical, chronological order is the order in which the events occurred. The stories that have a connection to the doctrine need to be listed in their chronological order.

3.4 For each separate story, make notes of the sequence of events that connect to the doctrine being analyzed

Each Bible story should be considered within its context. After considering the context, note the sequence of events that relate to the doctrine. Do not write down all the events. Include only those that connect to the doctrine being studied. When moving from one story to another, there may be changes in the historical circumstances. If needed,, include notes helpful to understand the historical circumstances surrounding each new story.

3.5 Discover life-lessons from the story that relate to the doctrine

Consider the sequence of events that relate to the doctrine. From those events, discover life-lessons that are connected to the doctrine and write them down. Include only life-lessons that relate to the doctrine being analyzed.

3.6 Develop conclusions

The conclusions should express a summary of the doctrine by condensing, rearranging and combining all the life-lessons in order to make a composite statement or outline.

DOCTRINAL ANALYSIS USING BIBLE STORIES

DOCTRINE:

STORIES IN CHRONOLOGICAL ORDER THAT RELATE TO THE DOCTRINE:

STORY:
TEXT:

Context:

Sequence of events that relate to the doctrine:

Life-lessons taught by the story that relate to the doctrine:

STORY:
TEXT:

Context:

Sequence of events that relate to the doctrine:

Life-lessons taught by the story that relate to the doctrine:

STORY:
TEXT:

Context:

Sequence of events that relate to the doctrine:

Life-lessons taught by the story that relate to the doctrine:

CONCLUSIONS:

EXAMPLE: DOCTRINAL ANALYSIS USING BIBLE STORIES

DOCTRINE: Overcoming past mistakes

People who have repented need to overcome the consequences of sins committed in the past.

STORIES IN CHRONOLOGICAL ORDER THAT RELATE TO THE DOCTRINE

STORY: The First Sin
TEXT: Genesis 3:1-24

Context:
Everything that God created was perfect. At the creation, man was created in the image of God (1:26). In the garden there was one tree whose fruit was forbidden. God had ordered: "You are free to eat from any tree in the garden, but you must not eat from the tree of the knowledge of good and evil" (2:16-17).

Sequence of events that relate to the doctrine:
■ The snake tempted Eve to eat the fruit of the forbidden tree (3:1-5).
■ Eve ate the fruit of the forbidden tree, gave some to her husband, and he also ate it (3:6).
■ The eyes of both of them were opened; they realized they were naked; they sewed fig leaves together to cover themselves (3:7).
■ Adam and Eve heard the sound of the Lord God in the garden, and they hid from him among the trees (3:8-10).
■ Adam blamed the woman (3:10-12), and the woman blamed the serpent (3:13).
■ God promised that one of the offspring of the woman would crush the head of the snake (3:15).
■ God made garments of skin for Adam and Eve and clothed them (3:21).
■ Adam and Eve were driven out of the Garden of Eden (3:22-23).

Life-lessons taught by the story that relate to the doctrine:

1. The act of sin is simple, but the results are disastrous. It is impossible to overcome past mistakes without suffering the consequences of one's sins. It was easy for Eve to take the forbidden fruit, eat it and give it to Adam (3:6). However, the consequences were tremendous.
2. Past mistakes may not be overcome by fleeing from God. Adam and Eve could not hide themselves in the midst of the trees (3:8-9).
3. The sinner cannot overcome past mistakes on his own. God did not accept Adam and Eve with the clothes they made from fig leaves. God made them garments of animal skins (3:21). A person is only accepted by God when by faith he accepts the plan established by God.
4. It is impossible to overcome past mistakes by blaming others for one's sins. Adam blamed the woman and God for his sins (3:10-12), and Eve blamed the snake (3:13).
5. God's actions on behalf of the sinner, give the one who has sinned hope that he can overcome past mistakes. God made the first prophecy about Jesus when he promised Adam and Eve that they would have children, and one offspring would crush the snake's head while the snake would strike his heel (3:14-15). God also provided clothes from skins for the couple (3:21).

STORY: The Tower of Babel - Seeking to Overcome Past Errors without Obeying God
TEXT: Gen 11:1-9

Context:
After the flood, all the people were descendants of Noah. God ordered the descendants of Noah to scatter over the earth (9:1, 7).

Sequence of events that relate to the doctrine:
■ The whole world had one language (11:1).
■ The men settled in a plain and said: "Come, let us build ourselves a city, with a tower that reaches to the heavens, so that we may not be scattered over the face of the whole earth" (11:4).
■ God confused their language so they could not understand each other (11:7).
■ That was how God scattered them over the face of the whole earth (11:8).

Life-lesson taught by the story that relate to the doctrine:
1. Seeking to overcome past mistakes while disobeying God's commands, brings God's judgment and punishment. When Noah's

descendants refused to obey God's orders to scatter (9:1), God gave different people different languages (11:6-7).

STORY: Abraham, Lot and Hagar
TEXT: Gen 12 - 25

Context:
After the flood, God ordered Noah's descendants to scatter over the face of the earth (9:1,7). However, they built the Tower of Babel to keep from scattering. God stopped the building of the tower by giving different languages to the people. Since the people could not understand one another, they separated and scattered to different places.

Sequence of events that relate to the doctrine:
■ The Lord told Abram to leave his country, his people and his father's household (12:1-2).
■ Abram left, taking his nephew Lot with him (12:4-9).
■ When quarreling arose between Abram's herdsmen and Lot's herdsmen, Abram let Lot choose the land he wanted (13:1-13).
■ God promised Abram many descendants (13:14-17).
■ God promised Abram a son (15:1-4), that he would have many descendants (15:5); and God established a covenant with him (15:6-21).
■ Sarai, Abram's wife, had borne him no children (16:1).
■ Abram had a child, called Ishmael, with Hagar, Sarai's maid (16:1-6).
■ God established a new covenant with Abram, changed his name to Abraham, and changed Sarai's name to Sarah (17:1-16). God promised to give Abraham a son through Sarah (17:16-19).
■ God helped Sarah become pregnant, and Abraham and Sarah had a son they called Isaac (Gen 21:1-7).
■ Sarah wanted Abraham to get rid of the slave woman, Hagar, and her son Ishmael (21:10).
■ Abraham sent Hagar and Ishmael away with a little food and some water (21:8-16).
■ Hagar and Ishmael left without direction and wandered in the desert (21:14). When they were without water, the boy cried, and Hagar was without hope. God heard the boy's cry, spoke to Hagar about her responsibility to care for the boy, and opened her eyes to see a well with water (21:17-19).

Life-lessons taught by the story that relate to the doctrine:
1. To overcome past mistakes, it may be necessary to give up one's rights. To overcome his problems with Lot, Abraham, the oldest and chief of the family, gave up his rights to choose the land he would occupy and gave Lot the choice (13:1-12).
2. Seeking to overcome past mistakes without assuming responsibilities for consequences of one's sins results in injustice. When Sarah became jealous of Hagar and her son Ishmael, Abraham washed his hands of the results of his sleeping with Hagar and thus committed injustice in his own home. He was a rich man, so sending Hagar and Ishmael away with little food and water was an act of injustice (16:1-6; 21;8-21).
3. The victim of injustice must overcome the mistakes committed by others. Hagar's behavior is an example of the suffering of a rejected lover. She did not choose to have sex with Abraham. After having the son, she was rejected. She and her son were sent away into the desert with only a little food and water (21:8-21). She left without direction. She was angry, depressed and lonely (21:16). She received help from two sources:
   1° God. God opened Hagar's eyes to see the well that was nearby. Rejection generates anger, and anger generates depression. Often the rejected and abused person only sees his own problem and misses solutions that are obvious. God opened Hagar's eyes to see the well that was at hand.
   2° The responsibilities with the child helped Hagar recovery. Life does not end when a person is rejected. Also, one's responsibilities do not go away. Although Hagar was rejected by Abraham, that did not prevent God from giving her the resources to live and to recover her life.

STORY: David: Forgiven, But, Suffering the Consequences of Past Mistakes
TEXT: 2 Samuel 11 - 24

Context:
God chose Saul as the first King of Israel. He had a good beginning, but when he became disobedient, God rejected Saul and chose David to take Saul's place as king.

Sequence of events that relate to the doctrine:
■ David was made king over all the tribes of Israel (5:1-5). He conquered Jerusalem and lived there (5:6-9).
■ David's strength as king kept growing (5:10-25).

- The Lord gave David victory wherever he went (8:6). David governed Israel, doing what was right and just for all his people (8:15).
- David slept with Bathsheba, his neighbor's wife, and then ordered her husband murdered (11:1-27).
- The prophet Nathan rebuked David; David recognized and confessed his sin. A consequence of David's sin was that there would always be violence in his own family (12:1-15).
- David confessed his sin to God (Ps 32:5; 51:3-4), prayed for a pure heart (Ps 51:10) and taught sinners to return to obeying God's laws (Ps 51:13).
- David's son Amnon sexually abused his half-sister Tamar (13:1-22).
- Another son, Absalom, killed Amnon and fled (13:22-39).
- Absalom returned to Jerusalem and made peace with David (14:1-33).
- Absalom revolted against David (15:1-12).
- David fled Jerusalem with his followers (15:13-37).
- Absalom was killed in battle (18:1-18).
- David mourned the death of Absalom (18:19-19:2).
- David returned to Jerusalem and restored his kingdom (19:9-20:3).
- When David was an old man, his son Adonijah set himself up as king. However, David chose Solomon to be the king (1 Kg1:1-53).

Life-lessons taught by the story that relate to the doctrine:
1. One cannot overcome past mistakes without suffering the consequences of one's sins. Sin is forgiven by God when it is confessed; however, its consequences in this life continue. Although David confessed his sin and was forgiven, he had to suffer the consequences. The child, fruit of adultery, died (2 Sam 12:18). David's son, Amnon, saw his father take the wife of another man. When Amnon was filled with lust for his half-sister, and he took her by force (2 Sam 13:1-23). Absalom knew his father ordered an innocent man killed, so he murdered his half brother, who was guilty of incest (2 Sam 13:28-29). Absalom saw his father take Uriah's rightful place with Bathsheba (2 Sam 11:3), and he wanted to take his father's place as king (2 Sam 15:1-13). Another son, Adonijar, sought to make himself king (1Kg. 1:5-10) and was murdered (1Kg. 2:25).
2. Overcoming past mistakes involves assuming responsibilities for one's sins, and also using one's testimony on the results of sin as a means to teach others to return to God. David confessed: "I have sinned against the Lord" (2 Sam 12:13), and he taught sinners to return to God (Ps 51:13).

STORY: The Sinful Woman - Overcoming Past Mistakes with Faith in Jesus
TEXT: Lk 7:36-50

Context:
At the beginning of his second year of public ministry, the popularity of Jesus with the people was increasing; however, the religious leaders began to resist him.

Sequence of events that relate to the doctrine:
- A Pharisee named Simon invited Jesus to have dinner with him. A sinful woman went to the house with an alabaster jar of perfume. She stood behind Jesus at his feet, weeping. Her tears wet his feet, and she wiped them with her hair, kissed them, and poured perfume on them (7:36-38).
- Simon judged that Jesus could not be a prophet, or he would know that the woman was sinful (7:39).
- Jesus told a parable about two men who owed the same moneylender. One had a small debt, and the other a large one. Both were forgiven. The one who was forgiven the largest debt loved the moneylender the most. Jesus told the woman that her sins were forgiven and that her faith had saved her (7:40-50).

Life-lessons taught by the story that relate to the doctrine:
1. Anyone can overcome past mistakes, even those despised within their culture. Jesus had compassion for those who were rejected and despised by their society. He accepted and forgave a prostitute (Lk 7:36-50).
2. The self-righteous, religious person who values tradition more than people raises barriers that hinder others from overcoming past mistakes. The Pharisee Simon was religious but had no tolerance for the prostitute (Lk 7:39).
3. The first step to overcoming past mistakes is to have faith that Jesus accepts and forgives the repentant sinner. Recognizing that one is forgiven produces a manifestation of love toward Jesus. The parable of the moneylender who forgave the two debtors teaches that recognizing that one is forgiven, produces actions that manifest love for Jesus (Lk 7:40-48).

STORY: The Wayward Son - An Undeserved New Beginning
TEXT: Lk 15:1-31

Context:
Jesus' third year of public ministry began with the death of John the Baptist. When King Herod killed John the Baptist, the people were furious with their king. After Jesus multiplied the fish and bread to feed five thousand, the multitude wanted to revolt against Herod and crown Jesus as king (Jn 6:15). When Jesus refused to lead a popular movement against King Herod, the multitude felt deceived and Jesus lost his popularity (Jn 6:60-66). The conflicts between Jesus and the religious leaders increased.

Sequence of events that relate to the doctrine:
- The Pharisees and religious teachers accused Jesus of socializing with sinners. Jesus responded with three parables of things that were lost and found: the sheep (Lk 15:1-7), the coin (Lk 15:8-10), and the son (15:11-31).
- The youngest son of a father took all his father gave him and went to a far country where he wasted his wealth in wild living (15:11-13).
- Becoming hungry, he obtained a job feeding pigs (15:15).
- He came to his senses, decided to return to his father's home, confessed his sins, acknowledged that he no longer deserved to be a son, and requested that his father accept him as a hired man (15:17-19).
- The father saw the son when he was still a long way off, ran to him, hugged and kissed him, welcomed him home as a son, and gave him a party (15:20-24).

Life-lessons taught by the story that relate to the doctrine:
1. Past mistakes are overcome when the sinner returns to God the Father. Returning to God involves:
   - 1st Repentance, feeling shame for past sins (Lk 15:18).
   - 2nd Confession, acknowledging one's sins (Lk 15:18, 21).
   - 3rd A turning over of oneself to God, depending on his mercy and not on one's own merits (Lk 15:19, 21).
   - 4th A change in one's attitudes and actions; the one that left the father returned to him (Lk 15:13, 20).
   - 5th Faith, expressed by the confidence the son had in his father (Lk 15:20).
2. One may overcome past mistakes because God is in a hurry to forgive the repentant sinner. The father in the parable represents God the Father (Lk 15:11-32). The only time the Bible reveals God being in a hurry is when the father of the prodigal son ran to meet his repentant son (Lk 15:20).

STORY: Jesus and Zacchaeus - Paying Back Those Cheated
TEXT: Lk 19:1-10

Context:
Jesus was on his way to Jerusalem to experience his death and resurrection. The disciples were wanting to know who would be the most important in Jesus' kingdom. The religious leaders were planning to kill Jesus.

Sequence of events that relate to the doctrine:
- Zacchaeus as a chief tax collector was wealthy (19:2).
- Being short, Zacchaeus could not see Jesus because of the crowd, so he climbed a sycamore-fig tree (19:3-4).
- Jesus went to Zacchaeus' house (19:5).
- Zacchaeus stated that he would give half of his possessions to the poor, and if he had cheated anybody, he would pay them back four times the amount cheated (19:8).
- Jesus said that salvation entered Zacchaeus' house because he came to seek and to save those who were lost (19:9).

Life-lessons taught by the story that relate to the doctrine:
1. The first step to overcoming past mistakes is to seek Jesus, who himself seeks to save those who are lost. Zacchaeus climbed the tree to see Jesus (19:3).
2. To overcome past mistakes, whenever possible, the sinner needs to pay back those who suffered loss because of his sins. Zacchaeus paid back to those he exploited four times the amount he had cheated (19:8).

STORY: Peter - Restored by Jesus
TEXT: Mt 26:31-75; Mk 14:32-54; Lk 22:39-52; Jn 18:1-27; 21:1-24

Context:
The arrested Jesus was being judged.

Sequence of events that relate to the doctrine:
- Jesus was betrayed by Judas and arrested on the Mount of Olives (Mt 26:47-50; Lk 14:43-50; Lk 22:47-48; Jn 18:1-9).

- Peter, with a sword, cut off the right ear of a servant of the high priest (Mt 26:51-54; Lk 22:49-53; Jn 18:10-11).
- The disciples abandoned Jesus (Mt 26:55-56; Mk 14:51-52).
- While Jesus was being judged, three times Peter denied that he knew Jesus (Mt 26:58, 69-75; Mk 14:54, 66-72; Lk 22:55-62; Jn 18:15-18, 25-27).

Context:

On the Sunday of his resurrection, Jesus appeared to Mary Magdalene, some other women, two disciples on the road to Emmaus, and the disciples, with Thomas being absent. The following Sunday, Thomas was present with the other disciples when Jesus appeared.

The third time that Jesus appeared to his disciples was near the Sea of Tiberias where seven disciples went fishing.

Sequence of events that relate to the doctrine:
- Seven of the disciples, including Peter, went fishing (Jn 21:2-3).
- Jesus appeared on the shore and told the fishermen to throw their net on the right side. They caught a large number of fish (Jn 21:4-11).
- After the disciples came to the shore and ate, three times Jesus asked Peter: "Do you love me?" Each time Peter answered that he did love him and Jesus replied for Peter to feed his sheep (Jn 21:15-19).
- Jesus indicated the kind of death Peter would experience (Jn 21:18-19).
- Peter wanted to know about "the other disciple," and Jesus responded that was not for Peter to know (Jn 21:20-24).

Life-lessons taught by the story that relate to the doctrine:
1. The Christian does not overcome past mistakes by abandoning Jesus. When Peter said: "I am going out to fish," he was disillusioned because time had passed without further news of the Resurrected Jesus. He was ready to return to his old life of fishing for fish (Jn 21:1-3). It appears that nature itself was against Peter. He fished all night and caught nothing.
2. The Christian who betrays Jesus by word or action can overcome past mistakes because Jesus seeks to restore the wayward follower. Jesus went to Peter (Jn 21:4). Jesus is the Good Shepherd who seeks the lost sheep (Mt 18:12).
3. To overcome past mistakes, the Christian must accept the road Jesus gives him, without complaining about the privileges given to others. When Jesus indicated the way Peter would die, Peter wanted to know about John. Jesus replied that it was not for Peter to know. Peter needed to follow Jesus (Jn 21:18-22).

STORY: Saul/Paul - Accepted and Transformed by Jesus
TEXT: Acts 8:1; 9:1-27; 26:17-20

Context:

After his death, Jesus appeared to his disciples several times during forty days. Jesus was taken up into Heaven and his disciples stayed in Jerusalem. On the day of Pentecost, the Holy Spirit came to rest on each of the followers of Jesus. Peter testified about Jesus, and three thousand people accepted his message and were baptized (Ac 3:29). In Jerusalem, the number of Jesus' followers increased daily.

A great persecution broke out against the church. Stephen was the first martyr. Saul began to persecute the church, trying to destroy it (Ac 8:3).

Sequence of events that relate to the doctrine:
- Saul approved the stoning of Stephen (8:1).
- Saul began to destroy the church, dragging off men and women and putting them into prison (8:3).
- Saul was going to Damascus to take as prisoners the followers of Jesus who lived there (9:2).
- As Saul neared Damascus, a light from heaven flashed and a voice said: "Saul, Saul, why do you persecute me?" Jesus revealed himself to Saul and told him to go to the city. When Saul got up from the ground, he could not see (9:3-9).
- For three days Saul was blind and did not eat or drink. He was praying (9:9-11).
- The Lord sent Ananias to Saul. Ananias put his hands on Saul, and his sight was restored. Saul was filled with the Holy Spirit. Ananias baptized Saul (9:17-18).
- Saul at once began to preach that Jesus is the Son of God (9:20).
- Saul went to Jerusalem, but the disciples of Jesus feared him. Barnabas helped Saul and brought him to the apostles (9:26-27).
- Saul, who later became known as Paul, received a ministry from Jesus to announce the Gospel to the non-Jews (26:17-18). Paul was faithful to do the job given to him (19:19-20).

Life-lessons taught by the story that relate to the doctrine:

1. The one who has destroyed the lives of others with violent acts can overcome past mistakes because Jesus seeks the sinner, transforms him, and gives him responsibilities that make him useful. Jesus transformed Saul, the destroyer of the church, into Paul, the church-planting apostle.
2. The sinner who has an encounter with Jesus and accepts the challenge to obey him will overcome past mistakes. Paul is an example of this.
3. God's actions on behalf of the sinner gives him hope that he can overcome past mistakes. Jesus came to Saul on the road to Damascus.

CONCLUSIONS:

1. The act of sin may be simple, but the results are disastrous. The simple act of Eve's eating the fruit or David's sleeping with Bathsheba brought disastrous results.

2. Past mistakes may be overcome, but not without suffering the consequences of sins committed. The sinner is forgiven when he confesses his sins, but the consequences of his sins continue in the life on earth.

3. Anyone can overcome past mistakes. Examples include: the sinful woman who washed Jesus' feet with her tears, and Saul/Paul.

4. The action of God in favor of the sinner enables him to overcome past mistakes. The sinner cannot overcome past mistakes on his own. Jesus came to seek and to save the sinner. He accepts the sinner as he is and then transforms him into a new person. Jesus also seeks to restore one of his followers who has abandoned him.

5. The sinner can overcome past mistakes only when he accepts God's plan for his life.

6. To overcome past mistakes, the sinner must:
   - Acknowledge and confess his sins;
   - Accept Jesus as his Lord and Savior;
   - Assume the responsibilities for his sins;
   - Assume the responsibilities for the results of his sins;
   - Seek to make peace with the people who have become his enemies as a result of his sins;
   - Seek to restore to others their losses suffered as a consequence of his sins;
   - Begin to do the will of God in his present situation.

7. The mistakes of the past can be overcome only in the present. A person cannot undo the past, but in the present he can:
   - Recognize and acknowledge his sins;
   - Assume the responsibilities for the consequences of his sins;
   - Forgive and receive forgiveness;
   - Experience the transformation from Jesus that will change his way of thinking, talking, acting and being, so he will not repeat in the future the mistakes made in the past.

DOCTRINAL SERMON USING BIBLE STORIES

1. A doctrinal sermon using Bible stories

The doctrinal sermon using Bible stories, consists of the storytelling-preacher making a trip through the Bible, following the historical chronological road, and stopping to visit the stories that have a connection with the selected doctrine. Each time he stops to visit a story, he presents life-lessons discovered there that relate to the doctrine. The storytelling-preacher tells only stories that relate to the doctrine, and he selects and presents some of the life-lessons that connect to the doctrine.

The most common type of literature in the Bible is the story. Bible stories are a never-ending treasure for teaching doctrine. Moses, Joshua, Samuel, Jesus, Stephen and Paul preached doctrinal sermons using Bible stories, and so can you.

2. How to prepare the doctrinal sermon using Bible stories

2.1 Analyze the doctrine using Bible stories in chronological order

Follow the plan given in the chapter (13) DOCTRINAL ANALYSIS USING BIBLE STORIES IN CHRONOLOGICAL ORDER.

2.2 Select the major stories that connect with the doctrine being studied

Some doctrines have multitudes of stories that relate to them. There would not be time in one session to tell all of them. Therefore, select the stories that emphasize the life-lessons that are essential to communicate the doctrine.

2.3 Consider the selected stories and choose the most important life-lessons that relate to the doctrine

From the selected stories, choose the most important life-lessons that relate to the doctrine. Then, determine the life-lessons that deserve the most emphasis. When preaching the sermon, some life-lessons may be only mentioned, while others will be emphasized by developing the **Preaching Cycle**.

IMPORTANT!!! Reduce to the minimum the number of life-lessons to be emphasized. The storytelling-preacher does not have time to develop all the great life-lessons taken from the stories that connect to the doctrine.

2.4 Prepare the Preaching Plan

The Preaching Plan presents the selected stories in chronological order. The part of the story that relates to the doctrine is told in detail; the rest is summarized. Chosen life-lessons that relate to the doctrine are presented. Some life-lessons are only mentioned; the key ones are developed using the **Preaching Cycle**.

When the same life-lesson, or others similar to it, are discovered in several stories, it will be emphasized only once with the **Preaching Cycle**. The life-lesson may be mentioned each time a story is told that connects to it. However, the **Preaching Cycle** is developed only one time.

After the storytelling-preacher tells one story and presents the life-lessons that relate to the doctrine, he advances to the next chosen story and repeats the same process. He keeps repeating the same process until he is ready to conclude the sermon.

THE PREACHING PLAN FOR THE DOCTRINAL SERMON USING BIBLE STORIES

INTRODUCTION:

The introduction presents the doctrine. Use only a few sentences to explain the doctrine.

STORIES SELECTED THAT RELATE TO THE DOCTRINE:

1st Story that relates to the doctrine
- Note the **sequence of events**. The part of the story that relates to the doctrine is told in detail, and the rest is summarized. Refer to the doctrinal analysis and begin copying or abbreviating the notes from the historical context and the sequence of events.
- Selected life-lessons taken from the story that relate to the doctrine will be presented.

OBSERVATION: *Some of the life-lessons may be mentioned without further comment. The most important ones will be developed by utilizing the Preaching Cycle.*

> 1st **DIVISION** (The first life-lesson presented becomes the first division of the sermon. If it is only mentioned or if it utilizes the **Preaching Cycle**, it is still the first division.)

Use the Preaching Cycle with each life-lesson that deserves a strong emphasis:

2nd Story selected that relates to the doctrine:
- When moving from one story to another, there may be changes in the historical circumstances. If needed, include notes helpful to understand the historical circumstances surrounding each new story.
- Note the sequence of events. The part of the story that relates to the doctrine is told in detail; the rest is summarized.
- Selected life-lessons taken from the story that relate to the doctrine will be presented. Some will only be mentioned; the most important ones will be developed using the **Preaching Cycle**.

3nd Story selected that relates to the doctrine:
- Note new historical circumstances surrounding the story as needed.
- Note the sequence of events.
- Selected life-lessons taken from the story will be presented.

Continue the plan of telling the stories and presenting life-lessons that are transformed into sermon divisions until the conclusion is reached.

CONCLUSION:

The conclusion should review the main aspects treated in the sermon and call for action on the part of the listeners. The conclusion should be short. It should consume about ten percent of the total sermon.

Conclude the sermon:
- Mentioning the stories told;
- Summarizing the life-lessons emphasized and the principal applications;
- Appealing to the listeners to do the will of God, as presented in the sermon.

EXAMPLE: DOCTRINAL SERMON USING BIBLE STORIES

OVERCOMING PAST MISTAKES

INTRODUCTION:

Learning how to overcome the consequences of sins committed in the past is a necessity for every person. In the Bible many examples are given of people who overcame past mistakes.

STORY: The First Sin

TEXT: Genesis 3:1-24

Context:
Everything that God created was perfect. At the creation, man was created in the image of God (1:26). In the garden there was one tree whose fruit was forbidden. God had ordered:

"You are free to eat from any tree in the garden, but you must not eat from the tree of the knowledge of good and evil" (2:16-17).

Sequence of events:
- The snake tempted Eve to eat the fruit of the forbidden tree (3:1-5).
- Eve ate the fruit of the forbidden tree, gave some to her husband, and he also ate it (3:6).
- The eyes of both of them were opened; they realized they were naked, so they sewed fig leaves together to cover themselves (3:7).
- Adam and Eve heard the sound of the Lord God in the garden, and they hid from him among the trees (3:8-10).
- Adam blamed the woman (3:10-12), and the woman blamed the serpent (3:13).
- God promised that one of the offspring of the woman would crush the head of the serpent (3:15).
- God made garments of skin for Adam and Eve and clothed them (3:21).
- Adam and Eve were driven out of the Garden of Eden (3:22-23).

1. **The act of sin is simple, but the results are disastrous.**

It is impossible to overcome past mistakes without suffering the consequences of one's sins. It was easy for Eve to take the forbidden fruit, eat it and give it to Adam (3:6). However, the consequences were tremendous. Adam and Eve were expelled from the Garden of Eden (3:22-23). *(Mention without developing the Preaching Cycle.)*

2. **God's actions on behalf of the sinner gives him hope that he can overcome past mistakes.**

God made the first prophecy about Jesus when he promised Adam and Eve that they would have children, and one offspring would crush the snake's head while the snake would strike his heel (3:14-15). God also provided clothes from skins for the couple (3:21). *(Mention without developing the Preaching Cycle.)*

STORY: Abram (Abraham) and Hagar
TEXT: Gen 12 - 25

Context:
After the flood, God ordered Noah's descendants to scatter over the face of the earth (9:1,7). However, they built the Tower of Babel to keep from scattering. God stopped the building of the tower by giving different languages to the people. Since the people could not understand each other, they separated and scattered to different places. God began a new relationship with mankind through one man, Abram and his family.

Sequence of events:
- The Lord told Abram to leave his country, his people and his father's household (12:1-2).
- God promised Abram many descendants (13:14-17).
- God promised Abram a son (15:1-4), and many descendants (15:5), and God established a covenant with him (15:6-21).
- Sarai, Abram's wife, had borne him no children (16:1).
- Abram had a child, called Ishmael, with Hagar, Sarai's maid (16:1-6).
- God established a new covenant with Abram, changed his name to Abraham and Sarai's name to Sarah (17:1-16). God promised to give Abraham a son through Sarah (17:16-19).
- God helped Sarah become pregnant, and Abraham and Sarah had a son they called Isaac (Gen 21:1-7).
- Sarah wanted Abraham to get rid of the slave woman Hagar and her son Ishmael (21:10).
- Abraham sent Hagar and Ishmael away with a little food and some water (21:8-16).
- Hagar and Ishmael wandered in the desert until their water ran out (21:14-15).

3. **Seeking to overcome past mistakes without assuming responsibilities for consequences for one's sins may result in injustice.**

When Sarah became jealous of Hagar and her son Ishmael, Abraham was quick to wash his hands of the results of his sleeping with Hagar and committed an act of injustice in his own home. He was a rich man, so sending Hagar and Ishmael away with little food and water was an act of injustice (16:1-6; 21;8-21). *(Mention without developing the Preaching Cycle.)*

STORY: David - Forgiven, But Suffers the Consequences of Past Mistakes
TEXT: 2 Samuel 11 - 24

Context:
God chose Saul as the first king of Israel. Saul had a good beginning, but when he became disobedient, God rejected Saul and chose David to replace him as king.

Sequence of events:
- David was made king over all the tribes of Israel (5:1-5). He conquered Jerusalem and lived there (5:6-9).
- David's strength as king kept growing (5:10-25).
- The Lord gave David victory wherever he went (8:6) and he governed Israel, doing what was right and just for all his people (8:15).
- David slept with Bathsheba, his neighbor's wife, and then ordered her husband murdered (11:1-27).
- The prophet Nathan rebuked David; David recognized and confessed his sin. A consequence of David's sin was that there would always be violence in his own family (12:1-15).
- David confessed his sin to God (Ps 32:5; 51:3-4), prayed for a pure heart (Ps 51:10) and taught the sinners to return to obeying God's laws (Ps 51:-13).
- David's son Amnon sexually abused his half-sister Tamar (13:1-22).
- Another son Absalom killed Amnon and fled (13:22-39).
- Absalom returned to Jerusalem and made peace with David (14:1-33).
- Absalom revolted against David (15:1-12).
- David fled Jerusalem with his followers (15:13-37).
- Absalom was killed in battle (18:1-18).
- David mourned the death of Absalom (18:19-19:2).
- David returned to Jerusalem and restored his kingdom (19:9-20:3).
- When David was an old man, his son Adonijah set himself up as king. However, David chose Solomon to be the king (1 Kg1:1-53).

4. One cannot overcome past mistakes without suffering the consequences of one's sins.

Explanation:

Sin is forgiven by God when it is confessed; however, its consequences in this life continue. The person who sows his wild oats and then prays for a crop failure will be disappointed.

David confessed his sin and was forgiven; however, he had to suffer the consequences. The child, fruit of adultery, died (2 Sam 12:18). David's son, Amnon, saw his father take the wife of another man and he took his half-sister by force (2 Sam 13:1-23). Absalom knew his father had ordered an innocent man killed; Absalom murdered his half-brother who was guilty of incest (2 Sam 13:28-29). Absalom saw his father take Uriah's rightful place with his wife (2 Sam 11:3); Absalom tried to take his father's place as king (2 Sam 15:1-13). Another son, Adonijah, sought to make himself king (1Kg. 1:5-10).

Illustration:
- The thief who confesses his sin to God is forgiven, but may be judged and sent to prison.
- A youth who was addicted to drugs was converted, married a Christian and later became a pastor. He and his wife had two children. His two children became sick with AIDS, then his wife, and then the pastor. God forgave the ex-drug addict, but he did not free him from the AIDS virus contracted when he used drugs.

Application:

When you confess your sins, God forgives you and will not remember your sin any more. However, the consequences of your sin continue on this earth.

STORY: The Sinful Woman - Overcoming Past Mistakes with Faith in Jesus
TEXT: Lk 7:36-50

Context:

At the beginning of his second year of public ministry, the popularity of Jesus with the people was increasing. However, the religious leaders began to resist him.

Sequence of events:
- A Pharisee named Simon invited Jesus to have dinner with him. A sinful woman went to the house with an alabaster jar of perfume. She stood behind Jesus at his feet, weeping. Her tears wet his feet, and she wiped them with her hair, kissed them, and poured perfume on them (7:36-38).
- Simon judged that Jesus could not be a prophet or he would know the woman was sinful (7:39).
- Jesus told a parable about two men who owed the same moneylender. One had a small debt, and the other a large one. Both were forgiven. The one who was forgiven the larger debt loved the moneylender the most. Jesus told the woman that her sins were forgiven and that her faith had saved her (7:40-50).

5. Anyone can overcome past mistakes, even those despised and rejected within their culture.

Explanation:

Jesus had compassion for sinners who were

rejected and despised by their society. He came to seek and to save the sinner.

He accepted and saved the prostitute who was despised by Simon (Lk 7:36-50).

Illustration:

The Samaritan woman would have been rejected by the disciples because of their racial prejudice. She was rejected by her own people because of a lifestyle that resulted in her marrying five times, then becoming another man's lover. That is the reason she went to the well at noon when other women went at sunrise. However, Jesus offered her "living water."

Matthew, the tax collector, was hated by the Jews because he collaborated with their enemies, the Romans. However, Jesus invited Matthew to become one of his disciples.

Application:

People who are rejected and despised by our society are targets of Jesus' compassion. We as Christians who follow him need to take the Gospel to them. That is the way we can help them overcome past mistakes.

If you are rejected and despised by others, Jesus has compassion for you and desires to have you follow him. He will give you an opportunity to have a new life.

STORY: The Wayward Son - An Undeserved New Beginning
TEXT: Lk 15:1-31

Context:

Jesus' third year of public ministry began with the death of John the Baptist. When King Herod killed John the Baptist, the people were furious with their king. After Jesus multiplied the fish and bread to feed five thousand, the multitude wanted to revolt against Herod and crown Jesus as king (Jn 6:15). When Jesus refused to lead a popular movement against King Herod, the multitude felt deceived and Jesus lost his popularity (Jn 6:60-66). The conflicts between Jesus and the religious leaders increased.

Sequence of events:
- The Pharisees and religious teachers accused Jesus of socializing with sinners. Jesus responded with three parables of things that were lost and found: the sheep (Lk 15:1-7), the coin (Lk 15:8-10), and the son (15:11-31).
- The youngest son of a father took an early inheritance and went to a far country where he wasted his wealth in wild living (15:11-13).
- Becoming hungry, the son obtained a job feeding pigs (15:15).
- He came to his senses, decided to return to his father's home, confessed his sins, acknowledged that he no longer deserved to be a son, and requested that his father accept him as a hired man (15:17-19).
- The father saw the son when he was still a long way off, ran to him, hugged and kissed him, welcomed him home as a son, and gave him a party (15:20-24).

STORY: Jesus and Zacchaeus - Paying Back Those Cheated
TEXT: Lk 19:1-10

Context:

Jesus was on his way to Jerusalem to experience his death and resurrection. The disciples were wanting to know who would be the most important in Jesus' kingdom. The religious leaders were planning to kill Jesus.

Sequence of events:
- Zacchaeus as a chief tax collector was wealthy (19:2).
- Being short, Zacchaeus could not see Jesus because of the crowd, so he climbed a sycamore-fig tree (19:3-4).
- Jesus went to Zacchaeus' house (19:5).
- Zacchaeus stated that he would give half of his possessions to the poor, and if he had cheated anybody, he would pay them back four times the amount cheated (19:8).
- Jesus said that salvation entered Zacchaeus' house, because he came to seek and to save those who were lost (19:9-10).

STORY: Peter - Restored by Jesus
TEXT: Mt 26:31-75; Mk 14:32-54; Lk 22:39-52; Jn 18:1-27; 21:1-24

Context:

Jesus had been arrested and was being judged.

Sequence of events:
- Jesus was betrayed by Judas and arrested on the Mount of Olives (Mt 26:47-50; Lk 14:43-50; Lk 22:47-48; Jn 18:1-9).
- Peter, with a sword, cut off the right ear of a servant of the high priest (Mt 26:51-54; Lk 22:49-53; Jn 18:10-11).
- The disciples abandoned Jesus (Mt 26:55-56; Mk 14:51-52).
- Three times Peter denied that he knew Jesus (Mt 26:58, 69-75; Mk 14:54, 66-72; Lk 22:55-62; Jn 18:15-18, 25-27).

Context:

On the Sunday of his resurrection, Jesus appeared to Mary Magdalene, some other women, two disciples on the road to Emmaus, and the disciples, with Thomas being absent. The following Sunday, Thomas was present with the other disciples when Jesus appeared.

Afterwards Jesus appeared to his disciples near the Sea of Tiberias where seven of them had gone fishing.

Sequence of events:

- Six of the disciples went fishing with Peter (Jn 21:2-3).
- Jesus appeared on the shore and told the fishermen to throw their net on the right side. They caught a large number of fish (Jn 21:4-11).
- After the disciples came to the shore and ate, three times Jesus asked Peter: "Do you love me?" Each time Peter answered that he did love him. Jesus replied for Peter to feed his sheep (Jn 21:15-19).

6. The Christian who betrays Jesus by word or action can overcome past mistakes because Jesus seeks to restore the wayward follower.

Jesus went to where Peter was (Jn 21:4). Jesus is the Good Shepherd who seeks the lost sheep (Mt 18:12). *(Mention without developing the Preaching Cycle.)*

STORY: Saul/Paul - Accepted and Transformed by Jesus
TEXT: Ac 8:1; 9:1-27; 26:17-20

Context:

After his death, Jesus appeared to his disciples several times during the next forty days. Jesus was taken up into Heaven and his disciples stayed in Jerusalem. On the day of Pentecost, the Holy Spirit came to rest on each of the followers of Jesus. Peter testified about Jesus, and three thousand people accepted his message and were baptized. In Jerusalem, the number of Jesus' followers increased daily.

A great persecution broke out against the church. Stephen was the first martyr. Saul began to persecute the church, trying to destroy it (Ac 8:3).

Sequence of events:

- Saul approved the stoning of Stephen (8:1).
- Saul began to destroy the church, dragging off men and women and putting them into prison (8:3).
- Saul was going to Damascus to take as prisoners the followers of Jesus who lived there (9:2).
- As Saul neared Damascus, a light from heaven flashed and a voice said: "Saul, Saul, why do you persecute me?" Jesus revealed himself to Saul and told him to go to the city. When Saul got up from the ground, he could not see (9:3-9).
- For three days Saul was blind and did not eat or drink. He was praying (9:9-11).
- The Lord sent Ananias to Saul. Ananias put his hands on Saul, and his sight was restored. Saul was filled with the Holy Spirit. Ananias baptized Saul (9:17-18).
- Saul at once began to preach that Jesus is the Son of God (9:20).
- Saul went to Jerusalem, but the disciples of Jesus feared him. Barnabas helped Saul and brought him to the apostles (9:26-27).
- Saul, who later became known as Paul, received a ministry from Jesus to announce the Gospel to the non-Jews (26:17-18). Paul was faithful to do the job given to him (19:19-20).

7. God's actions on behalf of the sinner gives him hope that he can overcome past mistakes.

Explanation:

The sinful person cannot overcome his own mistakes. The action of God in favor of the sinner gives him hope of overcoming his past mistakes. God so loves the sinner that he sent his son Jesus to the earth. Jesus so loves the sinner that he died on the cross to save him from the consequences of his sin. Jesus accepts the sinner as he is and transforms him. Jesus came to seek and to save the person who is lost from God because of his sin.

Jesus came to Saul on the road to Damascus.

Illustration:

In the Garden of Eden, God made the first prophecy about Jesus when He promised Adam and Eve that one of their offspring would crush the snake's head while the snake would strike his heel (3:14-15). God provided clothes from skins for the couple (3:21).

God sent the prophet Nathan to confront David about his sin with Bathsheba.

God sent Jesus to die on the cross to take the place of every sinner.

The father of the prodigal son was in a hurry to receive his repentant son.

Application:

We who are Christians need to co-operate with God who acts on behalf of the sinner. Let us tell the sinner about the God who acts on his behalf.

The person who is not yet a follower and who desires to overcome past mistakes needs to accept what Jesus, the Son of God, has done on his behalf.

CONCLUSIONS:

1. The act of sin may be simple, but the results are disastrous. The simple act of Eve's eating the fruit or David's sleeping with Bathsheba brought disastrous results.

2. Past mistakes may be overcome, but not without suffering the consequences of sins committed. The sinner is forgiven when he confesses his sins, but the consequences of his sins continue in the life on earth.

3. The action of God in favor of the sinner enables him to overcome past mistakes. The sinner cannot overcome past mistakes on his own. Jesus came to seek and to save the sinner. He accepts the sinner as he is, and then he transforms him into a new person. Jesus also seeks to restore one of his followers who has abandoned him.

4. To overcome past mistakes, the sinner must:
   - Acknowledge and confess his sins;
   - Accept Jesus as his Lord and Savior;
   - Assume the responsibilities for his sins;
   - Assume the responsibilities for the results of his sins;
   - Seek to make peace with the people who have become his enemies as a result of his sins;
   - Seek to restore to others their losses suffered as a consequence of his sins;
   - Begin to do the will of God in his present situation.

INVITATION:

1. Make a commitment to do your part in overcoming past mistakes.

2. Accept God's actions on your behalf that make it possible for you to overcome your past mistakes.

USING DRAMA WITH BIBLE STORIES

A storyteller can give life and breath to a listener's soul by the way he tells the story. Jesus communicated to the masses through storytelling. Jesus held thousands of people captive against their hunger pangs by storytelling. Lives were changed because Jesus told stories. The world was changed because Jesus told stories! The storyteller should live and breathe the drama of the story he narrates.

The essence of good drama is the story. Bible stories contain drama, personalities and conflict. Bible storytelling presents them the way they were first presented, as well-told stories. The narrator speaks as though he has seen or experienced the events described in the Bible story.

Scripture drama invites actors to make Bible characters come alive. The actors and the audience become aware of how they are similar to or different from each character. Drama helps the actors and the audience feel that they are eavesdropping on the private thoughts and actions of Bible characters.

Drama provides an opportunity for more people to participate in church activities. Those with musical talents or with the ability to teach have opportunities to participate in communicating God's Word. Drama allows more people to participate.

Do not use drama with Bible Storytelling to entertain; use drama to communicate God's truth. Scriptural drama, from the single storyteller to the multi-million dollar movie is useful only if it communicates truth that moves the participants and audience closer to God.

ROLE-PLAYING DRAMA

Role-playing is an effective method of helping a Bible story come alive. In role-playing, selected people act out a situation narrated in the Bible story. Actors are chosen to play the parts of individuals mentioned in the Bible story. The purpose of role-playing is to provide a close-to-reality base for understanding and gaining insights into the story.

Advantages of role-playing:
- It motivates the group;
- It results in spontaneous participation;
- It facilitates the understanding of the Bible;
- It excites children, youth and most adults;
- It helps the group to experience the biblical situation;
- It helps anchor the story in the group's mind.

For most stories, role-playing should portray only one scene from the Bible story. Choose a scene that anchors the story in the listener's mind. Almost every story can be dramatized by keying in on one essential scene and doing just that one scene.
- The scene of the snake talking to Eve would anchor the story of the first sin.
- The scene of two prostitutes before King Solomon, each claiming to be the mother of a baby, would anchor Solomon's wisdom in the listener's mind.
- The scene of a youth in ragged clothes clinging to a man's legs would anchor the parable of the Prodigal Son.

Role-playing drama that uses simplicity allows God to assume a more active roll. One does not have to use sets, props, lights or sound systems to touch hearts with messages born in heaven. The snake that tempted Eve can be a long sock covering an arm. The snake Moses raised on a pole in the desert can be as simple as a man's belt wrapped around a stick and held up. A child's doll put into a paper bag, with drawings of a fish, can portray Jonah being swallowed by a fish. Children on hands and knees, oinking like pigs, help portray the story of the Prodigal Son.

Role-playing drama may be a spontaneous presentation. Members of the listening group are chosen to become actors who, without previous rehearsal, play the parts of individuals mentioned in the Bible story. Or role-playing drama may be a rehearsed production with a director, stage, props and scripts that are memorized.

The storyteller-drama-leader should prepare his listeners to participate in the story. Listeners need to understand the story. The leader must establish the drama situation so that it is portrayable. He must instruct the

Bible Storytelling Tools © Jackson Day

actors on how to play their roles. He must instruct the observers as to how they will participate in the drama, or how they will participate in the discussion that will follow.

When drama is used as part of a storytelling event, as soon as the drama is finished, everybody may participate in a discussion time.

EXAMPLES OF ROLE-PLAYING DRAMAS

*EXAMPLE #1: **Adam and Eve** (Gen 3)*

ACTORS: Two adults: a male and a female

INSTRUCTIONS:
Imagine that you are Adam and Eve after they have been expelled from Eden. Adam is accusing Eve of getting them kicked out of Eden. Eve is defending herself and counter accusing Adam.

*EXAMPLE #2: **Isaac and Rebekah** (Gen 25:27-28)*

ACTORS: Two adults: a male and a female

INSTRUCTIONS:
Imagine that you are Isaac and Rebekah having a discussion about the children. Isaac is praising Esau and criticizing Jacob, while Rebekah is defending Jacob and criticizing Esau (Gen 25:27-28).

*EXAMPLE #3: **Siblings of Joseph** (Gen 37:3, 18, 26-28)*

ACTORS: Two men

INSTRUCTIONS:
Imagine that you are siblings of Joseph, and you have participated in selling him as a slave (Gen 37:3, 18, 26). You are having a discussion justifying your action.

*EXAMPLE #4: **Good Samaritan** (Lk 10:25-37)*

ACTORS: Actors representing: the victim, the thieves, the priest, the Levite, the Samaritan and the inn owner.

INSTRUCTIONS:
Present spontaneously, without previous rehearsal, the events of the parable of the good Samaritan.
As soon as the role-playing is finished, the leader asks the actors who represented the thieves, the Levite and the priest (as religious leaders) each to justify their actions.

QUESTIONS FOR GROUP DISCUSSION:
■ In what situations do we imitate the priest and the Levite?
■ What is the biblical message for:
  ● The thieves?
  ● The priest and the Levite?
  ● The Samaritan?

*EXAMPLE #5: **The Fight between Paul and Barnabas** (At: 15:36-41)*

ACTORS: Two men: one representing Paul, the other Barnabas

INSTRUCTIONS:
To represent spontaneously, without rehearsal, the events of the conflict between Paul and Barnabas because of John Mark.

QUESTIONS FOR GROUP DISCUSSION:
■ What were justifications for Paul's position and what were justifications for Barnabas'?
■ What does Paul and Barnabas' conflict teach us about resolving conflict?
■ What does Barnabas' position teach about the need to recover someone who failed in the past?
■ What does Paul and Barnabas' conflict teach us about a situation when two people are unable to work together because of strong convictions?

Bible Storytelling Tools © Jackson Day

USING MONO-DRAMA WITH BIBLE STORIES

A mono-drama is similar to a role-playing drama, except that only one actor presents a Bible character through a narration, a monologue or a dramatization, describing what happened through words and actions.

EXAMPLES OF MONO-DRAMAS

EXAMPLE #1: **Adam**

A man is invited to imagine that he is Adam. First he describes life in the Garden of Eden. Then he describes his adjustment to learning to live outside the garden.

EXAMPLE #2: **Mary, Jesus' Mother**

A woman is invited to imagine that she is Mary trying to explain to her other children why Jesus is different.

EXAMPLE #3: **Mother of James and John** *(Mt 20:20-28)*

A woman is invited to imagine that she is the mother of two adult men, James and John. She is explaining to them her plans for asking Jesus to give them privileged positions in his kingdom.

EXAMPLE #4: **Philemon**

Imagine that you are Philemon receiving Onesimus, the runaway slave. Imagine your reactions both before and after reading Paul's letter to you.

EXAMPLE #5: **Lazarus** *(Lk 16:19-31)*

An actor tells the following monologue.

My name is Lazarus. The greatest storyteller of all time told my story.

My body was covered with sores. I had leprosy, a disease that didn't have any cure in my time. Leprosy made me a social outcast and forced me to leave my family. Far away from my family, I was near starvation when I stopped by a very rich man's house. In those days, before eating, the rich would clean their hands with pieces of bread and then throw the bread under the table for the dogs to eat.

I was hungry. I wanted to eat some of that bread, but they wouldn't give me any. They gave it all to the dogs. My sores ached and itched, and pus would run out of them. I couldn't keep the dogs away that were determined to lick my wounds.

One day I died, and I was taken by the angels to Abraham's side. My arrival into heaven was treated as a celebration. That rich man also died and was buried, but he went to hell. When he looked up to heaven and saw me beside Abraham, he began to scream for Father Abraham to have pity on him. He asked for Abraham to send me to dip the tip of my finger in water to cool his tongue because of the agony of the fire in that place.

Father Abraham replied to the rich man: "Son, remember that in your lifetime you received your good things, while Lazarus received bad things, but now he is comforted here and you are in agony. And besides this, between us and you a great abyss has been fixed. No one can go to you from here to you, nor can anyone cross over from there to us."

What a pity! While the rich man was enjoying his life, he never gave thought that one day he would have to answer to God. I could not even cross the great abyss to give him water.

The man then asked for Abraham to send me to his parents' house to warn his five brothers so that they wouldn't go to the place of torment. Abraham answered that they have the books written by Moses and the Prophets.

The rich man replied: "Father Abraham, if they only had someone from the dead to go to them, they would repent."

Abraham answered: "If they do not listen to Moses and the Prophets, they will not be convinced even if someone rises from the dead."

If the man's brothers were unwilling to believe what is written in the Bible, they would never believe a warning that came from a dead man like me.

CONNECTING A BIBLE STORY TO THE LISTENERS' LIVES

The storyteller needs to make a connection between Bible stories and today's events. Connections can go in different directions.

- The storyteller can make connections between a Bible story and his own life.
- The storyteller can help the listeners make connections between a Bible story and their lives.
- A person can begin with circumstances in his own life and seek biblical stories that make connections with his own circumstances.
- A spiritual leader can begin with an episode from another person's life and then make connections to a Bible story that relates to similar situations.
- The storyteller can begin with contemporary stories and make connections to Bible stories that relate to similar situations.
- The storyteller can use contemporary stories to make Bible stories better understood.

1. The storyteller can make connections between a Bible story and his own life

The storyteller making connection between a Bible story and his own life allows the Bible story to establish the context for connections. He discovers what he has in common with experiences, events, emotions, and people presented in the Bible story. The story presents the situation, and the storyteller relates his own circumstances and experiences with those presented in the story.

The one who explores connections between Bible stories and his own life gives freedom for God's Spirit to internalize the story and bring about transformation. When events of one's life are connected and interpreted by a Bible story, God's story empowers, gives meaning to life and becomes a resource for one's own life's story. The chapter **TELLING A BIBLE STORY** gives suggestions that help the storyteller make connections between the narrative and his own life. I will repeat an example from that chapter.

In order to make a connection between the birth of Jesus in the manger and my experiences, I remember:

- The smell of the barnyard on the farm where I was raised;
- The disgust I felt when I stepped in fresh cow manure;
- The time I felt most alone. It was the first Christmas I spent in a city away from my family. I was in the university and had to work during the holidays;
- The most disagreeable night of my life. I was traveling with my wife, three small children and a lot of luggage through a semidesert area of Brazil. The motor of the car quit. After we waited on the side of the road for three hours, a lady gave my wife and children a ride into town, but she did not have room for our luggage, so I slept in the bushes by the car. The only hotel in town had no rooms available, and my wife and children slept on the floor of a restaurant-tavern with no mattresses;
- The difficulty of traveling with my wife when she was pregnant. She was more sensitive at that time;
- My first son was born in a sterilized room in a hospital, and I was afraid something would go wrong. When Jesus was born, Joseph must have experienced great fear in a filthy barnyard, without medical help and with poor lighting.

2. The storyteller can help his listeners make connections between a Bible story and their own lives

To make connections between the Bible story and one's listeners, it is necessary to allow the story to establish the context for the linkup. The storyteller helps his listeners discover what they have in common with experiences, events, emotions and people presented in the Bible story.

The storytelling teacher or preacher should use applications to make connections from the Bible story to current life. Applications help the listeners or students make connections between the Bible stories and their own lives. Applications give freedom to the Holy Spirit to internalize God's Word and provoke transformations.

The storyteller can also use planned activities to help listeners make connections from Bible stories to their own lives. The storyteller narrates the Bible story, following the sequence of events in chronological order. After telling the story, he asks questions or

Bible Storytelling Tools © Jackson Day

presents an activity that will help the listeners make a link between the Bible story and their own lives.

EXAMPLES: *Planned Activities to Help Listeners Connect Bible Stories to Their Own Lives*

EXAMPLE #1:   *Tower of Babel (Gen 11:1-9)*

Context:
After the flood, all the earth's inhabitants were descendants of Noah. God ordered Noah's descendants to multiply and scatter over the whole earth (Gen 9:7). Noah's descendants failed to remember God's plan.

Sequence of events:
- All the people spoke one language (11:1).
- The men found a plain, settled there and presented the challenge to build a tower that reached to the heavens (11:4).
- They wanted to be famous and not be scattered (11:4).
- God came down from heaven to see the men's activity. He confused their language so they could not understand each other, and the people scattered (11:5-7).
- Thus, God scattered them all over the earth (11:8).

Connection between the story and current life:
People who have high objectives, but who don't obey God, experience confusion. The inhabitants of the old world had high objectives. They wanted to be united and to enjoy harmony. The results of their disobeying God by refusing to scatter was the confusion of languages.

Give examples from your life when you had high objectives; however, you disobeyed God and the result was confusion.

EXAMPLE #2:   *The Sinful Woman who Anointed Jesus (Lk 7:36-50)*

Context:
In the second year of his public ministry, Jesus' popularity with the people was growing while the religious leaders increased their resistance toward him.

Sequence of events:
- The Pharisee Simon invited Jesus to dinner. A woman known for her sinful life appeared; her tears wet Jesus' feet. She dried his feet with her own hair and poured perfume on them (7:36-38).
- Simon judged that Jesus could not be a prophet because he allowed the sinful woman to touch him (7:39).
- Jesus told a parable of two debtors, one with great debt, another with a small one. Both were forgiven. Jesus asked the question: "Which of them will love the lender more?" Simon answered: "The one who had the bigger debt canceled" (7:40-50).

Connection between the story and current life:
Jesus accepted and gave salvation to the sinful woman, a prostitute who was cast aside by society and repelled by the Pharisee Simon. Who are some of the people who are cast aside by our society? How can we help them experience Jesus' compassion?

EXAMPLE #3:   *Two Doors, Two Roads and Two Foundations (Mt 7:13-14, 24-26)*

Context:
Jesus made the following comparisons in the Sermon on the Mount:

Sequence of events:
- A wide door and an easy road lead to destruction, and many take the easy road (7:13).
- A narrow door and a difficult road lead to life, and few find it (7:14).
- Jesus closed the Sermon on the Mount by telling the parable of the two foundations. The person who hears and obeys Jesus' teachings is like a wise man who built his house upon the rock. A heavy rain storm did not destroy the house (Mt 7:24-25). The person who hears Jesus' teachings and doesn't obey them is like a man without good judgment who built his house on sand. A rain storm destroyed the house (Mt 7:26-27).

Connection between the story and current life:
God recognizes only two classes of people in the world: his children or the children of Satan; believers or unbelievers; saved or condemned. How can Christians communicate this truth to people who believe that every religion is good, and it does not matter what one believes as long as he has a religious faith? How can Christians communicate the fact that only two classes of people exist from God's viewpoint? What contemporary stories or events illustrate this truth?

EXAMPLE #4: ***Jonah: The Reluctant Servant*** *(Jon 1)*

Context:

The prophet Jonah lived in the Kingdom of Israel. Assyria was Israel's great enemy. The capital city of Assyria was Nineveh. The inhabitants of Nineveh had multiplied their sins and wickedness to such a level that God decided to intervene. Before throwing Nineveh into judgment, God wanted Jonah to preach to the city and give the Ninevites an opportunity to repent.

Sequence of events:
- God commanded Jonah to go to Nineveh and to preach against it (1:1-2).
- Jonah tried to run away from the Lord by catching a ship going the opposite direction (1:3).
- God ordered a storm (1:4).
- The sailors were frightened. Each cried to his own god, and they threw cargo into the sea to lighten the ship. However, Jonah slept (1:4-5).
- Jonah admitted that he was responsible for the storm, the sailors threw him into the sea, and the sea became calm (1:6-15).
- The sailors were frightened and made promises to God (1:16).

Connection between the story and current life:

God wanted Jonah to go to Nineveh and preach. Jonah tried to flee from the presence of God. The result was that he suffered and the sailors in the ship suffered with him.

Divide those present into groups of three to five people. Ask them to describe quickly an experience of fleeing from God, and how that experience brought problems for others and to themselves. Give them ten minutes in their groups.

EXAMPLE # 5: ***Jesus Walks On Water*** *(Mt 14:22-32)*

Context:

In the beginning of the third year of his ministry, Jesus received the news that King Herod had killed John the Baptist. Jesus left Nazareth for the city of Capernaum. He entered a boat with his disciples to go to a solitary place. The crowds followed, going around the lake on foot. Jesus performed the miracle of feeding 5,000 people.

Sequence of events:
- After the miracle, Jesus ordered his disciples to get into the boat and go on ahead of him to the other side (Mt 14:22).
- Jesus went up the mountainside to pray alone (Mt 14:23).
- On the lake, a storm appeared, the waves beat with force and the wind blew against the disciples in the boat (Mt 14:24).
- Jesus went to the disciples, walking on the lake. The disciples saw him, were terrified and screamed: "It is a ghost" (Mt 14:25).
- Jesus said: "Take courage! It is I. Be not afraid!" (Mt 14:27).
- Peter replied: "Lord, if it is you, tell me to come to you on the water" (Mt 14:28).
- Jesus answered: "Come!" (Mt 14:29).
- Peter left the ship and began to walk on top of the water, but when he felt the wind he became afraid and began to sink. He screamed: "Master, save me" (Mt 14:29-30).
- Immediately Jesus extended his hand, caught Peter and said: "You of little faith, why did you doubt?" (Mt 14:31-32).
- Jesus and Peter entered the boat and the wind calmed down (Mt 14:32).
- The disciples worshiped Jesus (Mt 14:33).

Connection between the story and current life:

The disciples were terrified of a storm at sea. Their fear was unnecessary because Jesus is Master of Nature, and he has power over storms.

What makes you afraid? Also, what facts about God make your fear unnecessary?

Divide those present into small groups and ask them to share within their groups what makes them afraid. Then they are to mention the facts about God that makes their fear unnecessary. Give them seven minutes in their groups.

3. **A person can begin with circumstances in his own life and seek biblical stories that make connections with similar events**

The storyteller can begin with circumstances in his own life and seek biblical stories that make connections with similar events. He should teach others to begin with circumstances in their lives and to discover biblical stories that make connections with similar situations.

EXAMPLE # 1: ***Person Suffering Depression***

A woman, believer in Jesus Christ, often suffers problems with depression where she has low motivation, is pessimistic and feels that life is not worth living. She found several biblical characters who suffered depressions: Job, Moses, David, Jonah and Elijah. Elijah's story is a tremendous help to her. Elijah challenged the prophets of Baal to a spiritual battle on Mount Carmel. After God defeated Baal's prophets and they were killed, Jezebel threatened to kill Elijah. He was afraid and fled from her and prayed, requesting to die. God provided Elijah with water and food, allowed him to sleep and ordered him to travel to Mt Horeb. On the mountain Elijah had an encounter with God and had a victory over his depression (1 Kin 18 - 19).

Now when the woman feels threatened with depression, she reads the story of Elijah's battle with depression. She reads the story daily until the depression leaves her.

EXAMPLE # 2: ***The Involuntary Divorcee***

A man who was divorced against his wishes sought Bible stories of people who were rejected by others. The story that most helped him was of Abraham sending Hagar away.
- God promised Abram a son and established an alliance with him (Gen 15:1-21).
- Abram had a son, Ishmael, with Hagar, the maid of Sarai (Gen 16:1-6).
- Years later, God made a new alliance with Abram. Abram and Sarai had their names changed to Abraham and Sarah. God promised Abraham and Sarah a son (Gen 17:1-27).
- God gave Abraham and Sarah the son Isaac (Gen 21:1-7).
- Abraham sent Hagar and Ishmael out into the desert and provided them with food and water for one day (Gen 21:9-14).
- Hagar and Ishmael wandered in the wilderness. When the water was gone, Hagar left her son to die. God spoke to Hagar, told her to lift up the boy, promised that he would be the father of a great nation, and God opened her eyes to see a well of water (Gen 21:14-19).

The involuntary divorcee concluded Hagar's situation is an example of the suffering of a rejected spouse. Hagar was rejected and discarded by Abraham (Gen 21:9-21). She felt anger, depression and solitude (Gen 21:16).

She received help from two sources:
1) God opened Hagar's eyes, and she saw a well. Rejection generates anger, and anger generates depression. The rejected one only has eyes to see his own problems and does not see obvious solutions. God opened Hagar's eyes to see the near-by well.
2) The responsibility for her son helped her reconstruct her life. Life didn't end and her responsibilities for Ishmael were not terminated when Abraham sent them away. Hagar's rejection by a man did not remove God's divine resources that helped her survive and recover her life.

4. **A spiritual leader can begin with an episode from another person's life and make connections to a Bible story that relates to similar situations**

The spiritual leader often has the privilege of helping others find biblical solutions to their problems and circumstances. An effective way to help another deal with a situation is to make connections to a Bible story that relates to similar events.

For example, an evangelical psychologist is giving counsel to church youth who question if they have the right to have sex before marriage. The psychologist highlights the following stories and the life-lessons taught by them.

Story: **Dinah Was Sexually Abused**
(Gen 34: 1-31)
- Jacob was living in Canaan, close to the city of Shechem (Gen 33:18-20).
- Hamor was chief of that area (Gen 34:2).
- Dinah, Jacob's daughter, went to visit the young girls of the land (Gen 34:1).
- Schechem, Hamor's son, sexually abused Dinah (Gen 34:2).
- Schechem was attracted to Dinah and wanted to marry her (Gen 34:3-6).
- Jacob's sons deceived Hamor and took revenge by killing all the men from the city (34:1-31).

Life-lessons:
1) Youth with a spiritual inheritance who accept the world's lifestyle will suffer damages. Worldliness not only prevents spiritual blessing, it carries real danger (34:2,13, 30-31). Dinah was a descendant of Abraham, Isaac, and Israel and possessed a spiritual inheritance. But she chose to have a social life with the daughters of the land (34:1), who were pagans and didn't know God. Dinah accepted their lifestyle, choosing a permissive life that made it easy for her to be sexually abused (34:1-2, 13, 27).
2) Sex outside of the marriage brings disastrous consequences for the families involved. Jacob's sons didn't forgive Shechem and sought revenge against him and his city.

Bible Storytelling Tools © Jackson Day

Story: **Joseph Is Tempted by Potiphar's Wife** (Gen 39:1-21)
- In Egypt, Joseph was sold to Potiphar, captain of Pharaoh's bodyguard (37:36; 39:1).
- God was with Joseph and blessed him. Joseph became responsible for managing everything that belonged to Potiphar (39:2-6).
- Potiphar's wife invited Joseph to go to bed with her; Joseph resisted in order not to sin against God (39:7-10).
- One day Potiphar's wife seized Joseph's garment; he fled, leaving it in her hands. She used the garment to falsely accuse him (39:11-19).
- Potiphar put Joseph in jail, but the Lord was with him (39:20-21).

Life-lessons:
1) God's faithful servant will suffer temptations, yet victory is experienced when one is tempted without yielding. Joseph suffered strong sexual temptations without yielding (39:6-12).
2) The person responsible for tempting others probably will not respect those with higher standards who resist temptation. The tempter may even seek revenge on those who resist temptation. That was the reaction of Potiphar's wife (39:14-19).
3) It is important to think of positive reasons for resisting temptation instead of considering only its prohibitive character. Joseph's motivation for resisting temptation was: "How can I do this great evil, and sin against God?" (39:9).
4) It is better to suffer injustly than to suffer deserving punishment. Joseph suffered because he resisted sexual temptation (39:13-20). (See 1 Pet 3:14-17.)

Story: **Sexual Sins in David's House** (2 Sam 11 - 13)
- David had sex with Bathsheba, his neighbor's wife, and then David ordered Uriah, her husband killed (11:1-27).
- The Prophet Nathan rebuked David. David recognized his sin; however, one consequence of his sin was that there would always be violence in his family (12:1-31).
- The son who was the result of David and Bathsheba's adultery died (12:15-23).
- Amnon, David's son, sexually abused his half-sister Tamar (13:1-22).
- Absalom, another son of David and the brother of Tamar, killed his half-brother Amnon and fled (13:23-39).

Life-lessons:
1) God's servant is subject to strong temptations. David was sexually attracted to Bathsheba (2 Sam 11:2-4).
2) God is aware when a person sins. God saw what David did with Bathsheba and Uriah (2 Sam 11:22).
3) Sin: so simple the act, so painful the results. It was simple for David to go to bed with Bathsheba (2 Sam 11:4), but painful were the results (2 Sam 12:9-14).
4) A good-looking woman can gain privileges by using her body, though such a woman is a curse and not a blessing. The man who enjoys sexual pleasure with her is harmed and sows moral rottenness. Bathsheba was an unfaithful and ambitious woman who used sex to her advantage. She received a royal reward: she became the king's wife. Those who loved her were harmed: her husband was betrayed and killed, and David was punished because of his adultery with her.
5) Confessed sin is forgiven, but its consequences endure. The one who sows his wild oats and then prays for a crop failure will have his request denied by God. David confessed his sin and was forgiven, yet he suffered. The child who was the result of adultery died (2 Sam 12:18); David's daughter Tamar was sexually abused by her half-brother Amnon (13:10-17); Amnon was killed by another half-brother, Absalom (13:23-29); Absalom led a revolution against David (15:1-14); Absalom was killed in battle (18:14-15); another son, Adonijah, tried to take the throne by force (1 Kin 1:5-10) and was killed (1 Kin 2:25).
6) Uncontrolled sexual desires harm oneself as well as others. David observed a married woman taking a bath and yielded to his desires (2 Sam 11:1-4). His son Amnon did not control his desires for his half-sister, Tamar. He raped her, then despised her (2 Sam 13:1-19).

Story: **The Sinful Woman Who Went to Simon's House and Anointed Jesus** (Lk 7:36-50)
- Simon, a Pharisee, invited Jesus to dine with him. A sinful woman appeared, wet his feet with her tears and dried them with her own hair (7:36-38).
- Simon judged that Jesus could not be a prophet because he allowed such a woman to touch him (7:39).
- Jesus narrated a parable of two debtors, one with a large debt, the other with a small one.

Bible Storytelling Tools © Jackson Day

Both were forgiven. The one who was forgiven the larger debt loved the moneylender the most (7:40-50).

Life-lessons:
1) Jesus has compassion and desires to forgive those who are rejected by society because of their sexual sins. He accepted and saved the sinful woman, who was a prostitute (Lk 7:36-50).
2) Faith in Jesus, results in salvation and forgiveness of sins. The woman's faith in Jesus resulted in her salvation and forgiveness of her sins (Lk 7:50).
3) The person who is aware that his sins are forgiven manifests love to Jesus. That is the main life-lesson Jesus taught with the Parable of Two Debtors (Lk 7:40-48).

5. The storyteller can begin with contemporary stories and make connection to biblical truths

The Bible storyteller should also use stories from his own experience and those he hears others tell to make connection with Bible stories, his listeners' worldviews, and biblical teachings. The results will help God correct the worldview of the listeners with his divine view.

EXAMPLE #1:
Story: **The Night Watchman**
I was traveling with my wife and Marcos, a Brazilian pastor friend, going from Brasilia to Rio de Janeiro. We were going to lead a training clinic, and I was towing a trailer full of books. The highway was full of potholes. I continued driving after sunset. In the darkness of night, I hit a pothole and ruined a tire. We had difficulty changing the tire in the darkness. Shortly afterwards we discovered a small hotel, very simple yet clean. When I was registering, I told the clerk: "My car and trailer are full of books; do I need to remove them, or do you have a night watchman?"

The clerk answered: "We have a night watchman," and showed me a man sitting outside in a chair.

The following morning, I slipped out of bed, leaving my wife asleep in order to have the tire repaired before breakfast. But the front door of the hotel was locked, and I could not find an exit. I found a young lady in the kitchen preparing breakfast. I asked her how to get out. She answered: "The night watchman has the only key and he gets up at seven o'clock."

Connection with the Bible:
The man sitting outside the hotel had the title of night watchman. He earned the salary of a night watchman. He looked like a night watchman. But he did not fulfill his job of staying awake and watching the cars.

In John's Gospel, chapter ten, Jesus speaks about the mercenary who looks like a shepherd, has the responsibility of taking care of the sheep, but who does not do the job if a wolf appears. He is not willing to risk his life to protect the sheep. Regretfully, some men have the title of pastor, receive the salary of a pastor, but when they are unobserved, do not fulfill the job of a pastor.

EXAMPLE # 2:
Story: **The Home for the Innocent**
I was visiting an interior city in Brazil and read the local newspaper. The paper was full of irony. The page dedicated to crime told the story of a man's arrest the previous day. The man arrived home intoxicated and very angry. He released his anger by beating his two-year-old son. The neighbors heard the boy screaming and called the police. When the policemen arrived, the drunk could not understand the problem. The drunk father screamed: "The boy is mine, and I can do with him as I well please." The journalist concluded by saying: "The father was taken to jail, the home for the innocent."

Connection with the Bible:
God also has his "home for the innocent." People who proclaim their innocence and justify their actions will live there. The Bible calls the "home for the innocent" by the name of "hell." God is also preparing a "home for the guilty." There will live the people who confess their guilt and assume responsibility for their wrong actions. The Bible calls the "home for the guilty" by the name of "Heaven."

6. The storyteller can use contemporary stories to make Bible stories better understood

Sometimes, the telling of a contemporary story will help the listeners understand the implication of a Bible story better than trying to explain all that is involved in the story.

EXAMPLE: Stories to make connection with the impact of fear felt when Jesus resurrected the widow's son (Lk 7:11-17).

EXAMPLE #1:
Story: **Uncle John's Funeral**

When I was a little boy, my relatives went to my grandparents' home most Sunday afternoons and sat on the front porch swapping stories. I remember a story told about an event when my grandparents were young. An older man died while sitting in his chair. His body became stiff before neighbors realized he was dead. Ropes had to be used to tie his body down in the coffin.

During the funeral, a young niece was exaggerating her sorrow, constantly shouting: "O Uncle John, I never told you I loved you. If I could only see you one more time, I would tell you how much I love you!"

The rope holding Uncle John's body to the coffin broke. He sat up in his coffin, and the screaming niece was the first to jump out the window.

EXAMPLE #2:
Story: **The Sleeping Man in the Coffin**

When our family lived in an interior town in the country of Brazil, the newspaper told the following story. Someone died on a farm, and someone was sent in a truck to a city to buy a coffin. When the truck was returning to the farm, a young man flagged the truck down requesting a ride. He was told the coffin was empty. It started raining, and the youth climbed into the coffin to escape getting wet. He went to sleep. While he was sleeping, the truck stopped to give a ride to several others. The sleeping youth woke up, raised the lid of the coffin and asked: "Has it stopped raining?" Passengers started jumping off the moving truck and several broke their arms and several their legs.

Connection with a Bible Story: **Resurrection of the Widow's Son at Nain** (Lk 7:11-17)
- Jesus came to the city Nain, accompanied by a multitude (7:11).
- A funeral procession was coming out of the city. The dead man was the only son of a widow (7:12).
- Jesus said to the widow: "Do not weep." He touched the coffin and told the corpse: "Young man, I command you to arise" (7:13-14).
- The dead man sat up and began to speak (7:15).
- Fear gripped everyone! The multitude began glorifying God (7:16-17).

The contemporary stories of Uncle John's Funeral and the Sleeping Man in the Coffin make a connection to the resurrection of the widow's son at Nain. They help the listeners realize the impact of terror felt when the dead youth sat up and began to talk.

Conclusion:

The storyteller who makes connections between biblical stories and contemporary life builds bridges for the Holy Spirit to interiorize God's Word and transform lives. When connections are made from one's own situation to Bible stories, life develops a divine meaning, biblical stories have contemporary meaning, and the story becomes a resource for facing current situations.

CHRONOLOGICAL BIBLE STORYING TRACKS

One of the best methods to teach divine truths is to follow the historical sequence presented in the Bible. Tell the stories in the historical sequence order that the events took place. God revealed himself through his action in a historical sequence. Events registered in the Scriptures happened in time, space, and sequence. The Scriptures were progressively revealed by God within a structure and historical context. God is the God of history. The Christian faith is based upon the great acts revealed by God himself, beginning with the creation and climaxing with the life, death, resurrection and ascension of Christ, continuing with the expansion of the Church, and firming up by the expectation of the second coming of Christ.

The Bible is one complete book. The Old Testament is the logical introduction, the basis and the authority for an adequate understanding of Jesus Christ, who is presented in the New Testament. The Old Testament presents the foundation of Christ's redemptive work. It is essential to understanding the Old Testament in order to comprehend clearly the life and work of Christ. It is necessary to teach the background found in the Old Testament and its fulfillment in the New Testament. The best method to teach divine truth is to follow the chronological and historical presentation of Scriptural events.

Chronological Bible Storytelling uses the whole Bible; however, the storyteller will not narrate all the stories in the Bible. There are about two hundred well-known stories, plus many lesser known ones. Not all of the stories are essential to understand the Bible. A **Storying Track** is a plan for selecting stories to be told and possibly retold in chronological order to a specific group of people for specific purposes. The person organizing the *Storying Track* chooses Bible stories that are essential to reach his purpose, that relate to the local culture, and the spiritual needs of his listeners. He also considers the number of stories that can be presented in the time available. For each track, biblical truths are presented using stories in chronological order. Three different types of *Storying Tracks* will be presented.

1) The **Multiple Storying Track** is a plan for a group of stories to be retold or recycled to the same group of listeners for different purposes. It is cyclic in that some of the same stories are told more than one time.
2) The **Single Storying Track** is a plan for a group of Bible stories to be told once in chronological order and, with each story, truths are emphasized that connect with the needs of the listeners.
3) **Fast-tracking** follows a plan to tell a group of stories in chronological order in one setting with little exposition. It is done for the purpose of giving a panoramic view of the Bible.

I. A MULTIPLE STORYING TRACK

Many missionaries who minister to illiterate tribal people groups and people groups hostile to Christianity use *Multiple Bible Storying Tracks*. Also, church planters working with literate groups familiar with Christianity can take advantage of a *Church Planting Multiple Storying Track*.

The **Multiple Storying Track** is a plan for a group of stories to be told and retold to the same group of listeners. It is cyclic in that some of the same stories are repeated more than one time. Each track has a different purpose. Each track is a chronological group of stories selected to meet the needs of the hearers.

An example of a *Multiple Storying Track* would be:

Track #1: Evangelistic Bible Storying Track;
Track #2: Discipling Bible Storying Track;
Track #3: Leadership Equipping Bible Storying Track.

Traditional methods of witnessing are usually ineffective with oral communicators. The traditional method uses scripture texts to present the "*Plan of Salvation*" which declares: all are sinners; Jesus died to save the sinner and then rose from the grave; the sinner needs to repent and believe in Jesus in order to be saved; and only those who believe in Jesus are saved from hell and will go to heaven.

Bible Storytelling Tools © Jackson Day

I often use the traditional method of witnessing to literate people, and I train others to use it. However, I find several problems with the traditional method of witnessing with pre-literate tribal people and other oral communicators:

- Pre-literate tribal people express their religious convictions through storytelling. The history of the tribe and its teachings are handed down from generation to generation by an elder telling stories to the younger people. Presenting a factual "*Plan of Salvation*" disregards the storytelling method.
- The traditional method of witnessing uses "Christian vocabulary" with people who are unfamiliar with terms that are best understood by western evangelical church going people.
- The traditional method of witnessing rushes to the cross so quickly that many people don't have a foundation for making a commitment to follow Jesus.
- The traditional method of witnessing depends heavily upon the "Written Word." Tracts, literature and books are essential for witnessing, teaching and training. The question needs to be asked: Must oral communicators become literate in order to become followers of Jesus?
- The traditional method of witnessing does not deal with the fact that the mind-set or worldview of the pre-literate tribal people is different from that of the Western literate evangelical. The tribal people need to understand the difference between the worldview presented in the Bible and the one presented by their elders through stories.
- The traditional method of explaining isolated doctrines, such as the Trinity, or justification, etc. leaves pre-literate and other oral communicators confused and bored. However, they are not bored when stories are told and the doctrines reveal themselves through the stories of God acting in history.

There is one basic problem with the traditional method of witnessing to people groups hostile to Christianity. (Distinct cultural or ethnic groups of people are referred to as people groups.) When the Christian presents the "*Plan of Salvation*," the listener becomes angry, becomes an enemy and will never listen to the Christian message again. An example would be with Muslims. Missionaries have discovered that the traditional method of presenting the "*Plan of Salvation*" produces anger. Many Muslims, however, will keep returning to hear a series of Bible stories. Hearing about God at work in the lives of people and events, challenges listeners in a nonthreatening way to hear biblical teaching.

A child named Billy just couldn't swallow a pill. No matter what his mother tried, it just wouldn't go down. Threats of spankings or promises of candy made no difference; the pill always ended up right on the tip of his tongue. Finally, his mother discovered a method that worked. She cut a raisin open and inserted the pill. Then she gave it to Billy. He was able to swallow the raisin with its hidden pill, but was never able to swallow the pill alone, even though alone it was much smaller. Sometimes only by putting truths within a story will the preacher/teacher be able to get his listeners to swallow it. Stories are excellent *raisins* in which to place hard to swallow truths.

Stories are the best approach to modify the viewpoints of those who are predisposed to reject Bible teaching. Where head-on attack would certainly fail, the story becomes a *raisin* which contains the truth that is hard to swallow. The story gains a hearing that can then be used to change convictions which the listener would otherwise keep locked deep within a strong box, refusing even to examine. An example of this is found the Old Testament when Nathan told David a story about a rich man who had many sheep but stole the only lamb belonging to a poor man. David was enraged and Nathan confronted David with his sin problem (2 Sam 12:1-4). Stories are most effective with people who are not prepared to receive the truth. When confronting someone with the truth would transform the listener into an enemy, telling stories may change the person's life. This is the reason that telling Bible stories is the most effective tool discovered to present biblical truths to Muslims and Hindus.

For pre-literate tribal people, other oral communicators, or people groups hostile to Christianity, telling Bible stories in chronological order is the simplest and clearest method to teach them the Word of God and show them the road to salvation. Begin with the creation and continue until the ascension of Jesus, emphasizing the Bible stories that reveal the character of God and the sinful nature of man.

Stories create, maintain, and change worldviews. People express beliefs and behavior based upon stories heard from parents, relatives, elders, strangers, friends and even enemies. Stories influence how a person views his world. To change one's worldview, it is essential to replace the stories that influence one's life. Bible stories are effective tools to challenge and change the listener's worldview.

Bible Storytelling will result in listeners becoming followers of Jesus. The new believers in Jesus need to be taught the doctrines of their new faith and instructed in the behaviors God expects of his followers. The simplest and clearest method to teach the Word of God to new believers in Jesus or Christians with little biblical knowledge is to teach them the Scriptures in chronological order. Review stories already told and add new ones as needed, following the chronological order.

1. **TRACK #1: Evangelistic Bible Storying Track** (for non-believers or Christians with very little Biblical knowledge)

To make an *Evangelistic Bible Storying Track*, choose a group of basic Bible stories that will help teach the basic facts of the Gospel to those who are not followers of Jesus Christ. Give consideration to the cultural and spiritual needs of the listeners in the target group. The stories need to be presented in their chronological order. Begin with the creation in Genesis, continue through the life, death, resurrection and ascension of Jesus, and end with the first converts recorded in Acts. It is important to choose the stories that give a general summary of the Bible and those that serve as a foundation to give the non-follower of Jesus an understanding of the Gospel.

The basic structure of the Old Testament prepares the non-believer in Jesus to understand the history of Christ and the Gospel presented in the New Testament. Present the Scriptures in chronological order so the listeners will understand the history of Jesus and be adequately prepared for the evangelistic message. During the *Evangelistic Track*, present only the Old Testament stories that are fundamental to preparing listeners to understand the character of God, the sinful nature of the human heart, the inability of people to obey God's laws, and the history of Jesus.

During the *Evangelistic Storying Track*, emphasize the Old Testament stories that reveal:
- God as the creator, the law giver, judge and savior of all people;
- The character of God as being sovereign, all-powerful, all-knowing, all-present, holy, loving, righteous, merciful;
- The inability of people to please God through their actions, and their inability to obey the laws given by God;
- Humanity's desperate situation;
- Humanity's need for a liberator.

After completing the Old Testament stories; emphasize New Testament stories that give the fundamental history of Jesus, from his birth to his ascension, and the story of the first followers of Jesus in Acts. Emphasize:
- Facts about God the Father and Jesus Christ;
- The inability of people to obey God's laws;
- The inability of people to please God through their actions;
- The need of people for a liberator or a savior;
- The life of Jesus Christ from his birth until his ascension.

OBSERVATIONS:
1) When using *The Evangelistic Bible Storying Track* for pre-literate people and those with little knowledge of biblical truths, storytelling looks backward but never forward! At the beginning of each session, the storyteller may review stories already told, but he should never refer to stories yet to be told. When telling stories in the Old Testament, Jesus will never be mentioned.
2) Storytelling during the *Evangelistic Storying Track* is predominantly narrative with minimal exposition. The storyteller does not explain or emphasize life-lessons he discovered in the story. He may dialogue with his listeners, helping them to discover truths, but the storyteller does not expound on them.
3) Storytelling need not be done in a worship service. Discover the time, location, and method used by local storytellers, and do storytelling in a similar setting. Listeners are invited to organize a worship service only after the telling of the death and resurrection of Jesus and after they have become his followers.
4) An evangelical invitation is not given until after the telling of the crucifixion and resurrection story. Until the crucifixion and

Bible Storytelling Tools © Jackson Day

resurrection story, the listeners are not challenged to believe the stories, neither does the storyteller defend his convictions. The storyteller trusts the Holy Spirit to be the one who convinces his listeners of the truth of God's Word. Storytelling is a "win/win" method until the story of the crucifixion and resurrection. At that point, the listeners are invited to make a decision to become followers of Jesus.

2. **TRACK #2: Discipling Bible Storying Track** (for new believers, Christians with little biblical knowledge, and maturing Christians)

2.1 Review the Bible stories presented in the Evangelizing Track

Telling Bible stories will result in converts to the Christian faith. The new converts need a *Discipling Bible Storying Track*, a group of stories for new believers and Christians with little biblical knowledge. Review the stories presented in the *Evangelistic Track* while inserting some new stories in their proper chronological order. Go back to the creation in Genesis, continue through the Old Testament, then the life, death, resurrection and ascension of Jesus, and up to the first converts presented in Acts. Now add other stories from the Book of Acts.

During the Discipling Bible Storying Track:
- In the Old Testament, review the stories told and insert new ones as needed to emphasize the stories that reveal the relationship of God with his people and his provisions for them;
- Review the history of Jesus from his birth until his ascension. Emphasize stories that show the relationship and the demands of Jesus with his followers and stories that manifest the ministry of the Holy Spirit;
- Present the stories from Acts in chronological order, emphasizing the development and functions of the churches, expectations for the churches, as well as the spreading of the Gospel from the Jews to the Gentiles, from Jerusalem to Rome.

During the Discipling Bible Storying Track emphasize stories that manifest:
- God's relationship with his people;
- God's provision for his people;
- The importance of obeying biblical commands;
- The ministry of the Holy Spirit;
- The expected behavior of a follower of Jesus;
- The organization and function of a local church;
- How the Gospel of Jesus is spread.

2.2 Present the Epistles and the book of Revelation

After reviewing the Bible stories, present the epistles, emphasizing where each epistle would belong in the chronological order of Acts. Do a summary of each epistle and of Revelation with the purpose of establishing firm knowledge of the biblical teachings, the proper behavior of followers of Jesus, and the way a local church should function.

When communicating to oral communicators, special emphasis needs to be made to use concrete logic with all the Bible. Concrete logic refers to things that can be seen, heard, felt and experienced. About seventy per cent of the Bible is written in story form, including stories about people, events, history, parables and miracles. The Bible storyteller naturally uses concrete logic. However, oral communicators have problems understanding a speaker who uses abstract logic usually used by educated people and found in most published literature.

Part of the New Testament Scripture uses Greek rational logic. This is especially true of Paul's writings. He was an educated literate communicator. His writings were produced in agreement with the speech of a well educated literate communicator. It appears that Paul's chief work was to translate Gospel stories into abstract logic. In an effort to contextualize, Paul translated ideas expressed by Gospel stories into logical categories of Greek philosophy. Today, those who work with oral communicators need to do the opposite. They should take Paul's writings, illustrate them with stories, express his ideas in short proverbs, and use lots of repetitions.

My thesis is: in the same way that Paul took Gospel stories and converted them into abstract thinking, those who work with oral communicators should take Paul's abstract terms and transform them into concrete thinking by illustrating them with stories.

At times Paul reinforced his logical language by using practical, concrete illustrations. In Romans chapter four, he illustrated faith by describing Abraham's experience. In 2 Timothy chapter two, Paul speaks about the: "workman who does not need to be ashamed, handling accurately the word of truth" (v. 15). Paul illustrates his thoughts with the following concrete terms: son (v.1); soldier (v.3-4); athlete (v.5); farmer (v.6); workman (v.15); vases (v.20) and servant (v.24).

James wrote about speech in chapter three of his letter, giving a rich example of using concrete images to explain abstract thoughts. He illustrates using the following concrete images: horses' bits (v. 3), ships' rudders (v. 4), tongue (v. 5), fire (v. 5), species of animals (v. 7), fountain (v. 11), fruit trees (v. 12) etc.

The issue is not what kind of Bible literature to use with oral communicators. The issue is: when working with oral communicators, all speeches should use concrete logic that emphasizes: stories, history, parables, biblical miracles, metaphors, comparisons, allegories, similes, biographies, events, things, nature, etc.

Bible students need to study all the Bible. This means oral communicators also need to study the parts of the Bible that use abstract logic. Teach oral communicators to connect Paul's ideas (and others who wrote using abstract logic) to biblical stories. Then they will understand Paul's writings.

The oral communicator works with objects, facts and events while the literate communicator works with ideas. Thus the oral communicator navigates the world of stories while the literate-communicator navigates the world of ideas. Therefore, use stories and comparisons to illustrate abstract subjects to oral communicators.

2.3 Present topical studies teaching doctrine with Bible stories in chronological order

After reviewing the Bible stories in chronological order and after giving a panoramic view of the rest of the New Testament, it is time to teach doctrine by doing thematic studies. But Christians who are oral-communicators need an understanding of the Bible in chronological order before receiving doctrinal studies.

Doctrines at first should be taught by reviewing Bible stories in chronological order that are connected to the subject being studied.

EXAMPLES:
#1 To do a doctrinal study about "FAITH," review the stories in chronological order that are connected to faith and emphasize that part. The following stories could be used:
- Call of Abram;
- Abraham and Isaac;
- Joseph;
- Moses;
- Lack of faith of the Israelites who murmured in the wilderness wanderings;
- Samuel's birth in answer to prayer;
- David;
- Jesus and the sinful woman in Simon's house;
- Faith of the Centurion with the sick servant;
- Resurrection of Lazarus;
- Jesus and Thomas;
- First converts on the day of Pentecost.

#2 To do a thematic study about "TEMPTATION," review the stories that have something to do with temptation and emphasize that part. The following stories could be used:
- Adam and Eve;
- Cain and Abel;
- Abram in Egypt;
- Joseph and Potiphar's wife;
- David and Bathsheba;
- Jesus' temptation by Satan;
- Peter's denial of Jesus;
- Ananias and Sapphira;
- Peter's withdrawal from the Gentiles at Antioch.

2.4 Do analytical topical studies

All Christians need to be taught the great doctrines of the faith. They need to have analytical studies. But for oral-communicators, it is necessary to teach the Bible stories in chronological order before beginning topical studies. An understanding of the Bible stories in chronological order serves as a firm foundation to understand topical studies.

Even so; those who belong to a pre-literate tribal group, the illiterate who live among those who read and write, and other oral communicators have difficulty in understanding doctrinal studies done in outline form. They have difficulty understanding thematic studies made from the letters of Paul. However, after stories have been used to teach the doctrines, oral communicators can understand the doctrines as taught in the Epistles if they are presented using concrete logic. A person who likes to read and write uses abstract reasoning that relates to ideas. An oral communicator uses concrete reasoning that relates to daily life, stories, things and the nature; things that can be seen, heard, felt and experienced. A story, by its nature, is a type of concrete communication, because it is about people, things, places, experiences and events. For that reason, stories are the best way to impart knowledge to oral communicators. However, the traditional doctrinal topical study follows the logical model. It relates to educated people, but it is inadequate for oral communicators. One can elaborate topical studies for the oral communicators by structuring them with concrete illustrations. Always illustrate with stories all emphases of a topical study. The difference is not just to tell stories to oral communicators and use topical studies with literate communicators. Doctrinal studies for oral communicators need to be saturated with concrete logic that emphasizes: stories, history, parables, biblical miracles, metaphors, comparisons, allegories, similes, biographies, events, things, and nature. Every thought must be illustrated with a story or concrete object.

3. **TRACK #3: Leadership Equipping Bible Storying Track** (for mature Christians, potential leaders, and leaders)

The Bible storyteller does not wish the local followers of Jesus to depend on him always. The spreading of the Gospel to surrounding areas depends upon the development of local leadership. The *Leadership Equipping Bible Storying Track* is a group of stories for teaching doctrine and training mature Christians. While reviewing the Bible stories, emphasis is given to teaching skills that will qualify the student to be a spiritual leader. The non-narrative text or Bible text not presented in story form will be reviewed to give complete knowledge of the Scripture.

During the *Leadership Equipping Bible Story Track*, review the stories already told while adding new ones as needed. Review the New Testament Epistles and Revelation, review doctrinal studies using Bible stories, and then review analytical doctrinal studies using all of the Bible.

3.1 Types of Church Leaders
The plans for the leaders' training should be determined by:
- The types of church leaders needed;
- The number of leaders needed;
- The future leaders needed to implant new evangelistic outreach and churches;
- The time available for training that the trainers and the students have.

The church needs the following types of leaders:

Type 1: ■Leaders of the local church or mission congregation. These are the people that exercise functions within the local church such as: teaching, preaching, administration and evangelization. They are leaders of a local church. For example: Sunday School teachers, evangelists, outreach leaders, leaders of home Bible studies, deacons and church treasurers.

Type 2: ■Church planters, leaders of new evangelistic outreach projects, planters of new mission congregations, leaders of established mission congregations and small churches. The leaders included in this category are those who are responsible for planting a new church, participating in the leadership of a mission congregation or local church that is a distance from their home, or helping in the leadership of a church without a pastor. These are usually leaders who volunteer their time and do not receive a salary for their ministry.

Type 3: ■ Pastors of churches and missionary church planters. These leaders, usually, are paid a salary by a church or denomination and have had an opportunity to study at a biblical institute or a theological seminary.

Type 4: ■ Regional, national and international administrators. These are the presidents, executive-secretaries, administrators or supervisors that help the churches to unite their forces in fellowship and in reaching common objectives.

Type 5: ■ Theologians and teachers in the theological institutions. They teach theological disciplines with the purpose of training the leaders for the church. They should have an opportunity to do research and publish articles and books that benefit all within the church.

3.2 Review the Bible stories presented in the Evangelizing and Discipling Tracks

During the *Leadership Equipping Bible Story Track*, the Bible Storyteller becomes a teacher-trainer. The students are the more mature Christians who have leadership potential. To teach the more mature Christians and train leadership, review the Bible stories already taught and insert others in the proper chronological order as needed. While reviewing the Bible stories, teach skills that would qualify the students to be spiritual leaders. When a skill is taught related to communicating with Bible stories, the students will practice using the skill with the stories being studied. Other skills are taught by connecting the teaching of a skill that is related to a story being studied. Review is important, and each skill is emphasized on several occasions. Some skills that need to be taught:

■ How to analyze a Bible story;
■ How to tell a Bible story;
■ How to prepare and preach a sermon whose text is a Bible story;
■ How to prepare and teach a Bible study whose text is a Bible story;
■ How to evangelize;
■ How to disciple new believers in Jesus;
■ How to use the Bible in counseling;
■ How to lead a worship service, Bible study, or prayer meeting;
■ How to begin a new church.

During the Leadership Equipping Bible Storying Track plan, emphasize stories that manifest:

■ Fellowship within the family of faith;
■ The life and character of spiritual leaders;
■ Methods God uses to sanctify and mature his children;
■ The sanctification of the followers of Jesus;
■ The importance of obeying the leadership of God as revealed through the Holy Spirit;
■ Methods God uses to evangelize the non-converted;
■ Methods God uses to plant and grow churches.

Then the teacher/trainer needs to review the New Testament Epistles and Revelation, doctrinal studies using Bible stories, and analytical doctrinal studies using all of the Bible. At the same time he is training his student to teach them to others. Teach oral communicators who will be church leaders to connect Paul's ideas (and other New Testament writers who wrote using abstract logic) to biblical stories. Then they will understand Paul's writings and will be able to teach them to other oral communicators.

After the storyteller has completed the Multiple Storying Track, he is faced with an open-ended opportunity to teach or preach God's Word, using all the Scripture and different approaches. But as long as he is working with oral-communicators, following *Chronological Storying Tracks* will be a major emphasis. Repeatedly following *Chronological Storying Tracks* preserves the integrity of the Bible for oral-communicators.

MULTIPLE STORYING TRACK

TRACK I Evangelistic Bible Storying Track	TRACK II Discipling Bible Storying Track	TRACK III Leadership Equipping Bible Storying Track
Tell Bible stories beginning with the creation in Genesis through the life, death, resurrection, and ascension of Jesus to the first converts recorded in Acts.	Review the stories in their chronological order while adding new ones as needed. Begin again with the creation in Genesis and continue to the first converts presented in Acts. Then increase other stories from the Book of Acts. Summarize the New Testament Epistles and Revelation, and do doctrinal studies using Bible stories.	Review stories already told while adding new ones as needed. Teach skills that a spiritual leader needs. Study the New Testament Epistles and Revelation, do doctrinal studies using Bible stories, then do analytical doctrinal studies using all of the Bible.
Emphasize: ■Who God is; ■Character of God; ■Inability of people to please God; ■Humanity's desperate situation; ■Humanity's need for a liberator; ■Life of Jesus Christ; ■First believers.	**Emphasize:** ■God's relationship with his people; ■God's provision for his people; ■Importance of obeying biblical commands; ■Ministry of the Holy Spirit; ■Expected behavior of a follower of Jesus; ■Organization and function of a local church; ■How the Gospel of Jesus is spread.	**Emphasize:** ■Fellowship within the family of faith; ■Life and character of spiritual leaders; ■Methods God uses to sanctify and mature his children; ■Importance of obeying God; ■Methods God uses to evangelize; ■Methods God uses to plant and grow churches. **Train to:** ■Analyze a Bible story; ■Tell a Bible story; ■Preach and teach; ■Evangelize and disciple new believers; ■Counseling using the Bible; ■Lead a worship service, Bible study, or prayer meeting.

A MULTIPLE STORYING TRACK PLAN FOR PRE-LITERATE TRIBAL PEOPLES AND PEOPLE GROUPS HOSTILE TO CHRISTIANITY							
OLD TESTAMENT	GOSPELS	ACTS	EPISTLES AND REVELATION	TOPICAL STUDIES USING STORIES	ANALYTICAL TOPICAL STUDIES	LEADERSHIP SKILLS
TRACK I Non-believers			XXXXXXX	XXXXXXX	XXXXXX	XXXXXX	XXXXXX
Mixed group (non-believers with believers)			XXXXXXX	XXXXXX	XXXXXX	XXXXXX
Children				XXXXXXX	XXXXXX	XXXXXX	XXXXXX
TRACK II New believers and Christians with little Bible knowledge						XXXXXX	XXXXXX
Christians who are maturing							XXXXXX
TRACK III Mature Christian leaders							XXXXXX
Leaders and potential leaders							

4. Considerations for the Multiple Storying Track

Multiple Storying Tracks are usually used with pre-literate tribal people or people groups that are hostile to Christianity. However, there are other possibilities for *Multiple Storying Tracks*.

EXAMPLE # 1: A local church simultaneously using all three tracks

One church in Brasilia, the capital city of Brazil, uses a **Multiple Storying Track**. *An Evangelistic Track* (Track #1) is followed during the week for continuous Bible studies in the homes of church members where non-believer friends and family members attend. In another location an *Evangelistic Track* is being used to plant a new church at a mission congregation. On Sunday mornings during Sunday School, the church uses a *New Believers Track* (Track #2) where new Christians study the Bible in chronological order for six months. Then the pastor leads an eighteen-month, one night a week, training session to lead the *Leadership Training Track* (Track #3) for church leaders, Sunday School teachers, leaders of home Bible study groups and those involved in evangelistic outreach.

EXAMPLE # 2: An urban rehabilitation center follows a *Multiple Storying Two Track Plan*

An urban rehabilitation center needed a two-track plan. The center helps people recover from drugs and alcohol addictions. From three to six months the clients are isolated in a rural area and a ten-week track series of Bible stories is constantly repeated. When the clients leave the isolated rural area to go to a half-way house in the city, another fifteen-week track series of Bible stories is constantly repeated.

EXAMPLE # 3: A Church Planting Multiple Storying Track

The **Church Planting Multiple Storying Track** develops at least three tracks: the **Evangelistic or Basic Storying Track**, the **Discipling Storying Track** and the **Leadership Equipping Storying Track**.

The **Evangelistic or Basic Storying Track** chooses a group of basic Bible stories that together give a panoramic view of the Bible and an introduction to principal Bible teaching. Bible stories are presented in their chronological order beginning with the creation in Genesis, continuing through the life, death, resurrection and ascension of Jesus, and ending with the first converts recorded in Acts. It is important to choose the stories that give a general vision of the Bible and those that serve as a foundation to give the non-follower of Jesus a basic understanding of the Gospel.

The church planter who schedules one Bible Storytelling encounter per week should plan on two to nine months with the first Track. He can summarize several stories in one Storytelling session. For example during one Storytelling session, the church planter could give a summary of the lives of Abraham, Jacob and Joseph. He will give only a summary of each person's life and briefly refer to principal truths discovered in each life.

I recommend that after completing the Basic Storying Track, it should be repeated on a regular basis for those who in the future enter the church fellowship. A new class could begin every six months or at least once a year.

New converts and Christians with limited biblical knowledge need a **Discipling Bible Storying Track**, a more detailed telling of the stories with more time spent on life-lessons discovered from them. With the *First Storying Track*, several stories would have been summarized during a single encounter. For the *Second Storying Track*, the church planter will retell many of the stories already narrated, while entering into more details with each one. For example: if during the *First Storying Track* he gave a summary of the lives of Abraham, Jacob and Joseph during one encounter, with the *Second Storying Track* he could take from one to three encounters to consider the story of each of these three people. Some stories not mentioned the first time around could be inserted in their proper chronological order. Likewise, greater details will be given to treat biblical truths discovered from each story.

The church planter could plan on spending six months to two years with the *Second Storying Track*.

The **Maturing Christians and Leadership Equipping Bible Storying Track** brings together a group of stories for teaching doctrine and training mature Christians. While reviewing the Bible stories, emphasis is given to teaching skills that will qualify the students to be a spiritual leaders. The non-narrative or Bible text not presented in story form will be taught, to give complete knowledge of the Scripture. Special attention will be made to train mature Christians with leadership abilities to evangelize, teach, preach, organize Bible study groups and plant new churches.

During the *Third Bible Storying Track*, review stories already told while adding new ones as needed. Introduce Old Testament poetic literature, New Testament Epistles and Revelation. Do doctrinal studies using Bible stories, and then do analytical doctrinal studies using all of the Bible.

When the church planter begins the *Third Storying Track*, he is faced with an open-ended opportunity to teach or preach God's Word using all the Scripture and different approaches. However, if he is working with predominantly oral communicators, following chronological Storying Tracks will always be the principal method used. Repeatedly following chronological Storying Tracks preserves the integrity of the Bible for people with limited or no reading skills.

> **OBSERVATION**: For more information on Multiple Storying Tracks, consult: **Building On Firm Foundations** (Vols. 1-9) by Trevor McIlwain. This series of nine books presents the chronological approach as developed and used by McIlwain as a New Tribes missionary among tribal people on the Island of Palawan in the Philippines.

II. A SINGLE STORYING TRACK

A Single Storying Track is usually followed when ministering to a literate people group familiar with the Bible and with knowledge about Christianity.

The **Single Storying Track** is a group of Bible stories presented once and, with each story, truths are emphasized that connect with the needs of the listeners. The storyteller begins with the creation in Genesis, continues through the Old Testament, covers the life, death, resurrection and ascension of Jesus, continues through the Book of Acts, places the Epistles in their chronological order within Acts, and finishes with stories related to the end times. Afterwards, doctrines may be taught using Bible stories. The Single Storying Track is open-ended in that Bible stories in chronological order may continue and be repeated as needed. After going through the track, the storyteller identifies single stories or scripture texts as to where they belong in the chronological order.

The Single Storying Track is useful when evangelizing and teaching people groups who have a written language and are familiar with Christianity. The listeners in such a group usually have both followers and non-followers of Jesus. Some non-followers will have little knowledge about Jesus, while others will have a lot. Among the believers present, some will be new believers, while others will have a faith that is contaminated with tradition and legalism. Still others will be mature Christians, and some may be spiritual leaders. The listeners may also have different cultural backgrounds.

The *Multiple Storying Track* develops several tracks: the *Evangelistic Storying Track*, the *Discipling Storying Track* and the Leadership *Equipping Storying Track*. Stories emphasized in each of the tracks are chosen to meet the needs of the listeners whose spiritual condition places them with that track. But with the *Single Storying Track*, stories are chosen which give an overall view of the Bible and relate to the spiritual, cultural and social needs of the listeners present. The storyteller will consider the spiritual needs of his listeners and use the chosen story to emphasize truths that meet the needs of his particular listeners. One storytelling session may be used to emphasize truths related to the needs of non-believers, new believers, mature Christians and church leaders.

In Brazil, I found the *Single Storying Track* most helpful. The non-followers of Jesus are familiar with Christianity and have a vague knowledge of most of the Bible stories. Yet, many have never read the Bible themselves. The *Single Storying Track* is also useful in the rural poverty areas with few schools above elementary school level, and few can read. The *Single Storying Track* is useful in the urban slum communities. The *Single Storying Track* is useful in training preachers with little formal education.

In Brazil, many laymen are the spiritual leaders of home Bible study cell groups, preaching points with weekly worship services and mission congregations that will become future churches. Some only learned to read after becoming Christians. Some who cannot read have a child going to school who reads the Bible to them. After a short course in Chronological Bible Storytelling, they are able to use the Storying Track in their teaching or preaching in a most effective manner.

In Brazil, I have been in homes with dirt floors and have helped someone read the Bible for the first time. I have also been in the homes of the rich with post-graduate degrees and observed someone reading the Bible for the first time. In both situations the people were familiar with Christianity and had a vague

Bible Storytelling Tools © Jackson Day

knowledge of biblical stories, and chronological storytelling was most efficient.

I believe that the *Single Storying Track* would be helpful in all of South and Latin America.

The United States is producing a generation of high school graduates and university graduates who did not read or study the Bible at school. Therefore, it is possible to have a graduate degree and be biblically illiterate. The *Single Storying Track* could be productive for both evangelizing and teaching the biblically illiterate in the Western society.

Within a literate society, many are illiterate. Many who have learned to read and write prefer to learn with the oral approach. Many who are highly educated are biblically illiterate even though they claim to be Christians. A *Single Storying Track* where the Bible stories are told chronologically may be the ideal approach.

The *Single Storying Track* may be helpful to meet the needs of specific target groups. For example:
- A group of three people lead a weekly Bible study at a city jail where a prisoner seldom remains there for more than three months. A *Single Storying Track* with four to ten stories is adequate.
- A church that offers a six-week divorce recovery workshop twice a year could have a *Storying Track* with six stories that make connection with the needs of those suffering from divorce.

The *Single Storying Track* is open-ended in that Bible stories in chronological order may continue to be repeated as needed. After going through the track, the storytelling preacher or teacher identifies single stories or scripture texts as to where they belong in the chronological order.

III. FAST-STORYING TRACK

Fast-Storying Track follows a plan to tell a group of stories in one setting with little exposition. It is done for the purpose of giving a panoramic view of the Bible.

J. O. Terry, an emeritus Southern Baptist Missionary with the International Mission Board, often did Chronological Bible Storying Fast-Tracking in Asia, and I have done something similar in Brazil. Several times, I have also done a Fast-storying Track in the USA. Fast-tracking "stories" the entire Bible story in one setting with little exposition. Bible stories are told with no or few additional comments from the storyteller. The one setting may be done in several hours, or the stories may be told from one to several days. The storyteller moves from one story to another and keeps the stories coming, one after another.

J. O. Terry states he uses Fast-Tracking for the following situations:
- Where visitation time with a village or people is limited due to inaccessibility. He has walked to a village where neither he nor other evangelical Christians will return for years to come;
- For bedside presentations of the Bible in hospital ministry;
- For in-home visitation evangelism;
- To test worldview models with a target group before proceeding with in-depth story-by-story teaching guided by worldview issues;
- To initiate storytelling training during a leadership training seminar for preachers, Bible teachers, and church planters;
- To introduce a village or other target group to a panorama of the Bible story prior to story-by-story teaching;
- For fast-tracking the Old Testament stories to prepare people for viewing the JESUS film;
- For a refresher for discipling both new and mature believers in churches.

Fast-Tracking is similar to sharing the Bible with a sledge hammer blow. The comprehension may be low, but the emotional impact is great. There does need to be a follow-up to teach the stories at a slower pace. But, in many situations halitosis (bad smelling breath) is better than no breath. It is better for people to hear a Fast-Tracking presentation of the Gospel than to never hear.

When working with illiterate people groups who can only be visited from time to time between long intervals, Fast-Tracking can be done on each visit. Literate people have difficulty with hearing the same stories repeated; they like something new. Oral-communicators appreciate repetition. That is how they learn the Bible stories and make them theirs.

CONCLUSIONS

A **Storying Track** is a plan for selected stories to be told and possibly retold in chronological order to a specific group of people for specific purposes. The *Storying Track* considers the local background and spiritual needs of the listeners, as well as the time available. For each track, Storytelling presents biblical truths using Bible stories in chronological order. The storyteller begins with the creation in Genesis and goes through the Old Testament, covers the life, death, resurrection and ascension of Jesus, continues through the Book of Acts, places the Epistles in their chronological order within Acts, and finishes with stories related to the end times.

1) The **Multiple Storying Track** is a plan for a group of Bible stories to be told in chronological order and then recycled to the same group of listeners for different purposes. For pre-literate tribal people, people groups ignorant of biblical teaching, or people groups hostile to Christianity; teaching the Scripture with the *Multiple Storying Track* is the simplest and clearest method to teach them the Word of God. The *Multiple Storying Track* is also useful for church planters working with people from any educational level.

2) The **Single Storying Track** follows a one-time presentation of a group of Bible stories told in chronological order. With each story told, truths discovered from the story that connect with the needs of the listeners are emphasized. The *Single Storying Track* is most useful when evangelizing and teaching people groups who have a written language, schools that teach reading skills to the majority of the population, and, when the listeners are familiar with Christianity. The listeners in such a group usually include both followers and non-followers of Jesus.

3) **Fast-tracking** follows a plan to tell a group of stories in chronological order in one setting with little exposition. The *Fast Storying Track* is an excellent tool when the preacher/teacher has only a one-time opportunity, or when he is working with illiterate people groups who can only be visited from time to time with large intervals in between visits.

ORGANIZING THE STORYING TRACK

1. **Consider stories that connect to those basic biblical truths that need to be communicated to all people when organizing the Storying Track**

The Gospel requires a certain level of comprehension for an unbeliever to understand, believe and obey its implications. Some of the universal biblical truths that need to be communicated to all people are:
- The Bible is the inspired Word of God, and God is faithful to his Word.
- God is the creator of the world and all life. Everything God created is good.
- God is all-powerful.
- God created man in his image.
- God's perfect creation (including man) was contaminated and spoiled when man sinned.
- Satan, man's chief adversary, tempter, and the opponent for God's plan for mankind can only be overcome through the power of God.
- Man is a sinner who cannot liberate himself from the consequences of his own sin.
- God hates sin and punishes it by death (separation from himself).
- God loves man and wants fellowship with him.
- Man's only hope to be freed from sin is for God to liberate him.
- Jesus, the Son of God, is the only one who can liberate man from sin.
- Jesus' death on the cross paid the debt sinful man has with God.
- The Holy Spirit takes the place of Jesus on earth.
- One day Jesus will return to earth as the judge who will separate his followers from the others. His followers will go to live with him, and the others will go to the place prepared for Satan and his angels.

The storyteller should make a list of essential doctrines he desires to communicate. Then shorten the list to under twenty. Many issues can be combined into generalizations. This list will guide him in his selection of stories. Every essential doctrine should have at least six stories that relate or connect to it. A single story may be used to teach several different truths or abilities.

A core group of stories essential to communicate those universal truths would include most of the following:
- Creation;
- Sin of Adam and Eve;
- Noah and the flood;
- Abraham;
- Jacob/Israel;
- Joseph;
- Moses and the Exodus;
- God's covenant, the Ten Commandments;
- Twelve spies, rebellion of the people, the wilderness wanderings, the bronze snake and Moses' sin;
- Joshua, crossing of the Jordan, Jericho, and Rahab;
- King Saul, King David, and God's promise to David;
- Two kingdoms: Judah and Israel, the destruction of Israel, the exile of Judah in Babylonia, and the return of the remnant to Jerusalem;
- Jonah;
- Prophecies of the Messiah in Psalms, Isaiah, and Micah;
- Births of John the Baptist and Jesus;
- Jesus' baptism and temptations;
- Jesus and Nicodemus and, Jesus and the Samaritan woman at the well;
- Sermon on the Mount;
- Stories that show Jesus' power over evil spirits, nature, sickness and death;
- Stories of conflict between Jesus and the Jewish religious leaders;
- Jesus' last supper; betrayal, suicide of Judas, trial, crucifixion and burial;
- Jesus rose from the grave, appeared many times to many people and ascended;
- Pentecost and the first believers in Jesus;
- Promises of Jesus' return and events afterwards.

A useful rule of thumb is to list six stories that can make a connection to each essential doctrine that needs to be treated. A single story may be used to teach several different truths.

2. **Consider the worldview of the listeners when organizing the Storying Track**

The storyteller should consider his listeners' worldview. *Distinct cultural or ethnic groups of people may be called people groups.* A people group's worldview is developed by what they see, hear, smell, taste, touch and experience plus the explanations their elders gave for those experiences. Those experiences become a part of their thinking and value

Bible Storytelling Tools © Jackson Day

system. Their common way of thinking and common value system is their worldview. Those experiences and way of thinking become a set of filters through which a person processes, interprets, evaluates, accepts or rejects information. A worldview is a profile of the dominant trends that determine the way a specified group live, act, think, feel, work and relate. Their worldview determines their goals, values, behaviors, activities, thoughts, and emotions. It also determines things that are openly promoted and other things that are openly opposed.

Each people group has in their culture and religion certain general characteristics which are held in common with other people groups. Each group also has characteristics that are unique and contribute to their having an "oneness" in their way of thinking. Each culture has rules and values that guide its members, but which may be misunderstood by an "outsider." Each people group lives within its "cultural prison" with rules, regulations and walls that separate them from other cultures. The one who is transported to another "cultural prison" will judge the new culture by the guidelines and restrictions of his own "cultural prison."

An example of "culture prison": Islamic countries that have a theocratic system (governed by religious leaders) will not allow banks to charge interest. Islam prohibits charging interest on a loan. Islam considers that it is wrong to charge interest. There can be no argument and no appeal.

However, the Muslim considers the North American closed-minded and a prisoner to his "culture prison." When a Muslim from an Islamic country tells a North American that the United States is evil and should become a theocracy, the North American is closed-minded to the idea of the United States becoming a theocracy. Separation of church and state is a sacred precept established by the founding fathers of the United States of America. The North American "culture prison" prevents him from even considering the idea of the United States becoming a theocracy.

The people group that receives the "outsider" has its own way of thinking. The people have their own convictions as to the proper and improper way to live, act, think, feel, work, and relate. They also have convictions as to the proper behaviors both for men and for women. These convictions are usually latent, and the people may not be able to explain the convictions that dominate their lives. Their convictions are so conclusive in their own minds that they see no need to voice them. In fact, they are not even aware that anything needs to be explained to the "outsider." The storyteller needs to be aware of those specific issues which are unique to his listeners' cultural group.

I grew up in Alabama on a farm twelve miles from the small town of LaFayette. "Cotton was King." The planting, cultivating and picking of cotton influenced all areas of our lives. The winters were mild and short, but the summers were hot and long. In our part of Alabama, there were two people groups: the white Southern Americans and the Afro-Americans.

When I was a young adult, I moved to Pagosa Springs, Colorado, a small town in the high mountain country. The winters were long and cold with heavy snow, but the summers were short. Most of the men worked in saw milling, logging, or ranching. In Pagosa Springs, there were several distinct people groups, each with its own "way of thinking." There were three groups of old timers: 1) the old time Anglo families; 2) Indians who were natives to the area; and 3) descendants of Spanish Americans. There were two groups of newcomers: one group came to log the timber, work in the sawmills or construct homes; the other came to enjoy the recreation Colorado offered, to hunt, fish, and play in the snow. Each people group had its own distinct accepted way of thinking and doing things. Pagosa Springs, Colorado, was different than Alabama.

I moved to Brazil and discovered that the Brazilians have a different worldview from what I learned in the USA. One example is that people have two different ways of thinking about the clock. In the USA, people talk about time as though it were money, as something that can be "spent," "saved," "wasted," and "lost." The person who is late is considered "irresponsible." In Brazil, time is less important than relationships. A Brazilian who on his way to an appointment bumps into a friend, would opt to be late for his appointment rather than abruptly terminate the conversation before its natural conclusion. A Brazilian who would not have time to talk to a friend would be considered unreliable. If a Brazilian is late, it is assumed he has a good reason.

In the United States, I greet men friends with a handshake. In Brazil, I learned to greet men friends with bear hugs. When I visited

Uruguay, I learned to greet men friends with kisses on the cheek.

Your culture will influence your answer to the following question: "Which is the greater sin: to tell a lie or to lose your temper?"

If you have white skin and are from North America or Western Europe, your culture would place a high value on accuracy and truth. Lying would be the greater sin. But for most places outside of the Western world, greater value is placed on relationships. Losing your temper would be the greater sin because it would rupture relationships and destroy friendships.

Different cultures may discover different truths from the same Bible story. A pastor leading a Bible study with African pastors and western missionaries asked the group to write down what they believed to be the main message of the Old Testament story of Joseph. The Americans agreed that Joseph was a man who, no matter what happened, remained faithful to God. The Africans concluded that Joseph never forgot his family, no matter how far he traveled.

One who goes to another place within his own country where the same language is spoken needs to be aware that his listeners may have a different "way of thinking." An urban person from New York has a different way of thinking from a Tennessee mountain man. In the USA, a Texan may be impressed by how big something is, while the New Englander is more impressed by how old it is.

In Brazil, I discovered different people groups, each with its "own way of thinking." We moved to a small city situated in an agricultural area, Vitoria da Conquista. Producing coffee and raising cattle were the main activities. Farmers and ranchers in rural Brazil have a different way of thinking from those from the mega city of Sao Paulo. A Brazilian pastor raised in a middle class family complained that the uneducated poor could not understand his preaching. A pastor from the city of Rio de Janeiro moved to a town in the jungle of Equatorial Brazil, and he described how the people were so different from those in Rio.

The storyteller who is going to teach or preach to a people group that is different from his own should consider that his listeners have a different "way of thinking." He needs to learn how they live, think, feel, react, interact and behave. He should discover the things that contribute to their uniqueness. He should consider those things when he selects the stories that will make up his *Storying Track*.

It is important to consider worldview issues in order to prevent costly mistakes that result from being ignorant about a people group's spiritual receptivity and to better communicate spiritual truths to the target group.

3. **Presuppositions to consider when trying to understand the worldview of your target group:**

3.1 **The Bible presents a biblical worldview**

The Bible presents God's worldview. The only correct worldview is the one God gives us in the Bible. God chose to communicate his worldview to all cultures, people groups and times with his story. Within his larger story, are found many short stories. The Bible storyteller desires to communicate the biblical worldview to his listeners.

A conversion to Christianity requires replacing one's existing worldview. For people to change their worldview, they must hear and believe different stories. They must hear and believe the Bible stories. Those who hear and believe the Bible stories experience the Holy Spirit transforming their worldview.

Each people group forms its own "cultural prison" with rules, regulations and walls that separate them from other cultures. The biblical worldview is superior to all others. The rules and restrictions within the biblical worldview does not confine God's people group to a "cultural prison" but liberates those from all people groups to enjoy the freedom of following Jesus. The biblical worldview breaks down the walls of "cultural prisons" and gives freedom to the followers of Jesus.

3.2 **The storyteller has his own worldview that is not biblical**

The Bible storyteller's worldview is influenced by his experiences within the people group where he was born and raised. He takes with himself cultural baggage from his own background. People have a tendency to judge other cultures by the values of their own and to consider all other cultures inferior. Not everything that belongs to one's own culture and tradition is good. Much has been contaminated by sin and needs to be eliminated for one to work with another people group. One's own culture and worldview need to be examined by the biblical worldview. The storyteller may consider his mind-set a biblical worldview when, in fact, his viewpoints are contaminated by his native worldview. The storyteller needs to study the Bible to understand it and allow Jesus to break down the walls of his own "cultural prison" and free him to communicate God's message to people within another "cultural prison." Therefore, the storyteller needs to examine his own worldview by biblical teachings. He may be more influenced by stories from his native culture than by Bible stories.

Peter had difficulty breaking out of his own "cultural prison." Peter spent three years with Jesus, heard the Great Commission (Mt 28:19-20; Ac 1:8), was present at Pentecost, and yet it took voices, visions, angels, and the Holy Spirit to get him to enter the house of Cornelius (Ac 10). Yet once when he was with the apostle Paul at Antioch, he returned to his "cultural prison" and refused to eat with Gentiles. He experienced Paul's anger for not acting in line with the truth of the Gospel (Gal 2:11-21). Peter had difficulty escaping from his "cultural prison." It should be no surprise that today's cross-cultural Bible communicator has the same problem!

My own rural, Southern American background contributed to giving me cultural baggage that sometimes enters into conflict with God's views. There exists the danger that I may teach my Southern, rural American view to Brazilians and call it God's viewpoints.

3.3 The listeners to the storyteller have a local worldview that is not biblical

Each people group has their own way of thinking. They have their own convictions as to the proper and improper way to live, act, think, feel, work and relate. Since all people are sinners, each people group has a worldview that is contaminated and is contrary to the biblical worldview.

In northeastern Nigeria, two kinds of people herd sheep: young boys and mentally deficient adult men. When a foreign storyteller described Jesus as the "Good Shepherd," the Nigerians asked "What was wrong with Jesus?" They were getting the message that Jesus must have been mentally deficient. Jesus as the Good Shepherd communicates well to Hebrews and to the Western world, but not to certain tribal groups in northeastern Nigeria.

3.4 Evangelical Christians within the local community will have their worldview that is different from non-followers of Jesus

It is always a joy for the Bible storyteller to discover evangelical Christians within the target group. But the storyteller needs to be aware that the local Christians have a different worldview than non-followers of Jesus. Those privileged to be reared in a Christian home may not even be completely aware of the worldview of the non-believers in their community.

I grew up in rural Alabama where some men in our community had moonshine stills to produce illegal whiskey. My parents, as evangelical Christians, had little in common with them and did not socialize with their families. Therefore, I am unaware of the worldview of my former neighbors who had moonshine stills.

When a Christian is identifying the local worldview, he shouldn't get it from the local evangelical community, but from the typical, ordinary people within the culture.

4. Identify the issues that must be dealt with in order to establish a biblical worldview

The Bible storyteller needs to discover the worldview of the target group he is seeking to evangelize, teach and train. It is necessary to spend adequate time in pre-evangelism, getting to know the target group. He should become a friend to their literature and stories. It is essential to find out what they know and believe. It is important to learn what the target group believes, to encourage their beliefs when correct, and to avoid controversial viewpoints at first. It is necessary to identify the anti-Gospel beliefs the group has.

It is necessary to understand the storytelling customs of the target group in order to work within it. It is important to follow local customs of the target group concerning grouping of people (entire families together; women together in one group and men together in another; men seated together with the storyteller while women are behind a barrier, out of sight but within hearing distance; etc.). If the storyteller wants to be heard, he cannot put off local customs and mind-sets, but must utilize them.

A missionary visited an African people that give respect to the old leaders by letting them speak first. He asked the local Christians: "If you were to present the Gospel to the village council down under the tree where they meet, how would you do it?"

They answered: "We would stand up and ask the oldest, most respected man in the group: 'Father, what do our people believe about God?' He would start speaking and answer at length. Some other old men would chime in. Then we'd ask him another question, and he would answer. After a long time we would do most of the talking." In such a society, if the Bible storyteller does not give old leaders the proper respect, the Christian message will be rejected by them.

Jesus knew the people who were in his target group and their needs. On many occasions, Jesus proved he knew the spiritual needs and knew how to offer solutions correctly for those needs. Examples of Jesus' knowing the worldview or mind-set of his target person are:
- Nicodemus (Jn 3:1-12);
- Samaritan woman at the well (Jn 4:1-26);
- Father of the son with an evil spirit (Mk 9:14-29);
- Beggar born blind (Jn 9:1-8;35-41);
- Rich young ruler (Mk 10:17-23).

A good source for obtaining information on the culture of a target group is to collect life-stories, stories and proverbs from the culture. Collect the proverbs that are repeated, because they express the values of a people. Collect the life-stories from different age groups and gender. Collect the stories the parents use to teach and discipline their children. Before a people group changes its worldview, it must hear and accept different stories. Therefore, it is important to understand the stories that are part of the culture.

It is also important to understand the games they play and to discover who are the heroes they desire to imitate.

Anthropological and sociological documents and books go into in-depth instructions on understanding the worldview of target people. They can be most helpful in understanding the worldview of a given group of people.

5. Consider the barriers and bridges from the local worldview of the listeners when organizing the Storying Track

Barriers found in the local worldview will hinder the target group from becoming followers of Jesus. Barriers are the negative aspects of the culture which hinder the group in its hearing, understanding, or acting upon the biblical truths. On the other hand, bridges found in the local worldview connect to existing interests, concerns, convictions or circumstances which help the target group hear, understand and act upon the biblical truths. Bridges have a positive influence for helping a group accept the biblical teachings. With any culture, one can find both barriers and bridges. Some factors will hinder an understanding and acceptance of the Gospel. Other factors in the same culture provide a connecting point for presenting the Gospel.

The Bible storyteller should have a core set of stories that need to be included for all people everywhere. When he gains an understanding of the barriers of a specific group, he can avoid certain stories and determine others that would help overcome potential stumbling blocks. Certain issues should be avoided until the people are ready to hear them. Also, the storyteller will wish to include stories that serve as bridges to help his specific listeners accept the truth.

The "QUESTIONNAIRE: AN AID IN UNDERSTANDING THE WORLDVIEW OF THE TARGET GROUP" is included in this chapter. It will be helpful to discover the barriers and bridges of a people group. Also, the storyteller should interview new believers and ask them to describe the barriers and bridges they faced in coming to their decision to become followers of Jesus Christ.

6. Consider the barriers erected from the local worldview of the listeners when organizing the Storying Track

A people group's way of thinking can erect formidable barriers to God's Words and the Gospel. Barriers prevent people from understanding biblical truths, from obeying the Word of God and make it difficult for Christians to become responsible church members. Barriers enslave people's minds and emotions so they don't understand God's Word and often prevent them from even listening. Barriers result in the biblical teacher or preacher being misunderstood, resisted or even attacked as an enemy. If barriers are not overcome, the Gospel will not be heard.

6.1 Religious barriers erected by the local culture

Religious beliefs and practices (syncretism, superstition, idol worship, amulets) erect barriers. The national identity being equated with a prevalent religion is a strong barrier. Another strong barrier is the attitude that people should die with the religion with which they were born.

Many Roman Catholics believe Jesus is the obedient child of Mary, that they sit side by side on thrones in Heaven, and that he would never say "No" to his mother, the reigning queen of heaven. The cultural belief that Jesus is the obedient child of Mary is a religious barrier to the Gospel.

The belief that salvation is by good works and God would never send a man to hell who was a good husband, a good father and a good neighbor is a religious barrier to many.

The belief in reincarnation is a barrier raised by the local religious culture of spiritualists.

People groups usually resent those who introduce "outside religious teaching." The Gospel may be considered a religion of outsiders.

Religious barriers erected by the local culture result in an anti-Gospel barrier.

6.2 Barriers erected by the evangelicals

6.2.1 Barriers erected by the communicator of the Gospel

The communicator of the Gospel can erect barriers by his lack of understanding of the language and culture of his listeners. Certain words, gestures and actions have different meanings in different locations. For example: the OK gesture used in the USA is considered an obscene gesture in Latin America. The Storyteller may use the wrong words, gestures, or actions and be insensitive to their needs. He may also manifest prejudice and lack of respect to them.

The communicator of the Gospel may create barriers by his attitude towards the clock. People groups oriented toward event, rather than time, will not understand an attitude that makes arriving "on time" a requirement to hear Bible stories. Also, the time oriented person creates a barrier to forming friendships with listeners.

A missionary family moved to a tribal village, and they brought with them their children's pet, a cat. The only other person in the village who kept a cat was the local witch doctor. The tribe believed that at night the witch doctor's cat entered the huts to steal sleeping people's souls. When a member of the tribe asked the missionary why he came to live with them, he replied: "To gather souls and lay them at the feet of Jesus." The missionary, communicator of the Gospel, erected barriers by his ignorance of local culture.

A Brazilian missionary went to an Arab country where men have the custom of holding hands while walking through the streets. In the Brazilian culture, two men holding hands would be considered homosexuals. The missionary kept his hands in his pockets to avoid holding hands with another man. He finally realized that walking with his hands in his pockets was interpreted as a sign he did not wish friendship with Arab men.

The preacher/teacher can erect barriers by the way he presents the Gospel. With many non-evangelicals, it is not Jesus they reject; they reject the way that he is presented. Examples of presenting the Gospel with methods that erect barriers:

- <u>Harsh, critical speech</u>: in Athens, Paul didn't condemn idiolatry and attack idols. The preacher is not the unbelievers' shepherd and does not have the right to attack either their beliefs or their lifestyle.
- <u>Legalistic negative gospel</u>: "A Christian does not smoke, does not drink alcoholic beverages, does not go to dances. Women can not wear pants, can not use jewelry, cannot use makeup, etc." The negative message gives a wrong image of the Gospel and creates unnecessary barriers.
- <u>Attacking other religions</u>: the evangelical Christian is exhorted to announce the Gospel. He does not have the duty to speak evil of other churches, denominations or religions.
- <u>Using inflexible evangelistic programs</u>: some evangelicals use an evangelistic plan asking "correct questions" that evoke "correct answers" that imitates the art of salesmanship. The emphasis is on following the plan. The same approach used by a door-to-door vacuum cleaner salesman is used to present the Gospel.
- <u>Screaming and shouting</u>: they use screaming, shouting and pounding on furniture as a means to express authority and demand attention. For a message to have authority, one does not need to scream and shout; he only needs to get his message from the Bible.
- <u>Methods inappropriate for the target group</u>: a formal worship service with classical music is out of place in most rural communities. Also, a two-hour sermon is ineffective in most urban centers.
- <u>Communicating above the listeners' understanding level</u>: the teacher/preacher who elevates his language may not be understood. Teaching is effective when the students understand. Preaching is effective when the congregation comprehends the message.

6.2.2 Religious barriers erected by the local evangelical community

The local evangelical community can erect barriers with man-made legalistic traditions. For example, when the evangelicals become legalistic, they may erect barriers against ladies who wear makeup and against men who play sports. In Brazil, certain legalistic churches teach that the soccer ball is the "Devil's egg," and Christians are prohibited from playing ball.

6.2.3 "Judaizers" barrier

Being familiar with a type of Christianity that is contaminated with false teachings erects barriers. The teachings of today's "Judaizers" hinder the acceptance of the true Gospel.

6.3 Family barriers

Opposition from one's own family to the Gospel erects a strong barrier for any person who is interested in becoming a Christian. When parents, or siblings or a spouse strongly oppose the Gospel, that erects a powerful barrier.

6.4 Heart barriers

The things that people love can erect barriers against receiving the Gospel. The love of money, power, honor, pleasures (including sex), vices and the things of the world can erect barriers against the Gospel. The rich young ruler's love of money kept him from following Jesus (Mk 12:17-22).

6.5 Intellectual barriers

Intellectual barriers are barriers of the mind. They include reasoning ability, philosophies, principles, logic, literacy, and thought processes.

Misinformation about Christianity erects intellectual barriers based upon biases. The biases of the local spiritual leaders can contribute to popular misconceptions. This is a more serious barrier than ignorance of the Gospel. It implies a negative fixation that must be demolished, dissolved or overcome.

6.6 Ignorance barriers

Some people are ignorant because they have never heard the truth. Some people are ignorant because they refuse to hear the truth.

6.7 Indifference barrier

Some will listen to the presentation of the Gospel with complete apathy. Many different attitudes can cause indifference. For example:

- Indifference could be the result of one being resigned to his *fate* in life (also sex, birth defects, lingering or terminal illness, caste, religion).
- Indifference can be the result of moral insensitivity. A lifestyle of prostitution, gambling, crime, drunkenness, drugs, piracy, murder, etc. can lead to one's becoming insensitive to truth.
- Indifference can be the result of secularism (worldliness, materialism, the good life, success). The one who only has time for the things this world offers will be indifferent to spiritual truths.

6.8 Supernatural barriers

Demon possession, spirit mediums, witchcraft, charms, meditation (yoga), spiritism, and following the horoscope result in supernatural barriers being erected.

6.9 Cultural barriers

The customs that "everyone else does," which conflict with the teachings in God's Word and are inconsistent with Christian living, become barriers to the truth. Cultural traditions related to honor, wealth, the status of women, sexual morality, promiscuity, revenge, killing of enemies, and intoxicating beverages consumed at social events may erect strong barriers against the Gospel.

In some cultures, it is expected that teenage boys prove their manhood by becoming sexually active, but girls from good families remain virgins until marriage. That cultural expectation creates a barrier for young, unmarried men. If they refrain from sex until marriage, their peers will question their manhood.

The convictions that are ingrained in a culture can create a barrier to certain truths. In a culture that believes only criminal acts are sins, the storyteller would not want to tell the story of Cain and Abel at the beginning because it would enforce their belief that one must commit a serious crime in order to become a sinner. There may be the need to delay the telling of certain stories because certain worldview convictions will cause confusion or conflict in the minds of the hearers. Another example: in a certain Indian tribe in Mato Grosso do Sud, Brazil, when twins are born, both are buried alive. The tribe believes that one represents good and the other evil. Not knowing which will be good, both are murdered. The story of the twins, Esau and Jacob (Gen 25), would re-enforce such belief. The tribe would conclude that Jacob was the evil one. With that tribe, it would be better to delay mentioning that Esau and Jacob were twins.

The cultural beliefs of a people group may erect barriers that interfere with the teaching of biblical truths.

6.10 Christian "in name" only barrier

One of the most difficult barriers is that erected by people who falsely call themselves "Christian." Some consider themselves "Christians-by-birth." They may lead degenerate lives while masquerading as Christians. Destructive acts and even murder may be committed with the belief that violence is done for the glory of God and with his blessing. The one who considers himself a "Christian-by-birth" is often harder to reach than other unbelievers.

Also, those who suffer at the hands of so-called Christians may hate all who use the name of Jesus.

6.11 Fear barriers

In areas where a predominantly non-Christian religion is strong, becoming a follower of Jesus often results in physical harm and even death. Some people groups fear violent persecution (ridicule, family and peer pressure, threat of physical harm, destruction of property and crops, threat of death). Others fear losing material and social benefits (schooling benefits, medical benefits, burial place, relief aid, use of wells, etc.). Some fear becoming an outcast, an outsider.

In Rio de Janeiro, Brazil, a criminal gang member requested prayers from an Evangelical Christian. The criminal stated he desired to give up his life of crime; however, anyone who tried to leave his gang would be murdered. If the gang member could not be found, one of his family members would be murdered.

6.12 Physical barriers

Physical problems may so dominate a person's attention that no energy remains to consider spiritual concerns. Refugees of terrible natural disasters, victims of war, victims of prolonged violence, victims of extreme poverty, those facing starvation, or those suffering a terminal, painful disease may become imprisoned within physical barriers.

6.13 Social barriers

Family persecution, being part of a gang or club, peer pressure, status and power symbols can erect social barriers to the Gospel.

CONCLUSION: Consider the Barriers Erected from the Local Worldview

Consider the barriers from the local worldview of the listeners when organizing the *Storying Track*. The storyteller will want to be aware of these barriers, not in order to combat them head-on, but in order to select appropriate Bible stories. He does not wish to avoid a biblical truth because it raises a barrier. The barrier needs to be overcome. Understanding the barriers will help the teacher/preacher discover the pre-Gospel truths from the Old Testament that need to be taught before presenting the New Testament Gospel. However, if presenting a truth before the listeners are ready to hear it raises additional barriers, the storyteller may delay presenting the truth until the listeners are prepared to receive it. When appropriate Bible stories are chosen, he can trust the Holy Spirit to overcome the barriers to the Gospel in the hearts of his listeners.

The following goals should influence which stories are chosen to confront cultural barriers to the Gospel:
- Inform: the truth may be rejected because of a lack of knowledge. Use Bible stories to supply the needed knowledge.
- Clarify: a barrier may exist because certain facts are misunderstood. Use Bible stories to clarify what the Bible really says.
- Correct: a barrier may exist because people have inaccurate biblical information. Do not attack such barriers. Use Bible stories to correct the wrong information with the truth.
- Challenge: some convictions are held because they have never been examined. Use Bible stories to undermine and challenge beliefs that are in conflict with biblical teaching.
- Destroy: barriers of false beliefs and anti-truth doctrine need to be confronted and destroyed. Bible stories told in chronological order will slowly destroy false beliefs and anti-truth convictions.

The Bible storyteller by himself will never overcome the barriers. The Holy Spirit is the one who convicts the listener. When Bible stories are told that challenge the barriers to the Gospel, the storyteller can expect divine intervention to break down barriers and convict the listeners of God's truth.

Remember young Billy who just couldn't swallow a pill? Finally, his mother cut a raisin open and inserted the pill. Then she gave it to Billy. He was able to swallow the raisin with its hidden pill, but was never able to swallow the pill alone, even though alone it was much smaller. Cultural barriers often make certain biblical truths hard to swallow. Sometimes only by putting truths within a Bible story will the preacher/teacher be able to get his listeners to swallow it. Stories are excellent "raisins" to wrap truths in that are hard to swallow. The barriers must be faced and confronted to be overcome. The storytelling preacher/teacher needs wisdom in knowing when to face the barriers and how to choose the best stories for bringing them down.

7. Consider bridges to the Gospel that can be built for the local worldview of the listeners when organizing the Storying Track

Bridges are God-given opportunities for connecting to an existing interest, concern, situation or other factor which predisposes a person to the Gospel.

7.1 Supernatural bridges

The storyteller may encounter bridges that can only be explained by the fact that God is at work in an unusual way. Some bridges are built by divine interventions (signs and wonders), divine discipline and attention-getting answers to intercessory prayer.

Bridges are built when the sick are healed or drought ends with rain in answer to the prayer of the Bible Storytelling teacher/preacher. Missionaries were visiting an out-of-the-way village without any evangelical Christians. A respected farmer in the region told them: "Last week I had a dream that someone would bring me a message that would change my life." A man was thinking about the Bible stories he had heard and felt a constant breeze but noticed that the grass and trees were not swaying, and he interpreted this as a sign from God. A couple had burned incense and offered sacrifices to a local spiritualist leader to protect their son as he grew up, but the child suffered from epilepsy. An evangelical preacher prayed for the child and God healed the boy. Most of the boy's family burned their amulets and idols and became believers in Jesus.

Many redemptive analogies (examples of where God is already at work preparing a people or redemptive illustrations with words, events, or signs that point to salvation) occur that cannot be explained by human reason. An evangelistic team went to a mountain in Nigeria where members of the Fali people live and discovered that the Fali had a legend that one day God would send messengers to tell them of his Son.

7.2 Broken life bridges

God uses brokenness to turn people's hearts toward him. Those who don't come to God because of his love may come because of their pain. The brokenness may be physical (due to war, drought, famine, disease, handicaps, birth defects). It may be social (imprisonment, public disgrace, social stigma, becoming an unwed mother, divorce, occupation, rank or caste). It may be economic when a job is lost or financial ruin is threatened. Brokenness may be the result of hitting bottom because of alcohol or drug addiction. It may be spiritual (due to special work of the Holy Spirit). Brokenness may be emotional (a person experiencing depression is looking for a reason to continue living). Brokenness can reduce the quality of life, destroy all "safety nets," and serve to break the proud, self-sufficient spirit.

7.3 Social bridges

Testimonies or examples from peers or other respected persons are helpful social bridges. The non-believer who has relatives, friends or co-workers who are Christians has a bridge that facilitates his becoming a follower of Jesus. A friend or co-worker becoming a believer in Jesus builds bridges for becoming a Christian.

7.4 Family bridges

Opposition of the family erects a barrier for the Gospel. But when one or more family members become Christians, that facilitates the way for others in the family.

7.5 Cultural bridges

Cultural convictions from the listeners' worldview that parallel Bible stories (often with amazing similarity and detail) serve as bridges. The local culture may have shared items that strike an affirmative note with the biblical Worldview. For example, the Bororo (a tribal people group in Brazil) people assume a "truth" underlies all individual experience and knowledge. The Bible storyteller can use that conviction as a bridge by presenting Bible stories that clearly reflect individual experiences and guide the Bororo people to discover the truth of the Bible story.

The desire to improve one's own cultural knowledge may lead a person to hear the Gospel. There may be a curiosity to know about the Bible without any desire for salvation. The desire to learn English as a second language may open the door to tell Bible stories and discuss them in English.

Exposure to persistent, persuasive media Gospel messages on the radio, TV, or through the printed word facilitates the acceptance of God's message.

The love of music has attracted many to enter a church. After listening to the music, they have remained to hear the Gospel presented.

The teaching of Bible stories is facilitated when the culture of a people group contains knowledge about God, Jesus, and Christianity. The long history of the Catholic faith in Latin and South America has provided a significant base knowledge about God and Jesus which is not found, for example, in a Muslim or a Buddhist country. The knowledge about God is distorted and incorrect in most of South America, but there is the advantage that they do know about Jesus.

7.6 Emotional bridges

Enslavement to sin contributes to emotional instability. The desire for relief from fear, danger, or other oppressive factors, real or imagined, opens a person to hear the Gospel.

A mother prohibited her nine-year-old son George from playing with firecrackers during the summer holidays. But George bought some anyway. One day, when his mother was out of the house, George was on the front porch playing with firecrackers. His mother returned home without his realizing it. He had lit a firecracker when his mother stepped out the door and screamed: "George!" Without thinking, he threw the firecracker over his head and took off running. Hours later, when George returned home, he found his mother dead on the porch. The firecracker had gone off above her head and the fright provoked a heart attack. The trauma of being responsible for his mother's death and the accusations made by his father and other family members in the shock of grief left George with deep emotional pains. George thought he could never be forgiven. He became a lonely boy who stayed by himself. When he was a youth, he finally told his story to an evangelical Christian who befriended him. His friend told him stories from the Bible of people who had done great wrong but were forgiven by God, and he convinced George that God would forgive him for causing his mother's death.

7.7 Moral bridges

The person who is concerned about moral issues and desires to protect himself, his family and others from the consequences of low moral standards has a bridge for the Gospel. This bridge is constructed from a desire for a better way (search for peace, social stability, ethical concerns).

A young father with three daughters became concerned when two of his nieces became un-wed mothers. He heard about an evangelical church with a "True Love Waits" campaign. The campaign encourages youth to wait until marriage to become sexually active. The man took his family to that church because he wanted his daughters to be encouraged to wait until marriage to become sexually active.

7.8 Bridges over a "failed" religion

Some people become disillusioned with the religion of their people group because they realize that it failed them. They may seek to replace it with a religion perceived to be more powerful or responsible. Those who become disillusioned because the lifestyle of their own religious leaders conflicts with their teachings may seek a religion whose leaders are faithful to their teachings. When one's own religion does not answer life's most important questions, or fails to help one face a major crisis, he may look for a new religion.

7.9 Helpful bridges

Evangelical Christians being present and helping during a time of crisis, natural disaster, or sickness build bridges for those who were helped to hear the Gospel. Christians ministering through a labor of love, expressing kindness, providing medical helps and health care, providing agricultural training, or providing nutrition have built many strong bridges that helped the Gospel to be heard.

A strong bridge is built when a broken person receives aid from a relief ministry or some compassionate caring from a person testifying to the love of God. A medical doctor went to work among an unreached people group in Central Asia. At first the suspicious villagers called him a "Foreign Devil." But after he ministered to them for a few years he was called: "God's Angel."

Evangelical organizations build bridges when they contribute to improve community life with health care, schools, water supply or improved sanitary conditions.

7.10 Testimonial bridges

The testimonies or examples of evangelical Christians build bridges for the Gospel.

The testimonies may come from an "insider" or they can come from a respected "outsider." The testimony of an "insider" who is similar to the listeners assure them that they can have a similar experience. The testimonies and examples of slum dwellers speak to slum dwellers, leaders speak to leaders, ball players speak to ball players, un-wed mothers speak to un-wed mothers, and prisoners speak to prisoners.

The testimonies of respected "outsiders" who are perceived as better, stronger, or more desirable assures the listener that what they profess is good and desirable.

The testimony of a famous sports person impresses all who love sports. The testimony of a movie star or famous singer is heard by the masses.

7.11 "User-friendly" church bridges

In the same way as a "user-friendly" software program makes it easy for a beginner to start using a computer, a church that is "user-friendly" to those outside the evangelical family makes it easy for non-Christians to visit and feel welcome. Those outside the evangelical faith will be attracted by the music, worship, Bible teaching program and other activities of a "user-friendly" church. Entering the church, they cross a bridge to where they can hear the Gospel message. People seeking a purpose for life often visit churches and other religious organizations. The church that makes them feel welcome serves as a bridge to becoming a follower of Jesus.

8. Conclusion from considering barriers and bridges from the local worldview

The Bible storyteller should learn the worldview of his listeners and identify the barriers and bridges from their culture. The purpose of *Chronological Bible Storytelling* is not just to connect to barriers and bridges. The purpose in Chronological Bible Storytelling is to lead the listeners to hear, understand and accept God's message. Knowledge of barriers and bridges to the Gospel can be of tremendous help in selecting and preparing the stories, holding the attention of the listeners, and helping them understand and accept the truth. As the storyteller gains an understanding of the worldview of his target people, he should determine elements that connect as bridges and overcome barriers.

When evangelical Bible storytellers are in the target-group, the "outsider" should pay attention to the stories chosen by national evangelicals. The outsider would never select some of the stories chosen by nationals to connect with certain worldview issues. He may not even understand the reason a story is chosen, but he can assume that the national evangelical identify a connection from the Bible story with some barrier or a bridge inside of his culture.

9. Considerations for organizing an Evangelistic Bible Storying Track

I have prepared a questionnaire that may serve as an aid in helping a storyteller understand the worldview of his target people group. Research to understand the worldview of a target group should not be seen as an imposed burdensome task. The Bible storyteller should seek to understand the worldview of his target people group because he loves those whom God loves and he desires to know them better. An understanding of their spiritual beliefs, rituals, fears, hopes, previous knowledge of the Bible and also their misconceptions about biblical truths, will help him better choose Bible stories to use, select the biblical truths to emphasize and avoid syncretism that results when worldview issues are not understood.

QUESTIONNAIRE
AN AID IN UNDERSTANDING THE WORLDVIEW OF THE TARGET GROUP

The following questionnaire is an adaptation of one I prepared to use in Brazil to help church planters get to know people in the target area where they desired to plant a new church. The purpose of the questionnaire is to help church planters understand the worldview or mind-set of the people group they desire to reach with the Gospel. The interviewer should ask the questions and make notes. He should avoid making any comments or expressing negative responses to answers given. The interview is not to be used to share the convictions of the interviewer nor even to evangelize. The purpose is to get to know the people and their convictions, and then establish Bible studies and activities to evangelize, teach and train this target group. This questionnaire may serve as an example of some questions that could be adapted and used in helping one understand the worldview of his specific target group.

Ask the person being interviewed: "Would you please give me your opinion by answering some important questions?"

1) You live in what kind of dwelling?
2) Who lives in this dwelling with you?
3) Who makes up your family?
4) What people are most important to you?
5) What activities require most of your time?
6) In your opinion, where did the world come from (the stars, sun, animals, plants and people)?
7) Do you believe that God exists? (If the answer is "yes," ask: How do you imagine God to be?)
8) Do you believe that there exist invisible, spiritual powers in the world?
9) What is your opinion about evil in the world? (Why do people fight, rob, lie and kill?)
10) Why is there suffering and pain in this world?
11) Do you believe that there is a right and a wrong? Who or what has the authority to decide what is right or wrong?
12) What is your greatest fear?
13) Who do you seek help from when you have a serious problem?
14) What makes people good, or what makes them evil?
15) Who or what decides if a person after death goes to be rewarded or to be punished?
16) What do you think happens when a person dies?
17) In your opinion, who exercises control over the dead?
18) Do you believe the dead can enter into contact with the living and vice versa?
19) My church would like to help this community. How can we help you and your community?
20) What kind of church would you be interested in visiting?

A good source of obtaining information on the culture of a target group is to collect life-stories, stories and proverbs from the culture. Collect the proverbs that are repeated because they express the values of a people. Collect the life-stories of different people from different age groups and genders. Collect the stories the parents use to teach and discipline their children. Before a people group changes its worldview, it must hear and accept different stories. Therefore, it is important to understand the stories that are part of the culture. It is also important to understand the games they play and to discover who are their heroes they would like to imitate.

The storyteller from a culture different from his listeners should also pay close attention to the choice of stories from evangelical Bible storytellers within that people group.

The questionnaire **BARRIERS AND BRIDGES TO THE GOSPEL** is to be used to interview new converts. Interview at least five new converts and ask them to describe the barriers that hindered their accepting the Gospel and the bridges that facilitated their acceptance of the Gospel. Make notes of the answers. The chart that follows may be used with each one who is interviewed.

BARRIERS AND BRIDGES TO THE GOSPEL	
BARRIERS Things that hinder and make it difficult to accept the Gospel	**BRIDGES** Things that facilitate and make it easy to accept the Gospel

Take advantage of the two questionnaires **An Aid in Understanding the Worldview of the Target Group** and **Barriers and Bridges to the Gospel**. Also organize the following chart: **Worldview Considerations Connected to Bible Stories**. This chart is helpful in considering elements that serve as bridges and barriers. (A useful rule of thumb is to list six stories that can make a connection to each major worldview issue that needs to be treated.)

WORLDVIEW CONSIDERATIONS CONNECTED TO BIBLE STORIES				
	Worldview Issue	Is it a Barrier?	Is it a Bridge?	Connecting Doctrinal Teaching	Useful Stories
1					
2					
3					
4					

What are some doctrines or subjects that the **Evangelistic Bible Storying Track** should emphasize? Mark those that you consider essential.			
God	Biblical promises	Two groups: saved / condemned	
Jesus Christ	Humanity's need for a Liberator, a Savior	Forgiveness	
Satan and Demons	Biblical commandments	Problems / suffering	
Humanity's inability to obey God's laws	Humanity's inability to please God through works	OTHERS:	
God's leadership	Discipline / punishment		

OBSERVATIONS:
1) A useful rule of thumb is to list six stories that can make a connection to each major worldview issue that needs to be treated.
2) Consider issues that need to be avoided until people are prepared to hear them. (Example: If people believe that only a felony is sin, avoid the story of Cain and Abel at the beginning of Storytelling.)
3) Consider controversial issues that need to be avoided until a relationship has been established between storyteller and listeners.
4) Consider issues that need to be emphasized strongly.
5) Consider time limitations. Will the planting, cultivating and harvesting keep the people unavailable to meet at certain times of the year? How many weeks will the people be available to meet before bad weather or the rainy season prevents their getting out? In an urban center, vacations and school activities prevent families from participating at certain times.

10. Considerations for organizing the Discipling Bible Storying Track

The Discipling Bible Storying Track is for new believers and Christians with little biblical knowledge. The Bible storyteller should consider the worldview of the new converts to Christianity. He should identify the barriers that hinder their being faithful disciples and the bridges that help them follow Jesus. Consider the Bible stories that tear down the barriers and those that take advantage of the bridges. Some of the Bible stories used in the Evangelistic Track need to be retold and others need to be included. Select stories that help the new converts to understand: the relationship of God with his people, the importance of obeying biblical teachings; conduct that Jesus expects from his followers, and God's plan for a local church.

What are some doctrines or subjects that the **Discipling Bible Storying Track** should emphasize? Mark those that you consider essential.			
God's relationship with his people	Biblical commands	Discipline	
Salvation	God's leadership	Problems / Suffering	
Certainty of salvation	The disciples' responsibilities	Family	
Faith	Walking in Jesus	Stewardship	
Holy Spirit	Biblical promises	Legalism combated	
Trinity	Church	OTHERS:	
Eternal life	How a local church functions		
The end times	Fellowship in the family of faith		
Two groups: Saved / Condemned	Failures of God's servants		

What are some capacities or abilities that a Christian should obtain during the **Discipling Bible Storying Track**? Mark those that you consider essential.			
Study the Bible	Evangelize	Discover spiritual gifts	
Pray	Teaching new converts	OTHERS:	
Be a godly husband/wife	Believe God's promises		
Be a godly father/mother	Obey biblical commands		

A useful rule of thumb is to list six stories that can make a connection to each major doctrine or ability that needs to be treated. A single story may be used to teach different truths or abilities.

11. Considerations for organizing the Leadership Equipping Bible Storying Track

	RESEARCH Do research to collect data about the leadership needs in the region where the churches are seeking to minister. Obtain information by interviewing church leaders from the target area and consulting statistical reports kept by denominational leadership.	
	Region or geographical area where the leaders are to receive training:	
1	Number of churches, mission congregations, preaching points and home Bible study groups. Include all groups who meet regularly for the purpose of Bible study and worship.	
2	Total number of church members in the region. Include the members from all the churches, mission congregations, preaching points and other groups who meet regularly.	
3	Average number of church members who congregate in groups who meet regularly. Divide the total number of members of local churches by the total number of mission congregations, preaching points, and other groups who meet regularly.	
4	Total number of Type 1 leaders in the region who need training. (Leaders of local churches or mission congregations.)	
5	Number of places that need to have planted new churches, mission congregations or preaching points.	
6	Number of Type 2 leaders that need training. (Leaders included in this category are those who are responsible for planting a new church, those who are leaders in a mission congregation or local church that is a distance from their home, those who are the leaders of a church without a pastor.) The present number of Type 2 leaders would be the number of churches without pastors, plus mission congregations, and preaching points led by lay leadership. Add to that total the number of places that need a new church or evangelistic outreach start. How many of that number will need training?	
7	Number of Type 3 leaders that need training. (Pastors of churches and missionary church planters.) Determine the number of those leaders who need training.	

Decide which type of leaders will be primarily trained in the **Leadership Equipping Bible Storying Track:**

_____Type 1: Leaders included in this category are the people that exercise functions within the local church such as: teaching, preaching, administration and evangelization. For example: Sunday School teachers, evangelists, outreach leaders, leaders of home Bible studies, deacons and church treasurers.

_____Type 2: Leaders included in this category are those who are responsible for evangelistic outreach projects, planting a new church, participating in the leadership of a mission congregation or local church that is a distance from their home, or the leadership of a church without a pastor. These are usually leaders who volunteer their time and do not receive a salary for their ministry.

_____Type 3: Leaders included in this category are pastors of churches and missionary church planters. They usually, are paid a salary by a church or denomination.

The time available for training by the trainers and students:							
If once a week, mark the best time:							
	Sunday	Monday	Tuesday	Wednesday	Thursday	Friday	Saturday
Morning							
Afternoon							
Night							
If other times would be better:							
	A weekend every three months in the city or region?						
	A one-week training time in the city or region?						
	A one-week training at a camp or retreat place during vacation time or when the season gives a break in the work schedule? The best time is:						
	Are there other possibilities for scheduling training?						

What are some doctrines or subjects that the **Leadership Equipping Bible Storying Track** should emphasize? Mark those that you consider essential.			
God	Church	The life and character of leaders	OTHERS:
Jesus Christ	Fellowship within the family of faith	Expectations of a leader	
Holy Spirit	Methods God uses to plant churches	Sanctification	
Trinity	Local church organization and function	Failures of God's servants	
Satan and demons	Methods God uses to grow disciples and churches	The relationship between God and his people	
Sin	How God sanctifies and matures his children	Forgiveness	
Salvation	Methods God uses to evangelize	Church discipline	
Security of the believer	Walking in Jesus	Stewardship	
Eternal life	Legalism combated	Family	
God's leadership	Problems / suffering	Biblical commands	
Leadership of the Holy Spirit	Discipline	Biblical promises	
Faith	The end times		

What are some capacities or abilities that a Christian should obtain during the **Leadership Equipping Bible Storying Track**? Mark those that you consider essential.			
Analyze a Bible story	Lead a home worship or Bible study	Administrate a church or mission congregation	OTHERS:
Tell a Bible story	Make visits	Plant a new church or mission congregation	
Teach a Bible study	Evangelize	Administrate church finances	
Preach	Instruct new converts	Choose qualified leaders	
Lead a worship service	Disciple a potential leader	Train leaders	
Lead a prayer meeting	Counsel with the Bible		

A useful rule of thumb is to list six stories that can make a connection to each major doctrine or ability that needs to be treated. A single story may be used to teach several different truths or skills.

Bible Storytelling Tools © Jackson Day

PANORAMIC VIEW OF THE BIBLE IN CHRONOLOGICAL ORDER

I have prepared three charts, one for the Old Testament and two for the New Testament, which list stories in chronological order. The list of stories within the charts are helpful in selecting the stories and keeping them in their chronological order.

It would also be helpful to refer to the **List of Bible Stories with References** and the **Chart of Bible Stories and Doctrinal Objectives** that comes at the end of this book.

A CHRONOLOGICAL VIEW OF THE OLD TESTAMENT

ADAM ? BC	NOAH 2500 BC	ABRAHAM 2000 BC	MOSES 1500 BC	DAVID 1000 BC			500 BC	EZRA, NEHEMIAH 400 BC
HISTORY OF THE OLD WORLD		HISTORY OF ISRAEL						
Pre-Flood	Post-Flood	The People — Patriarchs	The Land: Going to, conquering and living in the land	The Kingdom				The Remnant
				United	Divided 931 BC	Partial 722 BC	In Exile 586 BC	Remnant 516 BC
Creation	Noah	Abraham	Moses:	Saul	**ISRAEL: NORTH**	**ONLY JUDAH**	**IN BABYLON**	**RESTORATION OF JUDAH**
Adam and Eve	Flood	Lot	■40 years in Egypt ■Burning bush	David ■Goliath	Jeroboam	Hezekiah	Daniel	Ezra
Cain and Abel	Babel	Hagar and Ishmael	■10 plagues ■Passover ■Escape from Egypt ■Crossing the Red Sea	■Jonathan ■Bathsheba ■Absalom	Ahab and Jezebel	Josiah		Nehemiah
Lamech		Sodom	■Manna	Solomon				Esther
Seth and Enosh		Isaac	■Water from the Rock ■10 Commandments ■Golden Calf	■Wisdom ■Temple ■Wives	**JUDAH: SOUTH**			
Enoch		Jacob/Israel	■Tabernacle ■Spies' report		Rehoboam			
Methu-selah		Joseph	■Punishment of rebellious Israelites ■Moses' sin ■Bronze Snake ■Balak and Balaam		Joash			
					THE PROPHETS			
			Joshua					
			Judges: ■Gideon ■Samson		■Elijah ■Elisha ■Amos ■Hosea ■Jonah	Isaiah Jeremiah	Daniel Ezekiel	Malachi
			Ruth					
			Samuel					

Bible Storytelling Tools © Jackson Day

PERIODS IN THE LIFE OF JESUS CHRIST

BIRTH AND INFANCY	YEAR OF PREPARATION	YEAR OF POPULARITY	YEAR OF OPPOSITION	RESURRECTED LIFE

Announcement and birth of John
 	
Predictions of the birth of Jesus
 	
Birth of Jesus
■ Angels and shepherds
■ Baby Jesus in the Temple
■ Visit of wise men
■ Escape to Egypt
 	
The child Jesus in the Temple
	■ John the Baptist preaching
	
	■ Baptism of Jesus
	
	■ Temptation of Jesus
	
	■ "Jesus the Lamb of God," says John
	
	■ Jesus with Andrew, Simon Peter, Philip and Nathaniel
	
	■ The wedding at Cana
	
	■ Jesus cleansed the Temple
	
	■ Jesus with Nicodemus
	
	■ Jesus with Samaritan woman
	
	■ Healing the official's son
	
	■ Jesus expelled from Nazareth
		■ John the Baptist imprisoned
		■ Jesus called four fishermen
		■ Paralytic lowered from the roof
		■ Matthew called
		■ Jesus and the Sabbath
		  • Invalid cured by the pool of Bethesda
		  • The disciples pick and eat grain
		  • Man with shriveled hand cured
		
		■ Jesus chose 12 disciples
		■ Sermon on the Mount
		■ Faith of centurion
		■ Jesus raised widow's son
		■ John the Baptist questioned Jesus
		■ Jesus at Simon's home
		■ Parables about the Kingdom's growth
		■ Cure of demon-possessed
		■ John the Baptist's death
			■ Feeding of 5,000
			■ Jesus walked on water
			■ Jesus abandoned by many disciples
			■ Peter's confession
			■ Transfiguration
			■ Demon-possessed boy healed
			■ Man born blind was healed, and parable of Good Shepherd
			■ Jesus sent out 70
			■ Parable: Good Samaritan
			■ Martha and Mary visited
			■ The Pharisees' blasphemy
			■ Parables: Lost and Found
			■ Lazarus' resurrection
			■ Ten cured of leprosy
			■ Jesus blessed the children
			■ Rich young ruler
			■ John and James' request
			■ Jesus and Zacchaeus
			■ Parable: Ten Talents
			
			PASSION WEEK
			■ Triumphal entry
			■ Jesus cleansed Temple
			■ Three warning parables:
			  • Two Sons
			  • Evil Tenants
			  • Wedding Banquet
			■ Three questions to trap Jesus
			■ Prophetic sermon on Mt of Olives
			■ Mary anointed Jesus
			■ Judas' betrayal
			■ Passover meal; feet washed; Lord's Supper
			■ Sacerdotal prayer
			■ Gethsemane: Jesus prayed, was betrayed and arrested
			■ Judgment
			■ Crucifixion
				■ Resurrection
				  • Empty tomb
				  • Mary Magdalene
				  • Two disciples on Emmaus road
				  • Disciples without Thomas and with him
				
				■ Peter reinstated
				
				■ The Great Commission
				
				(Jesus appeared ten times after his resurrection and was seen by many for 40 days.)
				
				■ Ascension of Jesus

Bible Storytelling Tools © Jackson Day

ACTS							
1	3	6:8	9:32	13	16	18:23	21:18 28
Ascension Matthias replaced Judas Pentecost	■Beggar healed ■Peter spoke in Temple ■Peter and John before Sanhedrin ■Believers shared ■Ananias and Sapphira ■Apostles persecuted ■Seven chosen	■Stephen, the first martyr ■The church persecuted and scattered ■Saul's conversion	■Peter and Cornelius ■The church in Antioch ■Peter escaped from prison	**First missionary journey** ■Cyprus ■Pisidian, Antioch ■Iconium ■Lystra and Derbe; the crippled healed and Paul stoned. ■Return to Antioch ■Jerusalem council ■Disagreement between Paul and Barnabas	**Second missionary journey** ■Timothy joined Paul and Silas ■Macedonian vision ■Lydia ■Paul and Silas in prison ■Thessalonica ■Berea ■Athens ■Corinth	**Third missionary journey** ■Priscilla, Aquila and Apollos ■Paul in Ephesus; the riot ■Troas: Eutychus raised from the dead ■Paul's farewell to Ephesian elders ■Trip to Jerusalem ■In Jerusalem	**Paul, the prisoner** ■Arrested ■Before the crowd ■Before the Sanhedrin ■Plot to kill Paul ■Imprisoned in Caesarea ■Before Felix ■Before Festus ■Before Agrippa ■Trip to Rome ■In Rome

CONCLUSION:

This chapter should help you prepare a Bible Storying Track. While Storytelling uses the whole Bible, the storyteller does not need to narrate all the stories in the Bible. There are about two hundred well known stories, plus many lesser known ones. Your listeners can understand the Bible without hearing all the stories. The storyteller will select his own groups of Bible stories that vary according to the Storying Track he selects, his purpose for telling the stories, the local spiritual needs, the cultural background of his listeners, and the time available.

1. A **Storying Track** is a plan for selected stories to be told and possibly retold in chronological order to a specific group of people for a specific purpose, according to and depending upon the local background, biblical knowledge, culture, and spiritual needs of the listeners as well as the time available.

2. The storyteller must determine the kind of **Storying Track** that is most appropriate for his listeners and situation. Three examples of **Storying Tracks** are:

2.1 The **Multiple Storying Track** is a plan for a group of stories in chronological order to be retold or recycled to the same group of listeners for different purposes. A Multiple Storying Track is most useful for pre-literate tribal people and people groups hostile to Christianity.

2.2 The **Single Storying Track** is a group of Bible stories in chronological order that is presented once. With each story, truths are emphasized that connect with the needs of the listeners. A Single Storying Track is most useful for a literate people group familiar with Christianity.

2.3 **Fast-tracking** follows a plan to tell a group of stories in one setting with little exposition, for the purpose of giving a panoramic view of the Bible.

3. Regardless of the Storying Track used, the storyteller needs to consider the following criteria in selecting his stories:

3.1 Select the stories that give an overview of divine history in chronological order.

3.2 Include Bible stories that are essential to giving an understanding of the Gospel of Jesus Christ and to introducing important doctrinal concepts.

3.3 Consider the cultural, spiritual background and biblical knowledge of the listeners. Consider Bible stories that make a connection with the worldview of people in the target group.

3.4 Consider the time limits available to both the storyteller and his listeners. Then select and streamline the stories that can be used within the time frame. Synchronize the presentation of the stories with the agricultural season and weather in rural areas and the school term, holidays, and vacation time in an urban setting.

LIST OF BIBLE STORIES WITH REFERENCES
In Chronological Order

Suggested Stories for Multiple Storying Track Marked

The **List of Bible Stories with References** should help the storyteller find the text for a story in the Bible.

Suggested stories for the Multiple Storying Track are marked for those who decide to use the following tracks: Evangelistic Storying Track, Discipling Storying Track, and Leadership Equipping Bible Storying Track. It should also help the one who chooses to create his own Multiple Storying Track.

The storyteller will select his own groups of selected Bible stories that vary according to the Storying Track he selects, his purpose for telling the stories, the local spiritual needs, the cultural background of his listeners, and the time available. The stories marked for the Multiple Storying Track in the chart **List of Bible Stories with References** are given as suggestions.

List of Bible Stories with References	TEXT	Evangelistic Storying Track	Discipling Storying Track	Leadership Equipping Storying Track
1. Old Testament Stories				
Creation	Genesis 1, 2	X		
First Sin	3:1-24	X	X	
Cain and Abel	4:1-10	x		
Flood	6:1-9:17	X	X	
Tower of Babel	11:1-9		X	
God Calls Abram	12:1-5	X	X	
Abram and Lot Separate	13:1-13		X	
God's Covenant with Abram	15:1-21; 17:1-27; 18:1-15	X		X
Hagar and Ishmael	16:1-15; 21:8-20			X
Sodom and Gomorrah Destroyed, Lot after Sodom	18:16- 19:38		X	
Isaac's Birth - Abraham Tested, Rebekah	21-24		X	X
Jacob, Esau, and Laban	26 -31	X		X
Joseph the Slave	37 - 41	X		X
Joseph Governor in Egypt	41:41 - 45		X	X
Jacob and Family in Egypt	46 - 50	X		
Joseph Forgives His Brothers	45:1-15; 50:15-21		X	
Moses' Birth, Moses the Young Man	Exodus 1 - 2	X		X
God Calls Moses to Return to Egypt	3:1 - 4:31			X
Moses and Pharaoh, Plagues 1-9	5 - 10	X		X
Passover and Exodus from Egypt	11- 12	X	X	
Crossing the Sea	13:17 - 14:31	X	X	
Bitter Water	15:22-27		X	
God Provides Manna, Quail and Water	16 - 17	X	X	
War Against the Amalekites	17:8-16		X	
Jethro Counsels Moses	18:1-27			X
Mount Sinai, the Ten Commandments	19 - 20	X	X	
Golden Calf	32:1-35	X	X	X
Making the Tabernacle	35 - 40		X	
Death of Nadab and Abihu	Leviticus 10:1-5			X
Miriam and Aaron Oppose Moses	Numbers 12			X
Spies with Little Faith	13:1-2, 17-33	X	X	X
Israelites Murmur, must Wander in the Desert	14:1-45	X	X	
Budding of Aaron's Staff	17			X
Moses Strikes the Rock at Meribah	20:2-13		X	X
Bronze Snake	21:4-9	X	X	

Bible Storytelling Tools © Jackson Day

List of Bible Stories with References	TEXT	Evangelistic Storying Track	Discipling Storying Track	Leadership Equipping Storying Track
Balaam and the Speaking Donkey	22 - 24			X
Worship of Baal, Peor and the Zeal of Phinehas	25:1-18	X		X
Midianites Destroyed, the Transjordan Tribes	31 - 32		X	
Joshua Replaces Moses	Joshua 1:1-9	X		X
Rahab and the Spies in Jericho	2:		X	
Crossing the Jordan	3 - 4	X		
Conquest of Jericho	6:1-27	X	X	
Achan's Sin	7:1-26		X	
Joshua Deceived by the Gibeonites	9:1-26			X
Victories of Joshua	10 - 12			
Joshua's Farewell	23 -24		X	X
Israelites Abandon God	Judges 2:6 - 3:6	X	X	
Deborah and Barak	4 - 5			X
Gideon	6 - 8		X	X
Samson	13 -16			X
Ruth	Ruth 1 - 4		X	
Hannah's Prayer and Samuel's Birth	1 Samuel 1:1 - 2::11		X	
Eli and His Sons	2:12-36; 4:12-22			X
God Speaks to the Boy Samuel	3:1-14		X	X
Philistines and the Ark of the Covenant	4:1 - 7:1			
Samuel Governs Israel	7:2-17	X		X
Saul Becomes King	8 - 11	X	X	
Samuel's Farewell Speech	12			X
Saul's Mistakes	13 - 15; 28, 31	X	X	X
Samuel Anoints David; David in Saul's Service	16:1-23		X	
David and Goliath	17:1-54	X		
David and Jonathan	1 Sam 18:1-5; 20:1-43; 2 Sam 9		X	
David Fleeing from Saul	1 Sam 19 - 31	X	X	X
David Becomes King	2 Samuel 1 - 5	X		X
God's Covenant with David	7:1-29	X		X
David's Victories	5, 8, 10		X	
David's Sin with Bathsheba; David Rebuked by Nathan	11, 12	X	X	X
Amnon and Tamar	13:1-22		X	
Absalom	13:23 - 19:43	X		X
Solomon Becomes King	1 Kings 1 - 2	X	X	X
Solomon's Wisdom	3:1-28; 10:1-13		X	X
Solomon Builds the Temple	5:13 - 8:66		X	
Solomon: Faithful to God	1 - 10		X	X
Solomon: Unfaithful to God	11:1-43	X	X	X
Division of the Kingdom: Judah and Israel	12:1-24	X		X
Idolatry of King Jeroboam in Israel	12:16-33	X		X
Prophet Elijah; King Ahab and Queen Jezebel	1 Kn 17 - 22; 2 Kn 9:30-37	X		X
Elijah and Baal's Prophets on Mount Carmel	1 Kn 18:17-46	X		X
Elijah Flees Jezebel; Mt Horeb; Call of Elisha	19:1-21			X
Ahab Takes Naboth's Vineyard	21:1-29		X	
Soldiers Killed by Fire	2 Kings 1:1-16			
Elijah Taken to Heaven	2:1-18			X
Prophet Elisha	1 Kn 19:19-21; 2 Kn 2 - 13		X	X
Elisha Purifies Water	2 Kn 2:19-22			
Elisha Multiplies the Widow's Oil	4:1-7		X	
Elisha Restores a Boy to Life	4:8-37		X	
Naaman Healed of Leprosy	5:1-27		X	X

List of Bible Stories with References	TEXT	Evangelistic Storying Track	Discipling Storying Track	Leadership Equipping Storying Track
Elisha Makes an Axhead Float	6:1-7			
Jonah	Jonah 1 - 4	X		X
Fall of Israel	2 Kings 17:1-41	X		
King Hezekiah of Judah	18:13- 20:21			X
Isaiah's Vision and Vocation	Isaiah 6:1-9		X	X
King Josiah of Judah	2 Kings 22:23-30			X
Conquest of Judah; Exile into Babylon	2 Kn 24:18 - 25:22	X		
Daniel's Education	Daniel 1:1-21		X	X
King Nebuchadnezzar's Dream; Daniel Interprets the Dream	2			X
Daniel's Friends; the Image of Gold and the Fiery Furnace	3:1-31		X	X
King Nebuchadnezzar Lives as a Wild Animal	4:1-37			X
Writing on the Wall	5:1-30			X
Daniel in the Lions' Den	6:1-28		X	X
Ezra: Exiles Return to Jerusalem; Rebuilding the Temple	Ezra 1 - 10	X	X	X
Nehemiah: Rebuilding the Walls for Jerusalem	Nehemiah 1 - 13			X
Esther	Esther 1 - 10		X	
2. Stories from the Life of Jesus				
2.1 Jesus' Birth and Childhood				
Birth of John the Baptist Foretold	Lk 1:5-25		X	
Mary Foretold Jesus' Birth	Lk 1:26-38	X		
Mary Visits Elizabeth	Lk 1:39-56		X	
Joseph Foretold of Jesus' Birth	Mt 1:18-25	X	X	
Birth of John the Baptist	Lk 1:57-80	X		
Birth of Jesus Christ	Lk 2:1-7	X	X	
Shepherds of Bethlehem	Lk 2:8-20	X		
Jesus Presented in the Temple	Lk 2:22-38		X	
Visit of the Wise Men	Mt 2:1-12	X		X
Escape to Egypt; Childhood in Nazareth	Mt 2:13-18	X		
Boy Jesus at the Temple	Lk 2:41-50		X	
2.2 First Year of Public Ministry; the Year of Preparation				
John the Baptist Prepares for Jesus	Mt 3:1-11; Lk 3:1-18	X		X
Baptism of Jesus	Mt 3:13-17	X	X	
Temptation of Jesus	Mt 4:1-11; Lk 4:1-13	X	X	X
First Disciples	Jn 1:29-51		X	X
Water Transformed into Wine	Jn 2:1-11		X	
First Cleansing of the Temple	Jn 2:13-22		X	
Jesus with Nicodemus	Jn 3:1-21	X	X	
Jesus with the Samaritan Woman	Jn 4:4-42		X	
Jesus Heals the Official's Son from a Distance	Jn 4:46-54			
2.3 Second Year of Public Ministry; the Year of Popularity				
John the Baptist Imprisoned; Jesus Preaches in Galilee	Mt 4:12-17	X		X
Jesus Rejected at Nazareth	Lk 4:16-30			X
Jesus Calls Four Fishermen	Mt 4:18-22; Lk 5:1-11		X	
Simon Peter's Mother-in-law Healed	Mk 1:29-33			
Calling of Matthew/Levi	Mt 9:9-13; Lk 5:27-32		X	
Parables in Defense of His Disciples Who Did Not Fast	Mt 9:14-17; Mk 2:18-22; Lk 5:33-39			X
Healing of the Invalid at Pool on Sabbath	Jn 5:1-47		X	
Jesus Defends His Disciples Who Picked Grain on the Sabbath	Mt 12:1-8; Mk 2:23-28; Lk 6:1-5		X	
Jesus Heals a Man with a Shriveled Hand on the Sabbath	Mt 12:9-14; Mk 3:1-6; Lk 6:6-11		X	
Jesus Selects Twelve Disciples	Mk 3:13-19; Lk 6:12-16	X	X	X
Sermon on the Mountain	Mt 5, 6, 7	X	X	X
Centurion's Faith; His Servant Healed	Mt 8:5-13; Lk 7:1-10		X	

List of Bible Stories with References	TEXT	Evangelistic Storying Track	Discipling Storying Track	Leadership Equipping Storying Track
Jesus Restores the Widow's Son O Life	Lk 7:11-17		X	
John the Baptist Asks; Jesus Answers	Mt 11:1-19; Lk 7:18-35		X	X
Sinful Woman Anoints Jesus; Parable: Two Debtors	Lk 7:36-50		X	X
Blasphemy of the Pharisees; Unforgivable Sin	Mt 12:22-37; Mk 3:20-30		X	X
Jesus' Mother and Brothers	Mk 3:21, 31-34		X	
Parables about Growth in the Kingdom of God	Mt 13:3-53; Mk 4:3-34; Lk 8:5-25		X	
Jesus Calms Storm on a Lake	Mt 8:23-27; Mk 4:35-41; Lk 8:22-25		X	
Healing of Two Demon-possessed Men	Mt 8:28-34; Mk 5:1-20; Lk 8:26-39		X	
Dead Girl Resurrected; Sick Woman Healed	Mt 9:18-26; Mk 5:21-43; Lk 8:40-56			
Jesus Instructs and Sends out the Twelve	Mt 10:1-16; Mk 6:7-13; Lk 9:1-6		X	X
Herod Kills John the Baptist	Mt 14:1-12; Mk 6:14-29	X		X
2.4 Third Year of Public Ministry; the Year of Opposition				
2.4.1 Semester of Retreats; a Time of Special Instruction for the Twelve				
5,000 Fed from Five Loaves and Two Fish	Mk 6:34-44; Jn 6:4-14	X		
Jesus Walks on Water	Mk 6:47-52; Jn 6:16-21	X		X
Jesus the Bread of Life; Many Disciples Desert Him	Jn 6:25-71	X		X
Jesus Disputes with the Pharisees about Traditions	Mt 15:1-20; Mk 7:1-23		X	
Daughter of a Syrophoenician Woman Healed	Mt 15:21-28; Mk 7:24-30			
4,000 Fed	Mt 15:32-39; Mk 8:1-10			
Blind Cured	Mk 8:22-26			
Pharisees and Sadducees Demand a Sign	Mt 15:39 - 16:4			X
Peter's Confession	Mt 16:13-20; Mk 8:27-30; Lk 9:18-20	X		X
Jesus Predicts His Death; Peter's Reprimand	Mt 16:21-28; Mk 8:31-9:1; Lk 9:22-27	X		X
Transfiguration	Mt 17:1-13; Mk 9:2-13; Lk 9:28-36	X	X	X
Demon-possessed Boy Healed	Mt 17:14-21; Mk 9:14-29; Lk 9:37-43		X	
Temple Tax; Coin in the Fish's Mouth	Mt 17:24-27			
Greatest in the Kingdom of Heaven	Mt 18:1-35; Mk 9:33-50		X	X
The Cost of Following Jesus	Mt 18:19-22; Lk 9:57-62	X	X	
2.4.2 Semester of Encounters in Jerusalem				
Jesus Rejects Advice from His Unbelieving Brothers	Jn 7:1-10			X
Rejection in a Samaritan Village	Lk 9:51-56			X
Jesus at the Feast of Tabernacles	Jn 7:11-52		X	
An Adulteress Brought to Jesus for Judgment	Jn 8:1-11	X		
Jesus Argues with Pharisees about Validity of His Testimony	Jn 8:12-58			X
Man Born Blind Healed on Sabbath; Parable of Good Shepherd	Jn 9:1 - 10:21		X	X
Mission of the Seventy	Lk 10:1-24			X
Parable: Good Samaritan	Lk 10:25-37		X	X
Martha and Mary Visited	Lk 10:38-41		X	
Jesus Accused of Being in League with Beelzebub	Lk 11:14-36			X
Jesus Pronounces Six Woes on Pharisees	Lk 11:37-54			X
Parable: Rich Fool	Lk 12:16-21		X	
Crippled Woman Healed on Sabbath	Lk 13:10-17	X		
Jesus at Feast of Dedication; Unbelief of the Jews	Jn 10:22-42			
At Pharisee's House; Parables: Honor, Great Banquet	Lk 14:1-24		X	
Cost of Being a Disciple	Lk 14:15-35	X	X	
Parables: Things Lost and Found– Sheep, Coin, and Son	Lk 15:1-31	X		
Parables on Stewardship: Unjust Steward; Rich Man and Lazarus	Lk 16		X	
Teaching and Parable: Sin and Forgiveness	Lk 17:1-10		X	
Lazarus Raised from Dead	Jn 11:1-44	X		X
Ten Healed of Leprosy; Grateful Samaritan	Lk 17:11-19		X	
Parables on Prayer: Persistent Widow; Pharisee and Publican	Lk 18:19-14		X	

List of Bible Stories with References	TEXT	Evangelistic Storying Track	Discipling Storying Track	Leadership Equipping Storying Track
Jesus Teaches Concerning Divorce	Mt 19:1-12; Mk 10:1-12		X	
Jesus and the Little Children	Mt 19:13-15; Mk 10:13-16; Lk 18:15-17		X	
Rich Young Ruler	Mt 19:16-29; Mk 10:17-31; Lk 18:18-30		X	
Parable: Workers in the Vineyard	Mt 20:1-16		X	
Selfish Request of James and John	Mt 20:20-28; Mk 35-45		X	X
Blind Bartimaeus and Companion Healed	Mt 20:29-34; Mk.10:46-52; Lk 18:35-43	X		
Jesus and Zacchaeus	Lk 19:1-10	X		
Parable: 10 Minas of Gold	Lk 19:11-27		X	
2.4.3 Holy Week				
Triumphal Entry into Jerusalem	Mt 21:1-17; Mk 11:1-11 Lk 19:29-44	X		
Barren Fig Tree Cursed	Mt 21:18-22; Mk 11:12-14, 20-24		X	
Cleansing of Temple	Mt 21:15-17; Mk 11:15-18; Lk 19:45-48	X		X
Greeks Desire to See Jesus	Jn 12:20-50		X	
Parables: Two Sons: Wicked Husbandmen; Marriage Feast of King's Son	Mt 21:28-22:14; Mk 11:27-12:12; Lk 20:1-19		X	
Three Ensnaring Questions: Tribute to Caesar; Resurrection; Great Commandment	Mt 22:15-40; Mk 12:13-34; Lk 20:20-40		X	
Jesus Gives Examples of Hypocrisy	Mt 23:13-36		X	X
Prophetic Words Spoken on Mt. of Olives	Mt 24:1 - 25:46		X	
Parables: 10 Virgins; Talents; Separation of Sheep from Goats	Mt 25:1-46		X	
Mary Anoints Jesus at Bethany	Mt 26:6-13; Jn 12:1-11	X		X
Judas Bargains with Rulers to Betray Jesus	Mt 26:14-16; Mk 14:10-11; Lk 22:3-6	X		
Passover Meal	Mt 26:17-25; Mk 14:12-17; Lk 22:7-30		X	
Jesus Washes Disciples' Feet	Jn 13:1-17		X	X
Jesus Predicts Judas' Betrayal and Peter's Denial	Mt 26:21-35; Mk 14:18-31; Jn 13:21-38	X		
Lord's Supper Instituted	Mt 26:26-29; Mk 14:22-25; Lk 22:17-23; 1 Cor 11:23-26	X	X	
Jesus' Farewell Discourse	Jn 14, 15, 16		X	
Jesus' Intercessory Prayer	Jn 17		X	X
In Gethsemane: Jesus Prays and Is Arrested	Mt 26:36-56; Mk 14: 32-52; Lk 22:39-53	X		X
Peter Denies His Lord	Mt 26:69-75; Mk 14: 66-72; Jn 18:15-27	X	X	X
Jesus' Judgments	Mk 26:57- 27: 31; Mk 14:53 - 15:20; Lk 22:63 - 23:25; Jn 18:12- 19: 16	X		X
Jesus' Crucifixion, Death, Burial, and Guards at Tomb	Mt 27:32-65; Mk 15:21-46; Lk 23:26-56; Jn 19:17-42	X	X	X
2.5 Resurrected Life of Jesus				
Resurrection	Mt 28:1-15; Mk 16; Lk 24:1-12	X	X	X
Jesus with Mary Magdalene	Jn 20:11-17	X		
Jesus with Two Disciples on Road to Emmaus	Lk 24:13-31		X	
Jesus Appears to Disciples with Thomas Absent	Lk 24: 36-43; Jn 20:19-25	X		
Jesus Appears to the Disciples with Thomas Present	Jn 20:26-31	X		X
Miraculous Catch of Fish; Peter Reinstated	Jn 21:1-24	X		X
Great Commission	Mt 28:16-20; Mk 16:15-18; Ac 1:6-8	X	X	X
Last Appearance and Ascension	Lk 24:44-53; Ac 1:9-12	X	X	X
Second Coming of Jesus	Mt 24:27-31; Ac 1:10-11; Rev 1:7-8	X	X	X
3. Events in the Life of the Early Church				
Holy Spirit Comes at Pentecost	Acts 2:1-13	X	X	X
Peter's Message	2:14-40	X	X	X
First Converts	2:37-45	X		X
Crippled Beggar Healed	3:1-10		X	
Peter and John Before the Sanhedrin	4:1-21		X	X
Believers Share Possessions	4:32-37		X	
Ananias and Sapphira	5:1-11		X	
Seven Helpers Chosen	6:1-7		X	X

List of Bible Stories with References	TEXT	Evangelistic Storying Track	Discipling Storying Track	Leadership Equipping Storying Track
Stephen: Seized; Tried; and Stoned	6:8 - 7:66		X	X
Philip, the Evangelist	8:4-40		X	X
Saul's Conversion	9:1-18		X	
Dorcas Restored to Life	9:36-43		X	
Peter and Cornelius	10:1 - 11:18		X	X
Church in Antioch Begins	11:19-30		X	
Peter Liberated from Prison	12:1-18		X	
First Missionaries: Barnabas and Saul	13:1-4			X
In Lystra: Crippled Healed; Paul Stoned	14:8-20			X
Council at Jerusalem	15:1-21	X		X
Paul and Barnabas Separate	15:36-41			X
Vision of Man from Macedonia	16:6-10			X
In Philipi: Conversions and Prison	16:11-46	X		
Paul in Athens	17:16-34	X		
In Ephesus: Apollos; Paul Teaches; Miracles; Riot	18:18 - 19:41	X		
Youth Falls from Window	20:7-12	X		
Paul's Farewell to Ephesian Leaders	20:13-36			X
Paul Arrested in Temple	21:27-36	X		
Paul Defends Himself	21:39 - 23:11	X		
Paul Before King Agrippa	25:13-32	X		
Paul in Storm at Sea	27:13-44	X		X
Paul Preaches at Rome under Guard	28:11-30	X		
Paul's Message	1 Cor 2:1-5		X	X
Division in Church at Corinth	1 Cor 1:1-17		X	X
Paul Opposes Peter at Antioch	Gal 2:11-14		X	X
Paul's Struggles for Church	Col 1:24 - 2:5		X	X

LIST OF MIRACLES
In Chronological Order

1. MIRACLES IN THE OLD TESTAMENT
Miracles in the Old Testament are grouped in three distinct time periods.

1.1 The Liberating of the People of God from Egypt and Their Establishment in Canaan

Ten Plagues	Exodus 7-12
Crossing the Red Sea	Ex 14:21-31
Bitter Waters at Marah Transformed	Ex 15:22-27
God Sends Manna	Ex 16:1-36
Water from the Rock at Rephidim	Ex 17:1-7
The Death of Nadab and Abihu	Leviticus 10:1-5
The Budding of Aaron's Staff	Numbers 17
Balaam and the Talking Donkey	Num 22:22-35
Crossing through the Jordan River	Joshua 3:14-17
Sun Stands Still	Jos 10:1-14

1.2 The Conflict Against Pagan Religions, Led by Elijah and Elisha

Elijah and the Drought	1 Kings 17:1-7
Elijah and the Widow at Zarephath	1 Kin 17:8-24
Elijah and Prophets of Baal on Mount Carmel	1 Kin 18:1-46
Soldiers Killed by Fire from Heaven	2 Kings 1:1-18
Elijah Taken up to Heaven in a Chariot of Fire	2 Kin 2:1-18
Water is Purified by Elisha	2 Kin 2:19-22
Elisha Multiplied Oil for Widow	2 Kin 4:1-7
Elisha Restored Shunammite's Son to Life	2 Kin 4:8-37
Naaman Healed of Leprosy	2 Kin 5:1-19
Elisha Makes an Ax-head Float	2 Kin 6:1-7
Jonah and the Fish	Jonah 1:15-2:10

1.3 The Time of Daniel, During the Exile in Babylon, When the Superiority of God Eternal above Other Gods, and the Faithfulness of Daniel and His Friends Was Vindicated

The Faithful Servants of God in Fiery Furnace	Daniel 3:1-31
Daniel in Lions' Den	Dan 6:1-28

2. MIRACLES IN THE NEW TESTAMENT

2.1 THE MIRACLES OF JESUS IN CHRONOLOGICAL ORDER

2.1.1 Miracles Performed During the First Year of Ministry

Water Transformed into Wine	Jn 2:1-11
Official's Son Cured from a Distance	Jn 4:46-54

2.1.2 Miracles Performed During the Second Year of Ministry

First Miraculous Catch of Fish	Lk 5:3-11
Jesus Drove Out an Evil Spirit at Capernaum	Mk 1:23-26; Lk 4:33-35
Peter's Mother-in-law Healed	Mt 8:14-15; Mk 1:30-31; Lk 4:38-39
Man with Leprosy Touched and Healed	Mt 8:2-4; Mk 1:40-45; Lk 5:12-15
Paralytic Lowered through the Roof	Mt 9:1-8; Mk 2:1-12; Lk 5:17-26
Invalid Cured on Sabbath at Pool	Jn 5:1-9
Man with a Shriveled Hand Cured on Sabbath	Mt 12:9-14; Mk 3:1-6; Lk 6:6-11
Centurion's Servant Healed	Mt 8:5-13; Lk 7:1-10
Jesus Restored Widow's Son to Life	Lk 7:11-17
Blind, Mute Demon-possessed Man Healed	Mt 12:22-37; Mk 3:12-30
Jesus Calmed Storm at Sea	Mt 8:23-27; Mk 4:35-41; Lk 8:26-30
Demon-possessed Man Healed and Pigs Drowned	Mt 8:28-34; Mk 5:1-20; Lk 8:26-39
Bleeding Woman Healed	Mt 9:20-22; Mk 5:23-34; Lk 8:43-48
Jairus' Daughter Restored to Life	Mt 9:18-34; Mk 5:21-24, 35-43; Lk 8:40-56
Two Blind Men Healed	Mt 9:27-31
Mute Demon-possessed Man Healed	Mt 9:32-33

2.1.3 Miracles Performed During the Third Year of Ministry

Five Thousand Fed	Mt 14:14-21; Mk 6:30-44; Lk 9:10-17; Jn 6:1-14
Jesus Walked on Water	Mt 14:24-33; Mk 6:47-52; Jn 6:15-21
Daughter of Syrophoenician Woman Healed	Mt 15:27-28; Mk 7:24-30
Deaf and Mute Man Healed	Mk 7:31-37
Four Thousand Fed	Mt 15:32-38; Mk 8:1-9
Blind Man at Bethsaida Healed	Mk 8:22-26
Demon-possessed Boy Healed	Mt 17:14-20; Mk 9:14-29; Lk 9:37-43
Coin in Mouth of a Fish	Mt 17:12-27
Man Who Was Born Blind Healed	Jn 9:1-41
Crippled Woman Healed on Sabbath	Lk 13:10-21
Man with Dropsy Healed on Sabbath	Lk 14:1-4
Jesus Raised Lazarus from the Dead	Jn 11:1-44
Ten Healed of Leprosy	Lk 17:11-19
Blind Bartimaeus and Companion Received Sight	Mt 20:29-34; Mk 10:45-52; Lk 18:35-43
Fig Tree Cursed and Withered	Mt 21:18-19; Mk 11:12-14
Malchus' Cut-off Ear Restored	Lk 22:49-51; Jn 18:10-11

2.1.4 Miracle Performed During Jesus' Resurrected Life

Second Miraculous Catch of Fish	Jn 21:5-11

2.2 Miracles Performed During the Time of the Early Church

Peter Healed Crippled Beggar	Acts 3:1-10
Ananias and Sapphira	Ac 5:1-11
Peter Healed Aeneas, a Paralytic	Ac 9:32-36
Peter Restored Dorcas to Life	Ac 9:37-43
Peter's Miraculous Release from Prison	Ac 12:6-19
Paul Healed Crippled Man in Lystra	Ac 14:8-11
Demon-possessed Fortune-teller Cured	Ac 16:16-18
Paul and Silas Released from Prison by Earthquake	Ac 16:19-34
Handkerchiefs from Paul Cured Sick	Ac 19:11-12
Youth Who Fell from Window Restored to Life	Ac 20:7-12

LIST OF JESUS' PARABLES

1. The Conflict of the New and the Old (First Year of Ministry)

Guest of the Bridegroom	Mt 9:14-15; Mk 2:18-20; Lk 5:33-35
New Patch and Old Garment	Mt 9:16; Mk 2:21; Lk 5:36
New Wine and Old Wineskin	Mt 9:17; Mk 2:22; Lk 5:37-39
Treasures, New and Old	Mt 13:51-52

2. Wisdom is Proved by Action (Second Year of Ministry)

Children at Play	Mt 11:16-19; Lk 7:31-35
Wise and Foolish Builders	Mt 7:24-27; Lk 6:46-49

3. Nature and Development of the Kingdom (Third Year of Ministry)

Sower and the Soils	Mt 13:3-8; Mk 4:4-8; Lk 8:5-8
Weeds Sowed Among Wheat	Mt 13:24-30, 36-43
Mustard Seed	Mt 13:31-32; Mk 4:30-32; Lk 13:18-19
Yeast	Mt 13:33; Lk 13:20-21
Hidden Treasure	Mt 13:44
Pearl of Great Value	Mt 13:45-46
Net that Caught All Kinds of Fish	Mt 13:47-50
Growing Seed: Spontaneous Growth	Mk 4:26-29

4. Counting the Cost of Discipleship

Empty House (Second Year of Ministry)	Mt 12:43-45
Uncompleted Tower (Third Year of Ministry)	Lk 14:25-30
King's Rash Warfare (Third Year of Ministry)	Lk 14:31-33

5. Forgiven and Forgiving

Two Debtors (Second Year of Ministry)	Lk 7:36-43
Unmerciful Debtor (Third Year of Ministry)	Mt 18:23-25

6. Prayer (Third Year of Ministry)
Persistent Friend at Midnight .... Lk 11:5-8
Persistent Widow .... Lk 18:1-8

7. Love for One's Neighbor (Third Year of Ministry)
Good Samaritan .... Lk 10:30-37

8. Humility (Third Year of Ministry)
Chief Seats .... Lk 14:7-11
Pharisee and Tax Collector .... Lk 18:9-14

9. Resourcefulness and Foresight (Second Year of Ministry)
Unjust Steward .... Lk 16:1-9

10. Worldly Riches (Second Year of Ministry)
Rich Fool .... Lk 12:16-21
Great Banquet .... Lk 14:16-24
Rich Man and Beggar .... Lk 16:19-31

11. Lost and Found (Third Year of Ministry)
Lost Sheep .... Mt 18:12-14; Lk 15:3-7
Lost Coin .... Lk 15:8-10
Prodigal Son .... Lk 15:11-24
Elder Son Remained Outside the Party .... Lk 15:25-31

12. Service and Reward (Third Year of Ministry)
Workers in Vineyard .... Mt 20:1-16
Talents (Passion Week) .... Mt 25:14-30
Ten Minas of Gold .... Lk 19:11-27
Unworthy Servants .... Lk 17:7-10

13. Watching for the Return of Jesus (Third Year of Ministry; Passion Week)
Ten Virgins: Wise and Foolish Bridesmaids .... Mt 25:1-13
Faithful and Unfaithful Servant .... Mt 24:45-51; Lk 12:41-48
Watchful Door Keeper .... Mk 13:32-37

14. The Kingdom and Judgment (Third Year of Ministry; Passion Week)
Two Sons .... Mt 21:28-32
Evil Tenants .... Mt 21:33-34; Mk 12:1-12; Lk 20:9-18
Unproductive Fig Tree .... Lk 13:6-9
Rejected Cornerstone .... Mt 21:42-45
Wedding Banquet of King's Son .... Mt 22:1-14
Separating Sheep from Goats .... Mt 25:14-46

Bible Storytelling Tools © Jackson Day

CHART OF BIBLE STORIES AND DOCTRINAL OBJECTIVES

The left side of the chart has a list of stories that I, the author of this book, consider to be some of the most important. The top of the chart has a list of doctrinal objectives, or important subjects.

The chart is useful to help one to study either a Bible story or a topic that is a doctrinal objective.

Example of using the CHART to discover doctrinal objectives within a Bible story:

Look at the Bible story: "Creation." Notice the **X** marks in the cells that relate to the doctrinal objectives. The story of the Creation can teach lessons related to the following doctrinal objectives:
- God the Father;
- Jesus Christ;
- Trinity;
- Characteristic of God;
- Family;
- Faith;
- Stewardship;
- Christian responsibility.

Example of using the CHART to discover the Bible stories that relate to a certain doctrinal objective:

A preacher wishes to use the chart for a specific situation. A church member sinned, and the preacher wishes to convince both the backslider and the church that a servant of God can fall into sin and recover to serve God again. The preacher discovers in the Doctrinal Objectives the column: "Christian in Sin," and he finds the following Bible stories that relate to the doctrine:
- Flood;
- Abraham;
- Jacob;
- Israel in the Desert;
- Moses Strikes the Rock at Meribah;
- David;
- Solomon;
- Elijah;
- Jonah;
- Ezra: Exiles Return to Jerusalem;
- Nehemiah;
- Jesus Calms Storm on a Lake;
- Demon-Possessed Boy Healed;
- Selfish Request of James and John;
- In Gethsemane: Jesus Prays and is Arrested;
- Peter Denies His Lord;
- Jesus' Appearances;
- Ananias and Sapphira;
- Seven Helpers Chosen;
- Peter and Cornelius;
- First Missionary Trip: Barnabas and Saul/Paul (John Mark);
- Paul Opposes Peter at Antioch.

The preacher who has as his doctrinal objective to show that a servant of God can fail and recover to serve God again will find several of the above stories helpful in reaching his objective.

The chart is useful to help one to study either a Bible story or to discover Bible stories that relate to a specific doctrinal objective.

Chart of Bible Stories and Doctrinal Objectives — Old Testament

Story	God the Father	Jesus Christ	Holy Spirit	Trinity	Characteristics	Savior verses Punisher	Satan and Demons	False Prophets	Problems and Suffering	Temptation	Sin	Idolatry	Consequences of Sin	Sinful Humanity	Conversion	Repentance	Decision Made	Called by God	Saved verses Condemned	God and His People	God and Leaders	Liberation / Salvation	Worship	Sanctification	Family	Employer / Employee	Government / Citizen	Christian / Non-Christian	Christian / Christian	Faith	Christian Service	Stewardship	Christian Responsibility	Walk with God	Devotional Life	Evangelism	Christian in Sin	Forgiveness	Overcoming Past Sins	Combating Legalism	Church	Last Things
Creation	X	X		X	X		X		X	X	X		X	X			X								X					X		X	X									
First Sin	X					X			X	X			X	X			X		X			X	X												X				X			
Cain and Abel	X					X					X		X	X				X	X				X		X									X	X		X					
Flood	X				X	X			X				X					X	X		X		X							X		X		X	X		X		X			
Abraham	X					X			X	X	X						X	X	X		X	X			X	X				X				X	X		X	X				
Jacob	X				X				X									X	X		X				X	X				X				X	X							
Joseph	X		X			X			X				X						X	X			X	X	X		X							X	X							
Moses and Pharaoh	X				X	X				X		X	X		X	X	X			X	X	X		X									X	X								
Exodus	X				X	X					X	X	X							X	X	X	X	X							X		X	X								
Ten Commandments	X		X									X				X				X		X	X											X								
Israel in the Desert							X		X	X	X	X	X	X						X	X	X									X			X								
Moses Strikes the Rock at Meribah										X			X				X		X		X																					
Bronze Snake		X										X	X							X		X																				
Joshua																		X	X	X	X		X											X	X							
Judges								X				X	X			X		X		X	X																					
Ruth									X											X					X						X											
Samuel			X					X				X	X					X		X	X			X	X										X							
Saul											X	X	X					X			X																X					
David					X	X			X		X		X	X		X	X	X	X	X	X		X	X	X					X				X	X	X	X	X	X			
Solomon												X						X		X	X						X								X							
Division of the Kingdom: Judah and Israel								X				X									X						X															
Elijah; King Ahab and Queen Jezebel								X	X			X	X							X	X					X	X	X						X			X					
Elisha									X												X						X															
Naaman Healed of Leprosy		X																									X	X		X						X	X					
Jonah														X				X				X						X								X				X		
Fall of Israel								X				X	X						X	X																						
King Hezekiah and Josiah of Judah	X				X	X						X									X		X				X							X	X		X					
Isaiah		X						X			X	X	X					X									X															X
Conquest of Judah; Exile into Babylon	X							X	X			X	X											X										X	X							
Daniel									X			X									X		X		X		X	X		X				X					X			
Ezra: Exiles Return to Jerusalem												X				X				X			X	X			X	X		X		X	X	X	X				X			
Nehemiah																X	X						X	X			X	X				X	X	X	X				X			
Esther									X								X			X				X	X		X	X					X									

Bible Storytelling Tools © Jackson Day

Chart of Bible Stories and Doctrinal Objectives

New Testament

	GOD	God the Father	Jesus Christ	Holy Spirit	Trinity	Characteristics	Savior verses Punisher	PROBLEM OF EVIL	Satan and Demons	False Prophets	Problems and Suffering	Temptation	Sin	Idolatry	Consequences of Sin	HUMANITY	Sinful Humanity	Conversion	Repentance	Decision Made	Called by God	RELATIONSHIP WITH GOD	Saved verses Condemned	God and His People	God and Leaders	Liberation / Salvation	Worship	Santification	RELATIONSHIPS	Family	Employer / Employee	Government / Citizen	Christian / Non-Christian	Christian / Christian	CHRISTIAN LIFE	Faith	Christian Service	Stewardship	Christian Responsibility	Walk with God	Devotional Life	Evangelism	Christian in Sin	Forgiveness	Overcoming Past Sins	Combating Legalism	CHURCH	LAST THINGS
Jesus' Birth and Childhood																																																
Birth of John and Jesus Foretold		X	X	X		X											X			X	X			X		X	X			X						X					X	X						
Birth of Jesus Christ			X								X															X	X			X		X				X		X			X							
Jesus as a Baby			X						X		X									X							X			X		X									X							
Boy Jesus at the Temple		X	X																											X																		
First Year of Public Ministry; The Year of Preparation																																																
John the Baptist Prepares for Jesus							X								X				X							X		X											X			X				X		
Baptism and Temptation of Jesus		X	X	X	X															X																			X									
Water into Wine; Temple Cleansed			X				X			X	X																X	X		X								X								X	X	
Jesus with Nicodemus; Samaritan Woman			X	X													X	X								X	X															X						
The Second Year of Public Ministry; The Year of Popularity																																																
John the Baptist Imprisoned											X		X							X				X	X					X		X				X				X								
Jesus Calls Four Fishermen; Matthew			X			X											X	X		X	X																		X			X				X		
Sabbath: Healings; Disciples Pick Grain						X				X														X	X			X									X		X							X		
Jesus Selects Twelve Disciples			X																	X	X			X	X															X								
Sermon on the Mountain		X	X			X	X			X		X	X							X			X	X	X		X										X		X	X	X			X		X		
Centurion's Faith; His Servant Healed											X																X				X					X					X							
John the Baptist Asks; Jesus Answers			X								X														X											X												
Woman Anoints Jesus; Parable: Two Debtors						X												X	X				X			X	X									X								X		X		
Parables: Growth in the Kingdom of God																				X			X															X				X						
Jesus Calms Storm on a Lake			X			X					X																X									X							X					
The Third Year of Public Ministry; The Year of Opposition																																																
5000 Fed from Five Loaves and Two Fish			X			X					X																									X	X											
Jesus Walks on Water			X			X					X										X						X									X												
Jesus the Bread of Life; Many Disciples Desert Him																				X			X													X			X									
Peter's Confession		X	X			X																														X											X	
Transfiguration		X	X			X																					X	X											X				X					
Demon-Possessed Boy Healed						X			X		X																									X	X			X	X		X					
Man Born Blind Healed; Parable of Good Shepherd			X			X	X			X	X								X	X			X	X		X	X													X						X		
Parable: Samaritan; Rich Fool; Things Lost/ Found		x				x	X				X	X	X		X		X	X		X	X		X			X				X							X	X	X					X	X	X		
Martha, Mary, and Lazarus			X			X					X																X			X						X	X						X					
Ten Healed of Leprosy; Grateful Samaritan			X								X							X		X			X			X	X									X			X					X				
Parables: Pharisee & Publican; Workers; 10 Pounds																	X		X				X		X	X																		X	X	X		
Jesus and the Little Children																					X			X						X									X									
Rich Young Ruler																	X						X			X	X										X		X			X						
Selfish Request of James and John													X																																			
Jesus and Zacchaeus			X			X											X	X	X	X	X		X			X	X											X	X						X	X		

Chart of Bible Stories and Doctrinal Objectives

New Testament

Story	God the Father	Jesus Christ	Holy Spirit	Trinity	Characteristics	Savior verses Punisher	Satan and Demons	False Prophets	Problems and Suffering	Temptation	Sin	Idolatry	Consequences of Sin	Sinful Humanity	Conversion	Repentance	Decision Made	Called by God	Saved verses Condemned	God and His People	God and Leaders	Liberation / Salvation	Worship	Sanctification	Family	Employer / Employee	Government / Citizen	Christian / Non-Christian	Christian / Christian	Faith	Christian Service	Stewardship	Christian Responsibility	Walk with God	Devotional Life	Evangelism	Christian in Sin	Forgiveness	Overcoming Past Sins	Combating Legalism	Church	Last Things
Holy Week																																										
Triumphal Entry into Jerusalem		X			X																		X												X							
Cleansing of Temple; Barren Fig Tree Cursed								X					X	X					X				X									X	X							X	X	
Parables: Two Sons; Wicked Husbandmen; Feast					X			X						X		X	X	X	X		X	X											X					X				
3 Questions: Tribute; Resurrection; Great Commandment																											X						X									
Prophetic Words Spoken on Mt of Olives						X	X		X				X	X					X									X	X				X	X	X	X	X					X
Parables: Virgins; Talents; Separation: Sheep & Goats						X											X		X										X		X		X									X
Passover Meal; Lord's Supper	X	X							X	X	X						X																									
Jesus' Intercessory Prayer	X	X																X										X					X									
In Gethsemane: Jesus Prays; His Arrest	X	X				X	X		X	X	X		X														X	X														
Peter Denies His Lord										X	X																															
Jesus' Judgments	X	X			X	X	X	X	X										X		X																					
Jesus' Crucifixion, Death, & Burial	X	X						X	X				X																													
The Resurrected Life of Jesus																																										
Resurrection	X	X	X						X																					X												
Jesus' Appearances		X	X		X																									X												
Miraculous Catch of fish; Peter Reinstated		X															X				X										X											
Last Appearance and Ascension		X																X			X												X									X
Events in the Life of the Early Church																																										
Pentecost: Holy Spirit; First Converts			X												X	X				X	X		X								X		X	X		X					X	
Sanhedrin Against the Disciples			X						X										X	X	X						X	X			X		X			X					X	
Ananias and Sapphira			X								X			X					X	X	X										X	X	X								X	
Seven Helpers Chosen			X																	X	X										X	X	X								X	
Stephen		X	X																X								X	X					X								X	
Philip, the Evangelist			X												X						X								X		X		X			X					X	X
Peter and Cornelius		X	X									X			X						X							X			X		X			X					X	X
Barnabas					X													X			X			X							X	X	X	X		X					X	
Saul/Paul		X	X					X	X					X	X	X	X	X																				X			X	X
First Missionary Trip: Barnabas and Saul/Paul								X	X												X										X	X	X	X		X			X		X	X
Council at Jerusalem																	X												X											X	X	
Second and Third Missionary Trips								X	X						X																X		X	X		X			X		X	X
Paul Arrested; His Defenses; in Rome		X							X																		X				X		X	X		X			X	X	X	X
Paul Opposes Peter at Antioch																													X		X		X	X		X		X	X	X	X	X

Bible Storytelling Tools © Jackson Day

www.ingramcontent.com/pod-product-compliance
Lightning Source LLC
Chambersburg PA
CBHW081223170426
43198CB00017B/2701